Objective-C for Absolute Beginners

iPhone, iPad, and Mac Programming Made Easy

Gary Bennett
Mitch Fisher
Brad Lees

Apress®

Objective-C for Absolute Beginners: iPhone, iPad, and Mac Programming Made Easy

ISBN-13 (pbk): 978-1-4302-2832-5

ISBN-13 (electronic): 978-1-4302-2833-2

9 8 7 6 5 4 3 2 1

President and Publisher: Paul Manning
Lead Editor: Clay Andres
Development Editor: Douglas Pundick
Technical Reviewer: James Bucanek
Editorial Board: Clay Andres, Steve Anglin, Mark Beckner, Ewan Buckingham, Gary Cornell, Jonathan Gennick, Jonathan Hassell, Michelle Lowman, Matthew Moodie, Duncan Parkes, Jeffrey Pepper, Frank Pohlmann, Douglas Pundick, Ben Renow-Clarke, Dominic Shakeshaft, Matt Wade, Tom Welsh
Coordinating Editor: Kelly Moritz
Copy Editor: Heather Lang and Tracy Brown
Compositor: MacPS, LLC
Indexer: BIM Indexing & Proofreading Services
Artist: April Milne
Cover Designer: Anna Ishchenko

Distributed to the book trade worldwide by Springer Science+Business Media, LLC., 233 Spring Street, 6th Floor, New York, NY 10013. Phone 1-800-SPRINGER, fax (201) 348-4505, e-mail orders-ny@springer-sbm.com, or visit www.springeronline.com.

For information on translations, please e-mail rights@apress.com, or visit www.apress.com.

Apress and friends of ED books may be purchased in bulk for academic, corporate, or promotional use. eBook versions and licenses are also available for most titles. For more information, reference our Special Bulk Sales–eBook Licensing web page at www.apress.com/info/bulksales.

The source code for this book is available to readers at www.apress.com.

I would like to dedicate this book to my wife Stefanie and to my children, Michael, Danielle, Michelle, and Emily. Thank you for always supporting me when I decide to do crazy things like write a book.

Also, I want to thank two of my friends, Mitch Fisher and Brad Lees, for co-authoring this book with me. They are two of the finest developers in the country, and are great friends. It was great being able to work with them again.

—Gary Bennett

I would like to thank all my family and friends who have patiently supported my work on this book. You know who you are. I would like to especially thank Lisa, Jade, Eric, and Patti for the long nights and forever-busy weekends that I was spending on this book and not with them.

—Mitch Fisher

I would like to thank my wife Natalie and my kids for the support and time they have given me to work on this book. I am also grateful for good friends who convince me to take on crazy endeavors.

—Brad Lees

Contents at a Glance

Contents

About the Authors

Gary Bennett is president of xcelMe.com. xcelMe teaches iPhone/iPad programming courses online. Gary has taught hundreds of students how to develop iPhone/iPad apps, and has several very popular apps on the iTunes Apps Store. Gary's students have some of the best-selling apps on the iTunes App Store. Gary also worked for 25 years in the technology and defense industries. He served 10 years in the U.S. Navy as a Nuclear Engineer aboard two nuclear submarines. After leaving the Navy, Gary worked for several companies as a software developer, CIO, and President. As CIO, he helped take VistaCare public in 2002. Gary also co-authored *iPhone Cool Projects* for Apress. Gary lives in Scottsdale, Arizona with his wife Stefanie and their four children.

Mitch Fisher is a software developer in the Phoenix, Arizona area. He was introduced to PCs back in the 1980s when 64K was a lot of memory and 1 Mhz was considered a fast computer. Over the last 25 years, Mitch has worked for several large and medium-sized companies in the roles of software developer and software architect, and had led several teams of developers on multi-million dollar projects. Mitch now divides his time between writing iOS applications and server-side UNIX technologies.

Brad Lees has more than 12 years' experience in application development and server management. He has specialized in creating and initiating software programs in real-estate development systems and financial institutions. His career has been highlighted by his positions as information systems manager at The Lyle Anderson Company; product development manager for Smarsh; vice president of application development for iNation; and IT manager at The Orcutt/Winslow Partnership, the largest architectural firm in Arizona. A graduate of Arizona State University, Brad and his wife Natalie reside in Phoenix with their five children

About the Technical Reviewer

 **James Bucanek** has spent the past 30 years programming and developing microcomputer systems. He has experience with a broad range of technologies, from embedded consumer products to industrial robotics. James is currently focused on Macintosh and iPhone software development. When not programming, James indulges in his love of the arts. He earned an Associate's degree from the Royal Academy of Dance in classical ballet, and occasionally teaches at Adams Ballet Academy.

Acknowledgments

We would like to thank Apress for all their help in making this book possible. Specifically, we would like to thank Kelly Moritz, our coordinating editor, for helping us stay focused and overcoming many obstacles. Without Kelly, this book would not have been possible.

Special thanks to Douglas Pundick, development editor, for all his suggestions during the editorial review process to help make this a great book. Thanks to Heather Lang and Tracy Brown, the copy editors who made the book look great.

We would also like to thank the Alice Community and Carnegie Mellon University for developing Alice and making learning object-oriented programming fun and easy!

Introduction

Over the last two years, we've heard this countless times: "I've never programmed before, but I have a great idea for an iPhone/iPad app. Can I really learn to program the iPhone or iPad?" We always answer, "yes, but you have to believe you can." Only you are going to tell yourself you can't do it.

For the Newbie

This book assumes you may have never programmed before. It is also written for someone who may have never programmed before using object-oriented programming (OOP) languages. There are lots of Objective-C books out there, but all of these books assume you have programmed before and know OOP. We wanted to write a book that takes readers from knowing nothing about programming to being able to program in Objective-C.

Over the last two years we of have taught hundreds of students at xcelMe.com to be iPhone/iPad developers. We have incorporated what we have learned in our first two courses, Introduction to Object Oriented Programming and Logic along and Objective-C for iPhone/iPad developers, into this book.

For the More Experienced

There are lots of developers who programmed years ago or programmed in a non-OOP language and need the background in OOP and Logic before they dive into Objective-C. This book is for you. We gently walk you through OOP and how it is used in iPhone/iPad development.

Why Alice: An Innovative 3D Programming Environment

Over the years, universities have struggled with several issues with their computer science departments:

- High male-to-female ratios
- High drop-out rates
- Longer than average time to graduation

One of the biggest challenges to learning OOP languages like Java, C++, or Objective-C is the steep learning curve from the very beginning. In the past, students had to learn at once the following topics:

- ■ Object-oriented principles
- ■ A complex Integrated Development Environment (IDE)
- ■ The syntax of the programming language
- ■ Programming logic and principles

Carnegie Mellon University received a grant from the U.S. government and developed Alice. Alice is an innovative 3D programming environment that makes it easy to create rich graphical applications for new developers. Alice is a teaching tool for students learning to program in an OOP environment. It uses 3D graphics and a drag-and-drop interface to facilitate a more engaging, less frustrating first programming experience.

Alice enables the students to focus on learning the principles of OOP without having to focus on learning a complex IDE and Objective-C principles all at once. We get to focus on each topic individually. This helps readers feel a real sense of accomplishment as they progress.

Alice removes all the complexity of learning an IDE and programming language syntax. It is drag-and-drop programming. You'll see it is actually fun to do, and you can develop really cool and sophisticated apps in Alice.

After the OOP topic has been introduced and readers feel comfortable with the material, we then move into Xcode, where readers get to use their new OOP knowledge in writing Objective-C applications. This enables readers to focus on the Objective-C syntax and language without having to learn OOP at the same time.

How This Book Is Organized

You'll notice that we are all about successes in this book. We introduce the OOP and Logic concepts in Alice and then move those concepts into Xcode and Objective-C. Most students are visual and learn by doing. We use both of these techniques. We'll walk you through topics and concepts with visual examples and then take you step-by-step examples reinforcing these.

Often we will repeat previous topics to reinforce what you have learned and apply these skills in new ways. This enables new programmers to re-apply development skills and feel a sense of accomplishment as they progress.

The Formula for Success

Learning to program is an interactive process between you and your program. Just like learning to play an instrument, you have to practice. You must work through the examples and exercises in this book. Just because you understand the concept, doesn't mean you will know how to apply it and use it.

You will learn a lot from this book. You will learn a lot from working through the exercises in this book. *But you will really learn when you debug your programs.* Spending time walking through your code and trying to find out why it is not working the way you want is a learning process that is unparalleled. The downside of debugging is it can be especially frustrating to the new developer. If you have never wanted to throw your computer out the window, you will. You will question why you are doing this, and whether you are smart enough to solve the problem. Programming is very humbling, even for the most experience developer.

Like a musician, the more you practice the better you get. You can do some amazing things as a programmer. The world is your oyster. It is one of the most satisfying accomplishments you can have, seeing you app on the iTunes App Store. However, there is a price, and that price is time spent coding.

Here is our formula for success:

- Believe you can do it. You'll be the only one who says you can't do this. So don't tell yourself that.
- Work through all the examples and exercises in this book.
- Code, code, and keeping coding. The more you code, the better you'll get.
- Be patient with yourself. If you were fortunate enough to have been a 4.0 student who can memorize material just by reading it, this will not happen with Objective-C coding. You are going to have to spend time coding.
- DON'T GIVE UP!

The Development Technology Stack

We will walk you through the process of understanding the development process for your iPhone/iPad apps and what technology is needed. However, it is helpful to briefly look at all the pieces together: a sample iPhone app, in a Table View. See Figure 1.

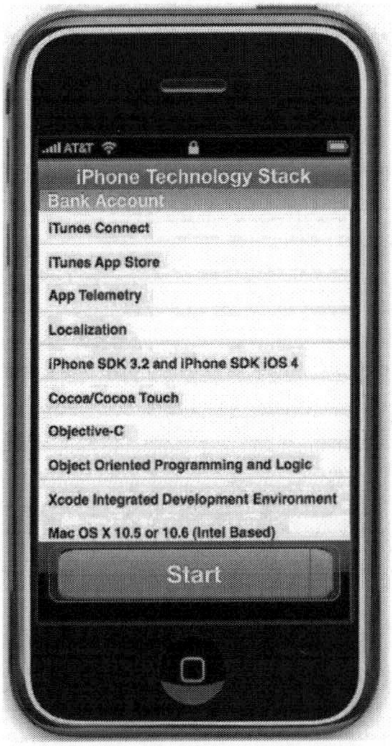

Figure 1. *The iPhone/iPad technology stack*

Required Software, Materials, and Equipment

One of the great things about Alice is it available on the three main operating systems used today:

- Windows
- Mac
- Linux

The other great thing about Alice is it is free! You can download Alice at www.Alice.org.

Operating System and IDE

Although you can use Alice on many platforms, the Integrated Development Environment (IDE) that developers use to develop iPhone/iPad apps Xcode, **has to be an Intel-based Mac!** The IDE is free and is available on your Mac DVD operating system. The operating system has to be 10.5 or later to develop iPhone apps, and 10.6 for iPad apps and iOS 4 apps.

Software Development Kits

You will need to download the iPhone/iPad IDE from Apple. This is available at `http://developer.apple.com/iphone`. You will need to register as an iPhone developer.

When you are ready to upload your app to the iTunes App Store, you will need to pay $99/yr to do this.

Dual Monitors

It is highly recommended that developers have a second monitor connected to their computer. It is great to step through your code and watch your output window and iPad simulator at the same time on dual, independent monitors. Apple hardware makes this easy. Just plug your second monitor in to the display port of any Intel-based Mac, with the correct mini display port adapter, of course, and you're able to have two monitors working independently from one another. See Figure 2. Note it is not required to have dual monitors. You will just have to organize your open windows to fit on your screen if you don't.

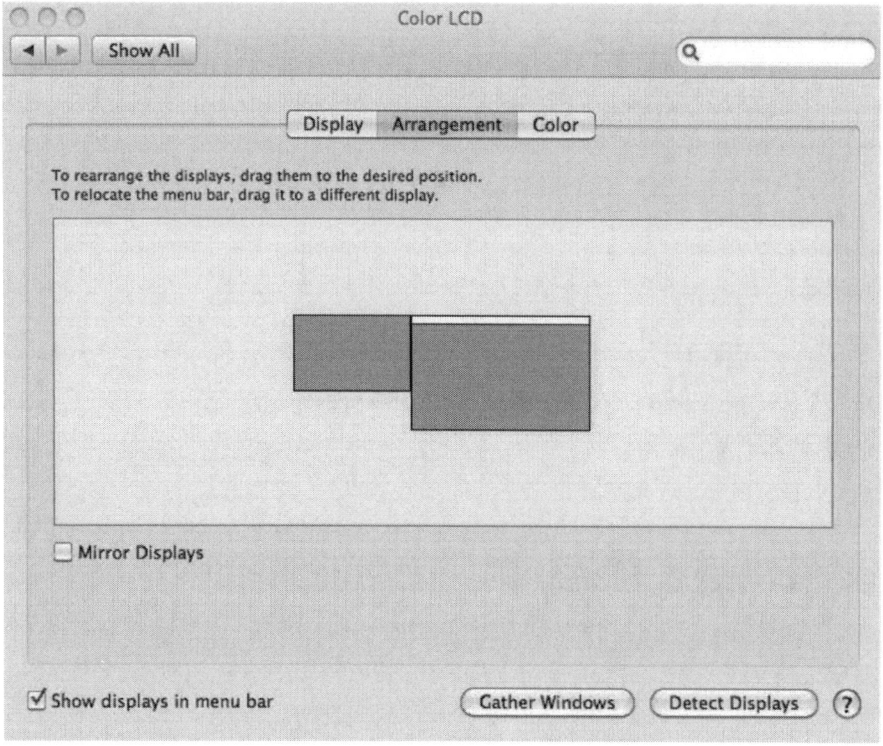

Figure 2. *Dual monitors*

Book Forum

We have developed an online forum for this book at http://forum.xcelme.com, where readers can go to ask questions of the authors while they are learning Objective-C. There you will find answers to the exercises and additional exercises to help you learn.

See Figure 3. Readers can also access answers to exercises and discover helpful links to help them be successful iPhone/iPad develops and great amazing apps. So let's get started!

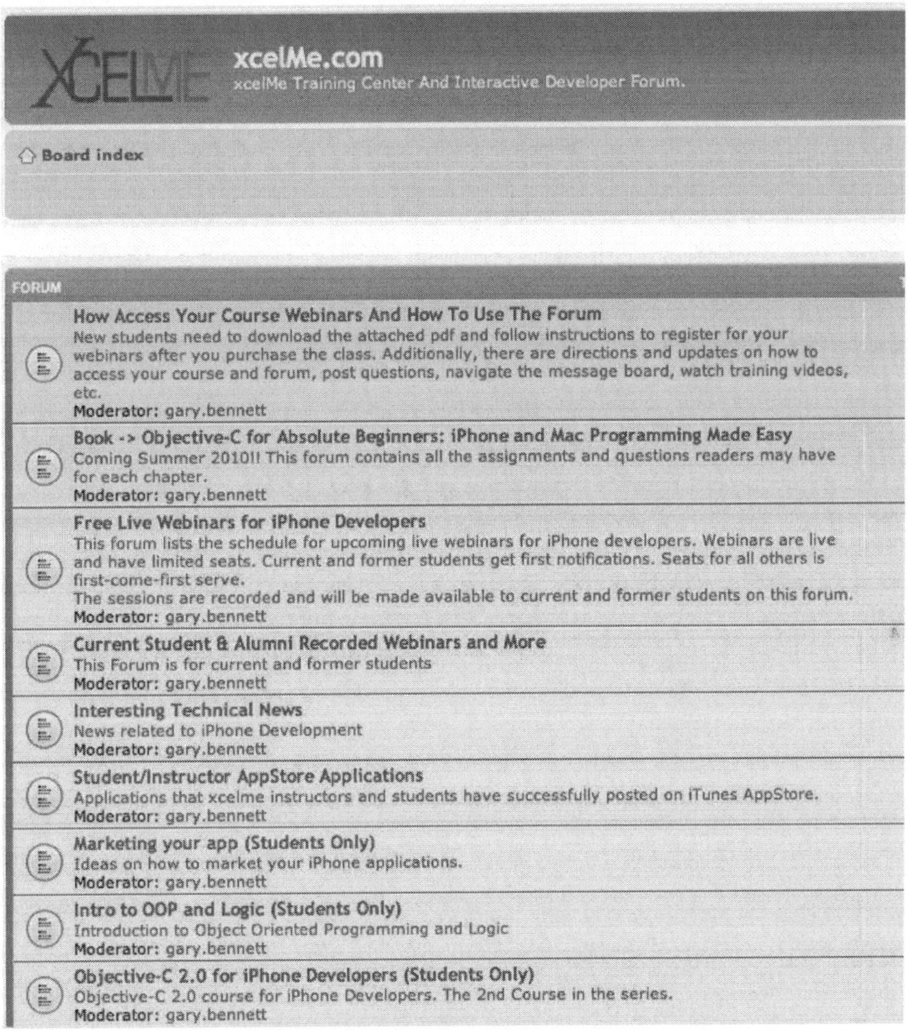

Figure 3. *Reader Forum for accessing answers to exercise and posting questions for authors*

Chapter 1

Becoming a Great iPhone/iPad or Mac Programmer

Now that you're ready to become a software developer and have read the Introduction of this book, you need to become familiar with some key concepts. Your computer program will do exactly what you tell it to do, no more and no less. It will follow the programming rules that were defined by the operating system and programming language. Your program doesn't care if you are having a bad day or how many times you ask it to perform something. Your program will do whatever you tell it to do. Often, what you think you've told your program to do and what it actually does are to different things.

> **NOTE:** If you haven't already, take a few minutes to read the Introduction to this book. You will better understand why we are using the Alice programming language and how to be successful in developing your iPhone/iPad and Mac apps.

Depending on your background, working with something absolutely black and white may be frustrating. Many times, programming students have lamented, "That's not what I wanted it to do!" As you begin to gain experience and confidence programming, you'll begin to think like a programmer. You will understand software design and logic, and you will experience having your programs perform exactly as you tell them to do as enormously satisfying.

Thinking Like a Developer

Software development involves writing a computer program and then having the computer execute the program. A **computer program** is the set of instructions that we want the computer to perform. Before we begin to write a computer program, it is helpful to list the steps that we want our program to perform, in the order we want them accomplished. This step-by-step process is called an **algorithm**.

If we want to write a computer program to toast a piece of bread, we would first write an algorithm. This algorithm might look something like this:

1. Take the bread out of the bag.

2. Place the bread in the toaster.

3. Press the toast button.

4. Wait for the toast to pop up.

5. Remove the toast from the toaster.

At first glance, this algorithm seems to solve our problem. However, our algorithm leaves out many details and makes many assumptions, for example:

1. What kind of toast does our user want? Does the user want white bread, wheat, or some other kind of bread?

2. How does the user want the bread toasted, light or dark?

3. What does the user want on the bread after it is toasted: butter, margarine, honey, or strawberry jam?

4. Maybe the user wanted another kind of toast, like French toast or garlic toast, which is prepared by means other than a toaster.

5. Does this algorithm work for all your users in their cultures and languages?

Now, you might be thinking we are getting too detailed for just doing a simple toast program. Over the years, software development has the reputation of taking too long, costing too much, and not being what the user wants. This reputation came to be because computer programmers often start writing their programs before they have really thought through their algorithms.

The key ingredients to making successful applications starts with **design requirements**. Design requirements can be very formal and detailed or a simple list on a piece of paper. The importance of design requirements is they help the developer flesh out what the application should do and not do when complete. Design requirements should not be completed in a programmer's vacuum but should be a collaboration between developers, users, and customers.

NOTE: If you take anything away from this chapter, take away the importance of considering design requirements and user interface design before starting software development. This is the most effective (and cheapest) use of time in the software development cycle. Using a pencil and eraser is a lot easier and faster than making changes to code because you didn't have others look at the designs before starting to program.

Another key ingredient to your successful app is the **user interface (UI)** design. Apple recommends that you spend over 50% of the entire development process focusing on the UI design. The design can be simple pencil-and-paper layouts created using the *iPhone Application Sketch Book* by Dean Kaplan (Apress, 2009) or on-screen layout created with the Omni Group's OmniGraffle software application with the Ultimate iPhone Stencil plug-in. Many software developers start with the UI design, and after laying out all the screen elements and having many users look at paper mock-ups, they then write out the design requirements from their screen layouts.

Once you have done your best to flesh out all the design requirements, laid out all the user interface screens, and had the client(s) or potential customers look at your design and give you feedback, coding can begin. Once coding begins, design requirements and user interface screens can change, but the changes are typically minor and easily accommodated by the development process. See Figures 1–1 and 1–2.

Figure 1–1. *This is a UI mock-up of the Account Balance screen for an iPhone mobile banking app before development begins. This UI design mock-up was completed using OmniGraffle.*

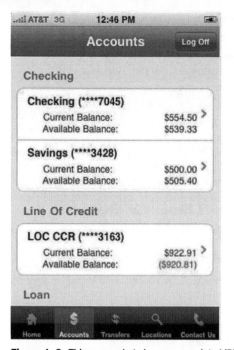

Figure 1–2. *This screenshot shows a completed iPhone mobile banking application as it appeared on the iTunes App Store. This app is called Woodforest Mobile Banking.*

Completing the Development Cycle

Now that we have our design requirements and user interface designs and have written our program, what's next? After programming, we need to make sure our program matches the design requirements and user interface design and that there are no errors. In programming vernacular, errors are called **bugs**. Bugs are undesired results of our programming and must be fixed before released to the App Store. The process of finding bugs in our programs and making sure the program meets the design requirements is called **testing**. Typically, someone who is experienced in software testing methodology and who didn't write the app performs this testing. Software testing is commonly referred to as **Quality Assurance (QA)**. Figure 1–3 shows the complete software development cycle.

> **NOTE:** When an application is ready to be submitted to the iTunes App Store, Xcode gives the file an .app extension, for example, appName.app. That is why iPhone, iPad, and Mac applications are called **apps**. We will use "program," "application," and "app" to mean the same thing throughout this book.

During the testing phase, the developer will need to work with QA staff to determine why the application is not working as designed. The process is called **debugging**. It requires the developer to step through the program to find out why the application is not working as designed. Figure 1–3 shows the complete software development cycle.

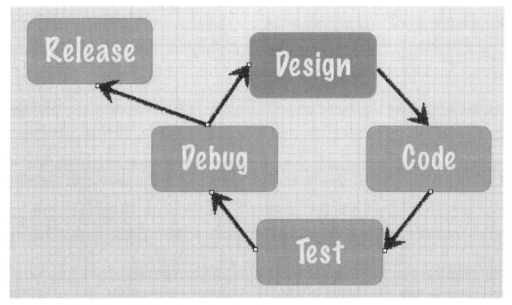

Figure 1–3. *The typical software development cycle*

Frequently during testing and debugging, changes to the requirements (design) need to occur to make the application more usable for the customer. Once the design requirements and user interface changes are made, the process begins over again.

At some point, the application that everyone has been working so hard on must be shipped to the iTunes App Store. Lots of considerations are taken into account when this happens:

- Cost of development
- Competition
- Stability of the application
- Return on investment

There is always the give-and-take between developers and management. Developers want the app perfect, and management wants to start realizing revenue from the investment as soon as possible. If the release were left up to the developers, the app would never ship to the App Store. Developers would continue to tweak the app forever, making it faster, more efficient, and more usable. At some point, however, the code needs to be pried from the developers' hands and shipped to the user, so it can do what it was meant to do.

Introducing Object Oriented Programming

As discussed in detail in the Introduction to this book, Alice enables us to focus on **object oriented programming (OOP)** without having to cover all the Objective-C programming syntax and complex Xcode development environment in one big step. Instead, we can focus on learning the basic principles of OOP and using those principles quickly to write our first programs.

For decades, developers have been trying to figure out a better way to develop code that was reusable, manageable, and easily maintained over the life of a project. OOP was designed to help achieve code reuse and maintainability while reducing the cost of software development.

OOP can be viewed as a collection of objects in a program. Actions are performed on these objects to accomplish the design requirements.

An **object** is anything that can be acted on. For example, an airplane, person, or screen/view on the iPad can all be objects. We may want to act on the plane by making the plane bank. We may want the person to walk or to change the color of the screen of an app on the iPad. Actions are all being applied to these objects; see Figure 1–4.

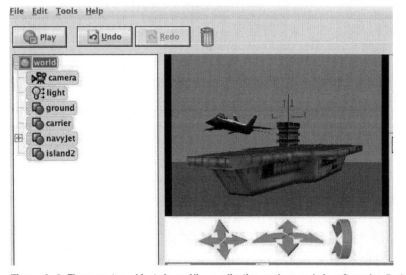

Figure 1–4. *These are two objects in an Alice application, a plane and aircraft carrier. Both objects can have actions applied—take off and landing for the plane and "turn to port" and "ahead flank" for the aircraft carrier.*

Like the play button in Alice, the Xcode **integrated development environment (IDE)** enables us to run our application from within our programming environment See Figure 1–5.

Figure 1–5. *This sample iPhone app contains UITableView objects. Actions such as "rotate left" or "user did select row 3" can be applied to this object.*

Actions that are performed on objects are called **methods**. Methods manipulate objects to accomplish what we want our app to do. For example, for our jet object in Figure 1–4, we might have the following methods:

```
goUp
goDown
bankLeft
turnOnAfterBurners
lowerLandingGear
```

For our iPhone application's UITableView object in Figure 1–5, we could have the following methods:

```
loadView
shouldAutorotateToInterfaceOrientation
numberOfSectionsInTableView
cellForRowAtIndexPath
didSelectRowAtIndexPath
```

All objects have data that describes those objects. Our properties hold values that describe the state of the objects. This data is defined as **properties**. Each property describes the associated object in a specific way. For example, the jet object's properties might be as follows:

```
altitude = 10,000 feet
heading = North
speed = 500 knots
```

```
pitch = 10 degrees
yaw = 20 degrees
latitude = 33.575776
longitude = -111.875766
```

For our UITableView object in Figure 1–5, these might be our properties:

```
backGroundColor = Red
selectedRow = 3
animateView = No
```

An object's properties can be changed at any time as our program is running, as the user interacts with the app, or as the programmer designs the app to accomplish the design requirements. The values stored in the properties of an object at a specific time are collectively called the **state of an object.**

State is an important concept in computer programming. When teaching students about state, Gary asks them to go over to a window and find an airplane in the sky. He then asks them to snap their figures and make up some of the values that the plane's property might have at that specific time. Those values might be

```
altitude = 10,000 feet
latitude = 33.575776
longitude = -111.875766
```

Those values represent the state of the object at the specific time that they snapped their fingers.

After waiting a couple of minutes, Gary asks the students to find that same plane, snap their fingers again, and record the plane's possible state at that specific point in time.

The values of the properties might then be something like this:

```
altitude = 10,500 feet
latitude = 33.575665
longitude = -111.875777
```

Notice how the state of the object changes over time.

Working with the Alice Interface

Alice offers a great approach in using the concepts that we have just discussed without all the complexity of learning Xcode and the Objective-C language at the same time. It just takes a few minutes to familiarize yourself with the Alice interface and begin writing a program.

The Introduction of this book describes how to download Alice. Once it's downloaded, you need to open Alice. See Figure 1–6

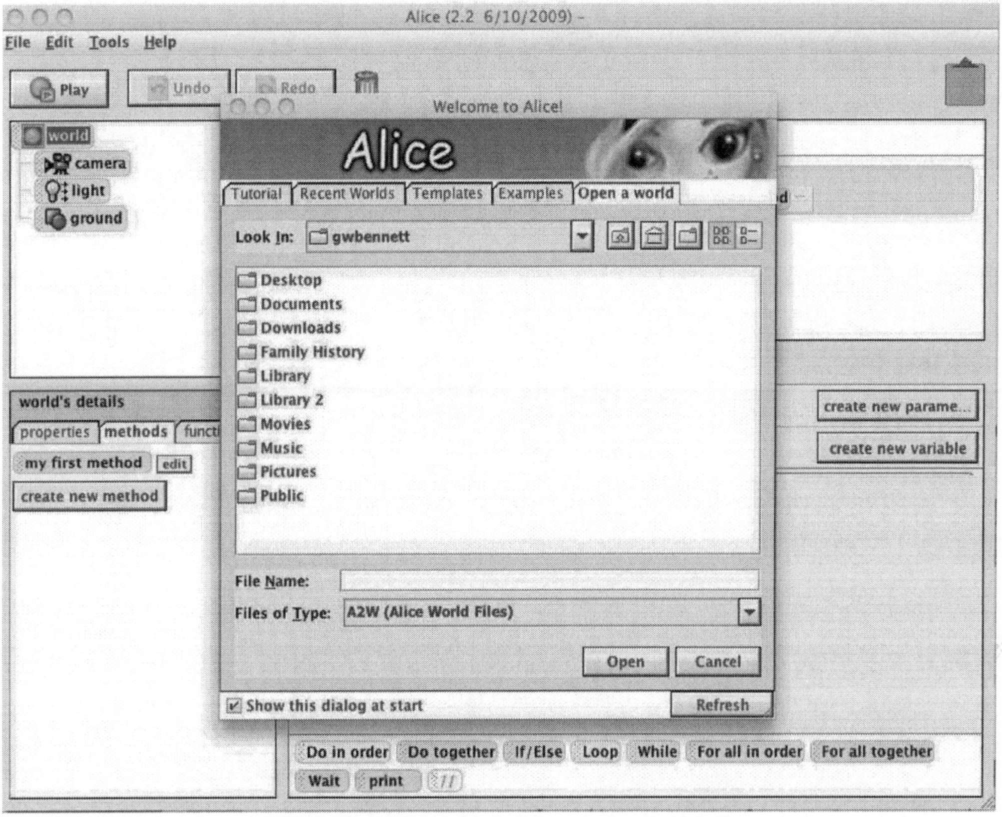

Figure 1–6. *It is worth your time to click on the Tutorial tab to familiarize yourself with the Alice application and user interface. Additionally, there are several great examples on the Examples tab.*

Alice has great tutorials and examples that are highly recommended for developers to work through, like the one shown in Figure 1–7.

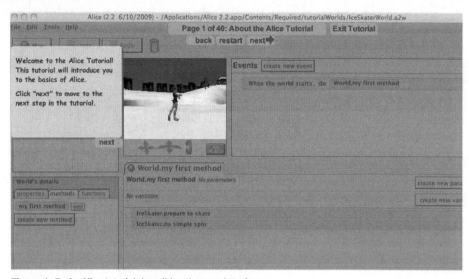

Figure 1–7. *An Alice tutorial describing the user interface*

Technically speaking, Alice is not a true IDE like Xcode, but it is pretty close and a whole lot easier to learn than Xcode. A true IDE combines code development, user interface layout, debugging tools, documentation and simulator/console launching for a single application; see Figure 1–8. However, Alice offers similar look, feel, and features to Xcode. This will serve you well later when we start writing Objective-C code.

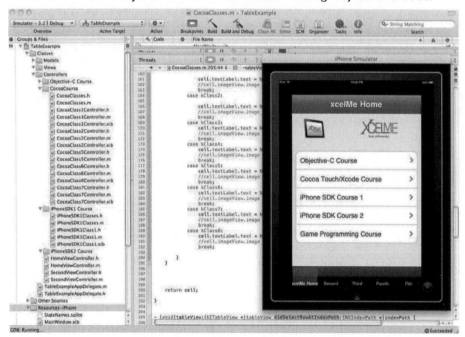

Figure 1–8. *The Xcode integrated development environment (IDE)) with the iPad Simulator*

In the next chapter, we will go through the Alice interface and write our first program.

Summary

Congratulations, you have finished the first chapter of this book. It is important that you have an understanding of the following terms, because they will be reinforced throughout this book:

- Computer program
- Algorithm
- Design requirements
- User interface
- Bug
- Quality assurance (QA)
- Debugging
- Object oriented programming (OOP)
- Object
- Property
- Method
- State of an object
- Integrated development environment (IDE)

Exercises

- Write an algorithm for how a soda machine works, from the time when a coin is inserted until a soda is dispensed. Assume the price of a soda is 80 cents.
- Write the design requirements for an app that will run the soda machine.

Programming Basics

This chapter will focus on the building blocks necessary to become a great Objective-C programmer. We are going to use the Alice user interface, write our first Alice program, explore some new OOP terms and write our first Objective-C program.

> **NOTE:** We want to introduce new concepts in Alice that later enable you to use these concepts in Objective-C. We believe this unique approach will help you learn the concepts quickly, without discouragement, and give you a great foundation to build on.

Taking a Tour with Alice

Alice's 3D programming environment makes it easy to write your first program using some of the principles that you learned about in Chapter 1. First, you need to learn a little more about Alice's user interface. When we first launch Alice, we are presented with a screen that looks like Figure 2–1.

You can start with the default blue sky and green grass template or pick another template with different backgrounds. Feel free to explore and have fun. This is where we will spend most of our time and write our first Alice application.

The Alice user interface is set up to help us efficiently write our applications. The user interface is very similar in form and function to the Xcode IDE. We will now explore the major sections of Alice.

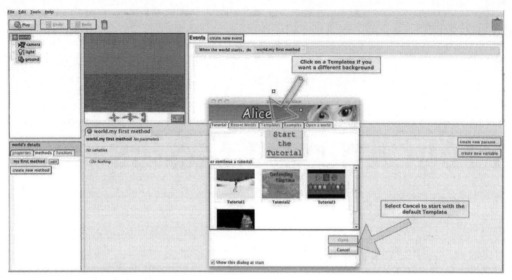

Figure 2–1. *Opening screen in Alice*

Navigation Menu

The Navigation menu, shown in Figure 2–2, enables us to open and close files, set our application preferences, and view world statistics, text output, and the error console. We can also access example worlds and Alice help.

> **NOTE:** It is important that you save your program frequently when using Alice. If Alice crashes and you haven't saved your work, you will lose all your code or changes since you last saved. Additionally, we recommend that you close Alice completely and reopen it when you want to open a new Alice program.

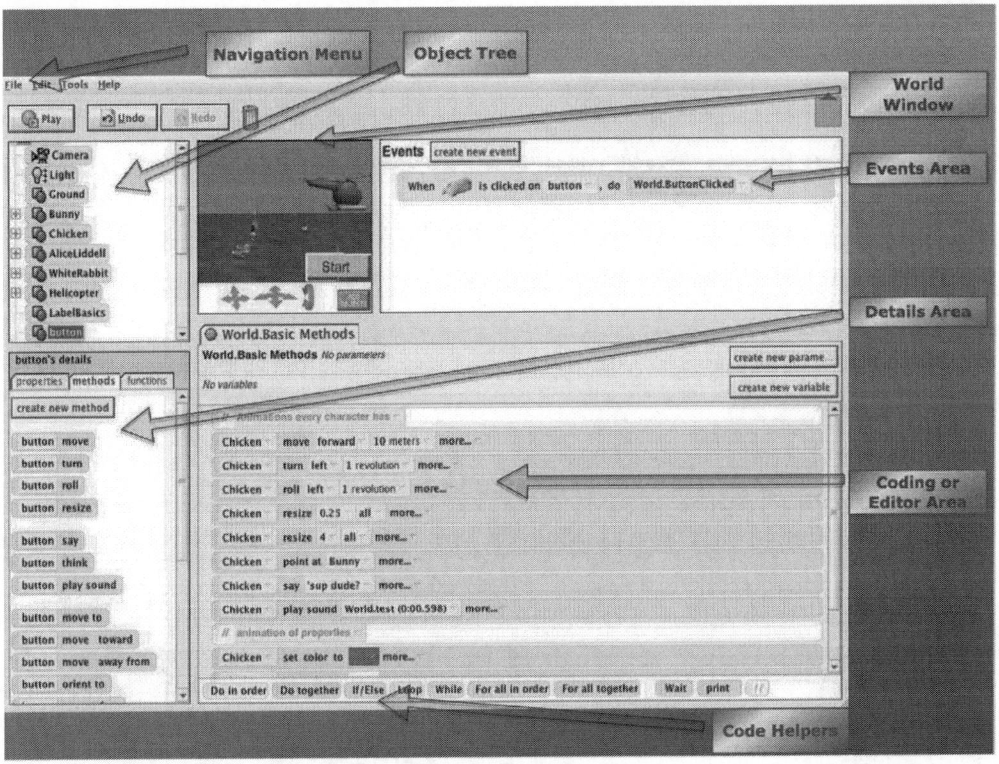

Figure 2–2. *This shows the Alice's user interface's main sections using the AlmostAllAboutAlice example included with Alice. Take some time to explore the user interface. You will see in this chapter how it compares with Xcode and how it will help us learn Objective-C.*

World Window

The World window shows what our virtual world will look like when it runs. This window is similar to the iPhone/iPad simulator we will use later to run our apps. The World Window enables us to take advantage of Alice's 3D user interface to model our application.

In the World Window, we can move the camera around and place the camera where we want for the viewing prospective we desire. Moving the three arrow tools in Figure 2–3 enables incredible flexibility for bringing our applications to life.

It is important to learn how to move the camera around your world to get the view you want the users to see.

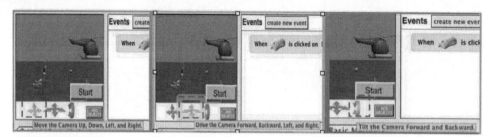

Figure 2–3. *Camera manipulation arrows to control the camera in World window.*

One of the most important Alice controls is the **Add Objects** control. See Figure 2–4. When we click the Add Objects button in the bottom-right corner of the World window, we launch the Alice's **Scene Editor**.

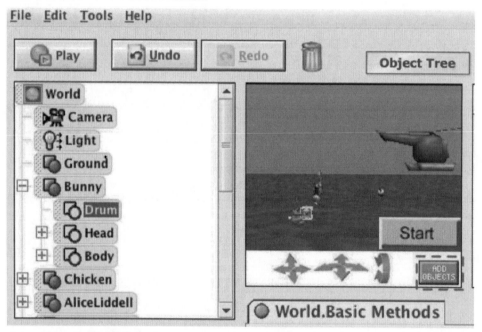

Figure 2–4. *The Add Objects button in the World Window is outlined with a box and is one of the most important controls. This button will launch the Alice's Scene editor and enable us to add objects to our Alice World.*

Take a minute to familiarize yourself with the Scene Editor, shown in Figure 2–5. The Scene Editor enables us to

- Add objects to our world from the gallery.
- Add objects to our world from the Internet.
- Position the object in our world.
- Adjust the camera for viewing our world.

We will spend a lot of time adding objects and setting the camera in our worlds using the Scene Editor.

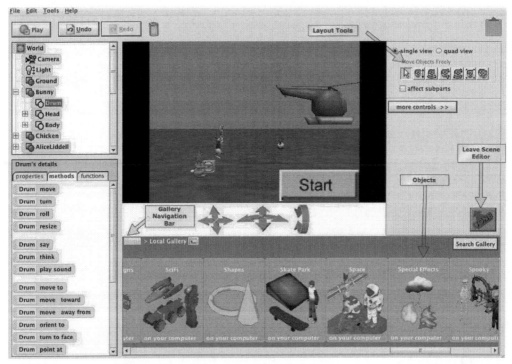

Figure 2–5. *Alice's Scene Editor*

Classes, Objects, and Instances in Alice

A group of objects with the same properties and same methods (actions) are called a **class**. For example, we could have a class called `Airplane`. In this class, we could have five objects:

```
boeing747
lockheedSR71
boeing737
citation10
f18Fighter
```

These objects are nearly identical. They are from the same `Airplane` class. They have the same methods:

```
land()
takeOff()
lowerLandingGear()
raiseLandingGear()
bankRight()
bankLeft()
```

The only thing that differentiates the objects is the values of their properties. Some of the properties of the values might be

```
wingLength = 20ft
maxThrust = 200,000lbs
numberOfEngines = 2
```

In your world, you may have two objects that are exactly the same. You may want two Boeing 737s in your view. Each copy is called an **instance**. Adding an instance of an object class to our program is called **instantiation**.

Object Tree

The **Object Tree** (see Figure 2–6) enables us to view all the objects in our Alice world. Additionally, if the object has subparts, you can view these subparts by clicking the plus sign or collapse the subparts by clicking the minus sign.

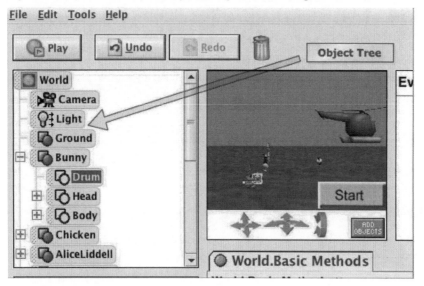

Figure 2–6. *The Object Tree*

Many of the Alice worlds come with several built-in objects that we will need for our apps. The world in Figure 2–6 comes with the Camera, Light, and Ground objects.

Editor Area

The Editor Area, the largest area of the Alice interface, is where we write our code. With Alice, we don't have to actually type code; we can drag and drop our code to manipulate our objects and properties.

NOTE: Don't forget the bottom of the Editor Area. The bottom contains a row of control and logic tiles for looping, branching, and other logical structures that we can use to control the behavior of our objects.

Details Area

The **Details Area** of the Alice interface contains the tabs for properties, methods, and functions that make up the object that is selected in the Object Tree.

- **Properties** contain the specific information of our selected object (e.g., weight, length, and height).

- **Methods** perform actions upon the object (e.g., take off and land).

- **Functions** and methods are similar. In Alice, the difference between the two is that a method does not return a value. A function will return a value.

Events Area

The Events Area of the Alice interface contains a listing of all the exiting events used by our app and provides for the ability to create new events. **Events** are conditions that trigger our methods. Methods that react to these events are called **event handlers**. These methods are specifically designed to handle these specific events. When a specific event occurs, it **triggers** a signal the event handler receives and handles.

Some examples would be the user touching a button on an iPhone. Touching or swiping, trigger events, and the methods that handle these events act on objects in our app. See Figure 2–7.

Figure 2–7. *Phonics Easy Reader 1, by Rock 'n' Learn running on the iPad Simulator in the left landscape orientation. Tapping the "Read to me" or "Let me try" button triggers events that methods receive and act on—in this example, reading to the child or having the child read the words of a sentence.*

Creating an Alice App—To the Moon Alice

We have covered some new terms and concepts, and now, it is time to do what programmers do—write code. It is customary for new developers to write a "Hello World" app as their first program. We will do something similar, but Alice makes it more interesting. We will then follow up our first Alice app with our first Objective-C app.

This Alice app will have three objects on the screen, the lunar lander object and two astronauts. One astronaut will say, "The Eagle has landed." The other astronaut will say, "That's one small step for man, one giant leap for mankind."

Alice really makes apps like this easy and fun to do. Make sure you follow these steps:

1. Click **File** and then **New**.

2. Click the **Template** tab.

3. Choose the **Space Template**, and click the **Open** button. See Figure 2–8.

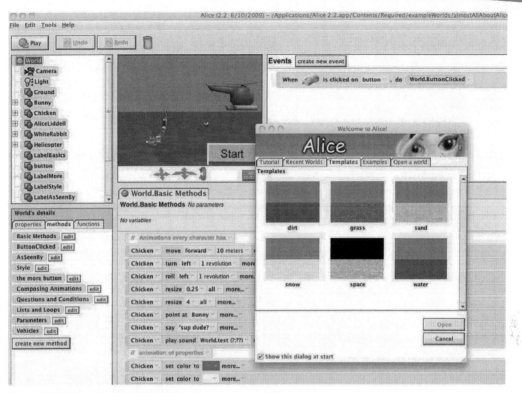

Figure 2–8. *Select the Space Template.*

4. Now, we need to add our objects. Click **Add Objects.** It was the important button in the World window shown in Figure 2–4.

5. In the Object Gallery, select the **Space Class**.

6. Right-click the **Lunar Lander** to view some of the information of the object. See Figure 2–9. We can click **"Add instance to world"** to add our objects to our world, or we can drag and drop from the gallery to the world.

> **NOTE**: You can see in this example why an instance is a copy of an object. We are making a copy of the object and putting it in our world. *Instantiation* is a big word for the process of making a copy of our object.

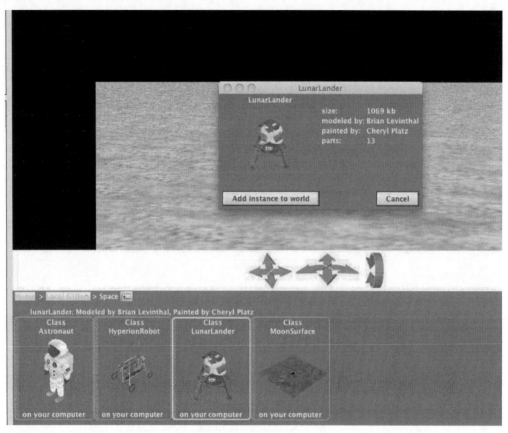

Figure 2–9. *Viewing and adding objects to our world from step 6.*

7. Click the Astronaut class twice to add our two astronauts to our world.

8. Use the **Camera Adjustment** and **Objects Adjustment** tools, outlined
    in boxes in Figure 2–10, to achieve the look and perspective you desire.

TIP: Sometimes when you add two objects, Alice places one object over the other. Drag the top
astronaut to the side of the other astronaut if this occurs. Your world should look like Figure 2–10.

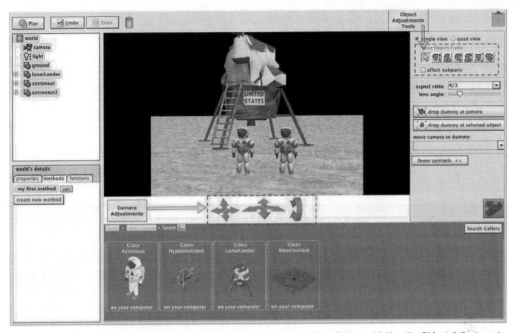

Figure 2–10. *Use the Camera Adjust tool to control the user perspective of the world. Use the Object Adjustment tools to shape and orientate your objects in your world.*

9. At the top right corner are the **Object Adjustment** tools. Hover the mouse over each tile to discover what each tile tool will do to the object. Notice the Object Tree in Figure 2–10. The ground, lunarLander, astronaut, and astronaut2 objects are in the Object Tree.

10. Click the **Done** button in the middle right of the screen. This will return us to the editor view.

11. Click the left astronaut in the World window. Make sure the methods tab is selected in the Details Area.

12. We are now going to make our astronauts say something. Remember actions to objects require methods. Drag the **Astronaut2|turn** tile from the Details Area to our Editor. Select **turn left**, **1/4 rotation** from the parameter list. See Figure 2–11. When we run our app, the left astronaut will turn to their left one-quarter rotation and face the other astronaut.

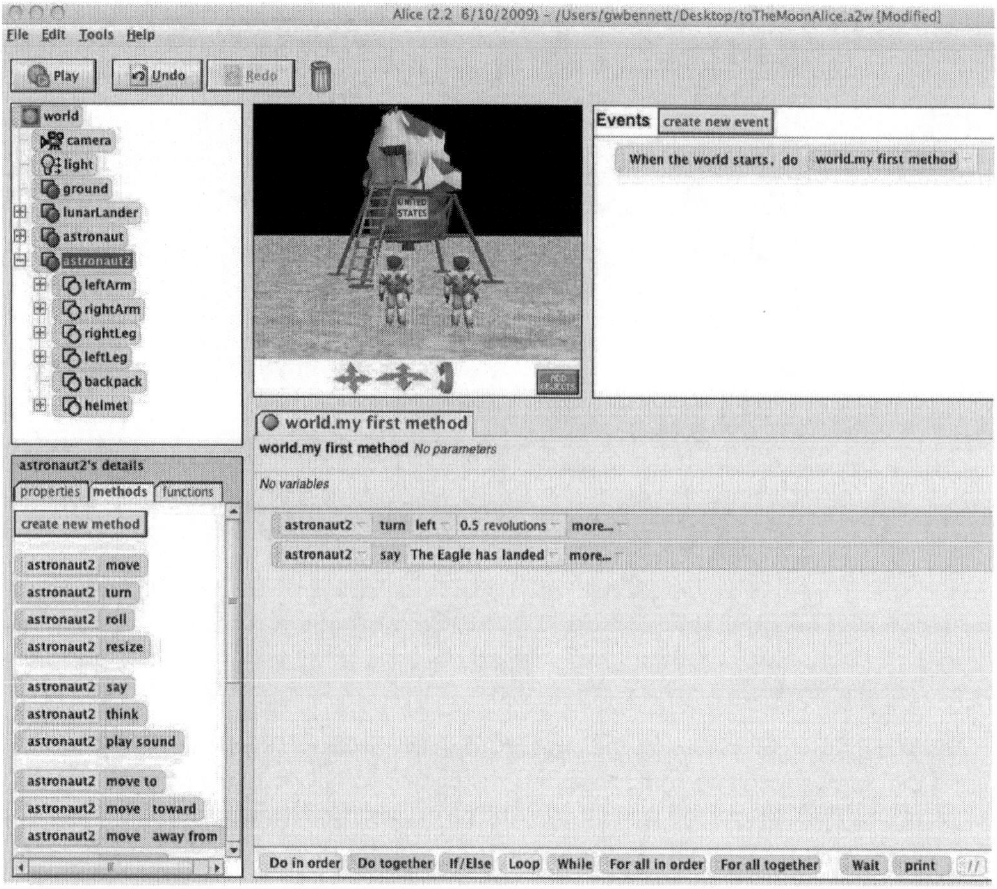

Figure 2–11. *The left Astronaut methods and parameters.*

13. Let's do the same thing for the other astronaut. Click the right astronaut. Drag the **Astronaut|turn** tile from the Details Area to our Editor. **Select turn right, 1/4 rotation** from the parameter list.

14. A **parameter** is the information a method needs to act upon the object. A method may need one or more parameters for a method. Click the right astronaut, and drag the **Astronaut2|say tile** to the editor, **select other** and then type **The Eagle has landed.** See Figure 2–12.

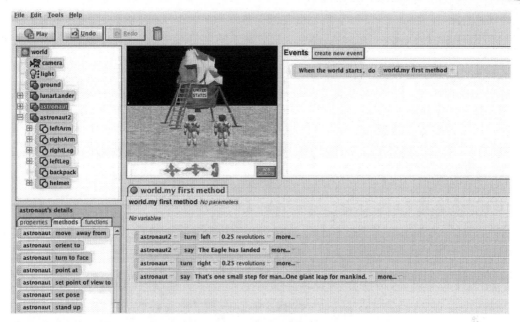

Figure 2–12. *Your editor should have these methods with the listed parameters.*

15. Click the right astronaut. Drag the **astronaut|say** tile to the editor, select
    other parameter and type **That's one small step for man. . .One giant
    leap for mankind**. Our app should like Figure 2–12.

16. Let's run our first program by clicking **Play**. If you have completed
    everything correctly, your app should look like Figure 2–13 when it runs.
    If not, you have some debugging to do.

17. Save the app as toTheMoonAlice.a2w. We will be using this app later.
    Click **File ➤ Save World or File ➤ Save World As.**

Figure 2–13. *From the top portion of the World Running window, we can rerun our program, pause, resume, restart, stop, and take a picture of our app. We can also speed up or slow down our app depending on how slow or fast our application is running.*

Your First Objective-C Program

Now that you have learned a little about OOP and have your first Alice program completed, it's time to write your first Objective-C program and begin to understand the Objective-C language, Xcode, and syntax. First, we have to install Xcode. Xcode is the IDE that we use when developing Objective-C apps. It is the equivalent to Alice's interface.

If you haven't already installed Xcode, you need to do that now. Unlike other commercial compilers that you have to buy, Xcode is included with the Mac operating system. As described in the Introduction to this book, you must use either Leopard or Snow Leopard on an Intel-based Mac to build iPhone apps. iPad apps require Snow Leopard. For the projects in this book, it doesn't matter what version of Xcode or Mac hardware you are using. However, you may notice slightly different options available in Xcode than described in this book.

Installing Xcode

Follow these steps to install Xcode:

1. Insert your operating system DVD, which may have come with your Mac. When you insert your DVD, you will see Mac OS X Install DVD window, as shown in Figure 2–14.

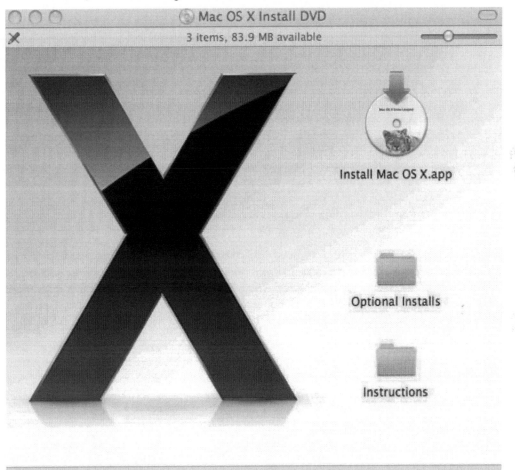

Figure 2–14. *Mac OS X Install DVD*

2. Click **Optional Installs**. You will then be presented with the Optional Installs window. See Figure 2–15.

Figure 2–15. *Optional Install Window.*

3.   Click the Xcode.mpkg icon in Figure 2–15 to install the Xcode package.

NOTE: This package has everything we need to write Objective-C and Mac apps. To be able to develop iPhone apps, you will need to apply for the iPhone Developer Program, pay $99, and download the iPhone SDK from Apple at http://developer.apple.com/iphone. You will not have to download the iPhone SDK for projects in this book, only if you want to write iPhone and iPad apps later.

4.   You will then be presented with the Xcode Installer; see Figure 2–16. The installer will walk you through the process of installing Xcode to completion.

After installation, you can find the Xcode app under your Mac HD directory. See Figure 2–17. We're not sure why the installer doesn't place it under Applications like other app installers, but Mac HD is where it is. Because you are going to be using Xcode a lot, save yourself some time and drag the app to your Dock where you can easily access it.

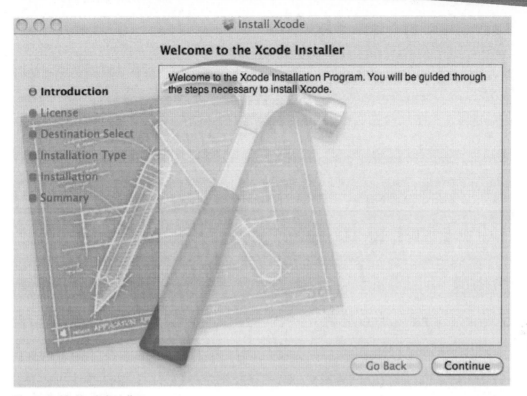

Figure 2–16. *Xcode Installer.*

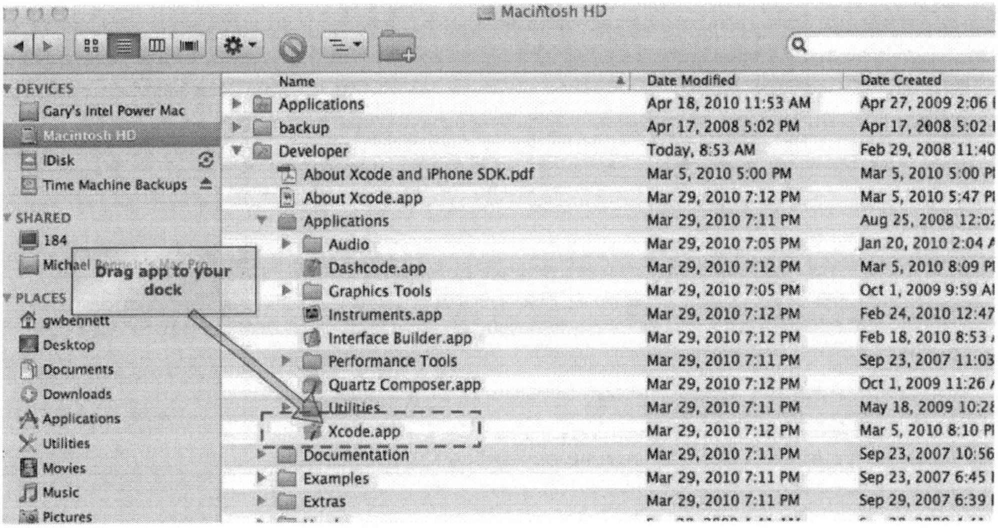

Figure 2–17. *The Xcode.app installation location.*

Launching and Using Xcode

Now that we have everything we need to begin writing Objective-C applications, let's get started. After launching Xcode, follow these steps:

1. Click **Create a new Xcode Project**. See Figure 2–18.

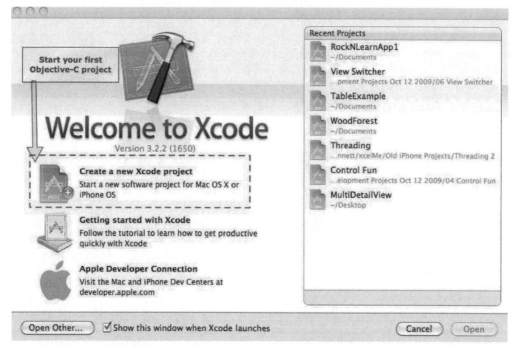

Figure 2–18. *Creating our first Objective-C project.*

> **IMPORTANT:** This is where many beginners get stuck depending on their version of Xcode and if they have the iPhone SDK installed. In Figure 2–19, you can see that we have the iPhone SDK installed. We also have the Snow Leopard version of Xcode installed. If you don't have these installed, that is OK. Just navigate in the left pane of your template options to **Applications** and look for command line tool.

2. Select **Applications** on the left side pane, and select the **Command Line Tool** template. See Figure 2–19.

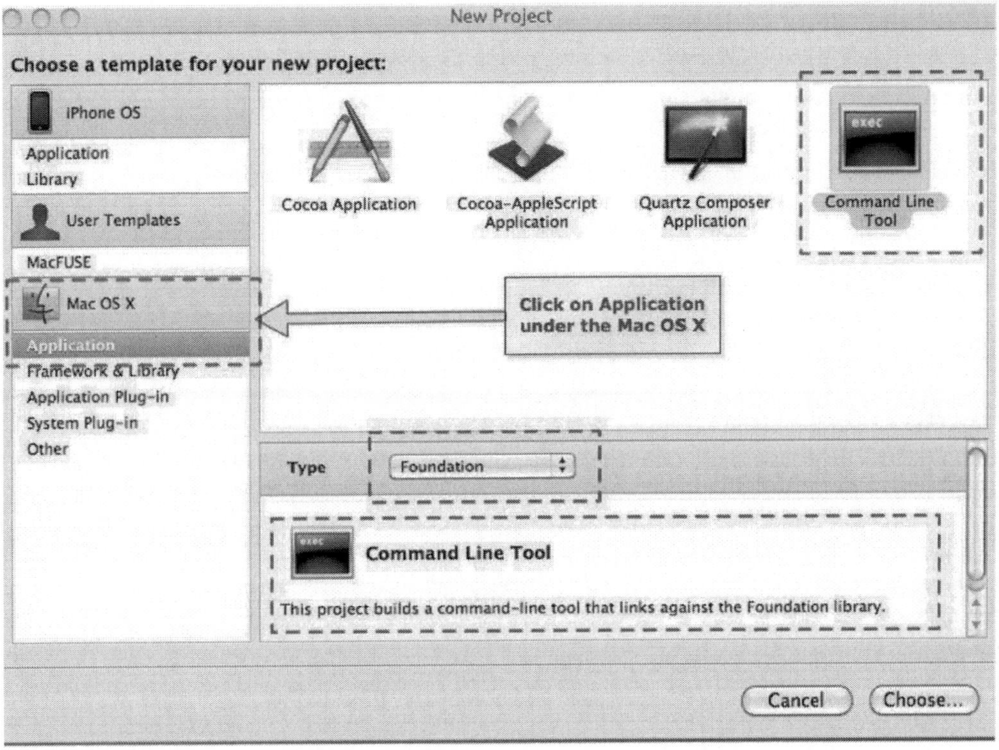

Figure 2–19. *Select Command Line Tool. You may have to navigate to an equivalent screen with other versions of Xcode. The bottom line is to navigate to Command Line tool.*

3. Let's name our app HelloWorld, as shown in Figure 2–20.

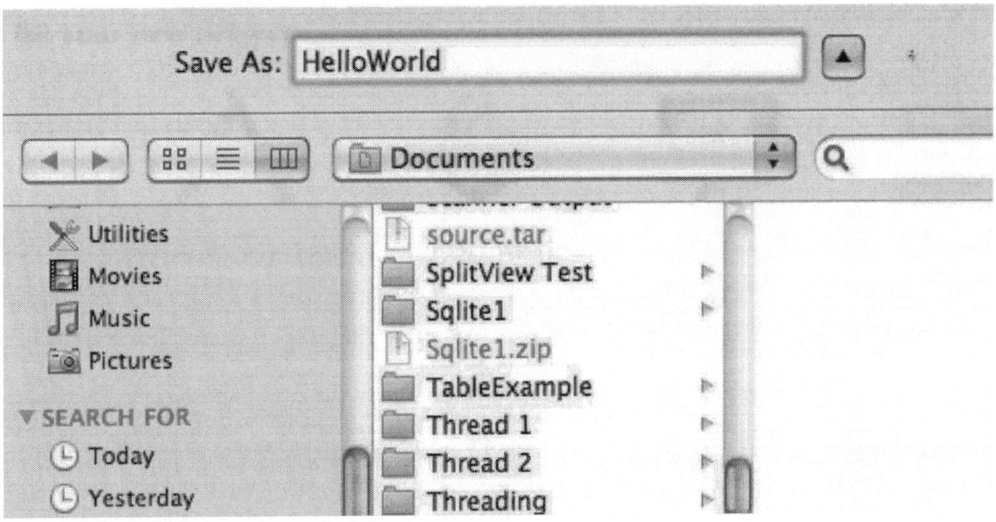

Figure 2–20. *This is our first app, so we practically have to name it HelloWorld.*

Xcode does a lot of work for us and creates a directory with files and code ready for us to use. That is what Xcode templates do—they save us a lot of time.

We need to become familiar with the Xcode IDE. Lets look at three of the most often used features (see Figure 2–21):

- Groups & Files section
- Editor section
- **Build and Run** button

These sections should look similar to what we used in our Alice Interface. The **Groups & Files** section contains files needed to build our apps. It will contain our classes, methods, and recourses.

The **Editor** section is the business end of the Xcode IDE, where our dreams are turned into reality. The editor section is where we write our code. You will notice that as you write your code, it will change colors. Sometimes, Xcode will even try to auto-complete words for you. The colors have meanings that will become apparent as we use the IDE. The editor section will also be the place where we debug our apps.

> **NOTE:** Even if we've mentioned it already, it is worth saying again. You will learn Objective-C programming by reading this book. You will really learn Objective-C by debugging your apps. Debugging is where developers learn and become great developers.

The **Build and Run** button turns our code from plain text to a `.app` that our Macs, iPhones or iPads know how to execute. With our Alice interface we used the play button to run our Alice app.

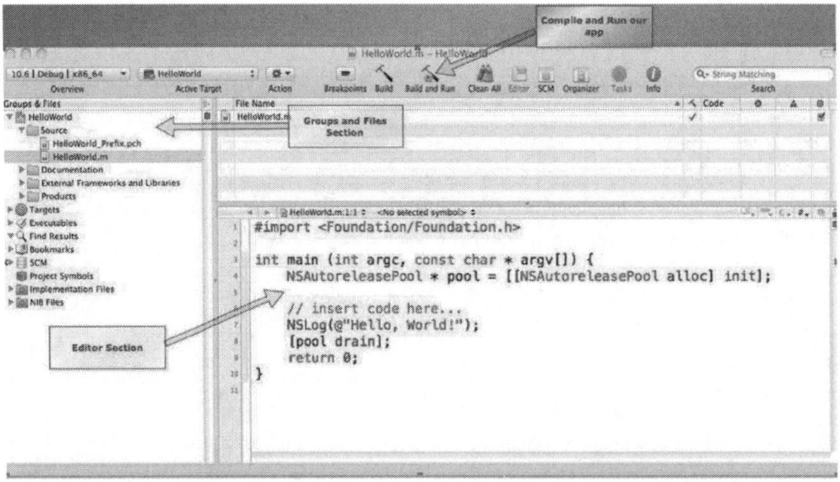

Figure 2–21. *The first three items we will be using in Xcode are the Editor section, Groups & Files section, and the Build and Run button (to compile and run our app). You can run the app right after creating the project by clicking the Build and Run button and seeing "Hello World!" printed out to the console.*

To run our first program, simply click the **Build and Run** button. Xcode checks our code syntax, compiles our app, and if no errors are found, makes a .app file and runs it. This application runs in a console or terminal.

When the app runs, it prints out "Hello World" to the console. Also, in the console window, we can see if the application terminated and why it terminated. In this case, it terminated normally. We can see this with the message, "Programmed exited with status value:0", meaning our app didn't crash. See Figure 2–22.

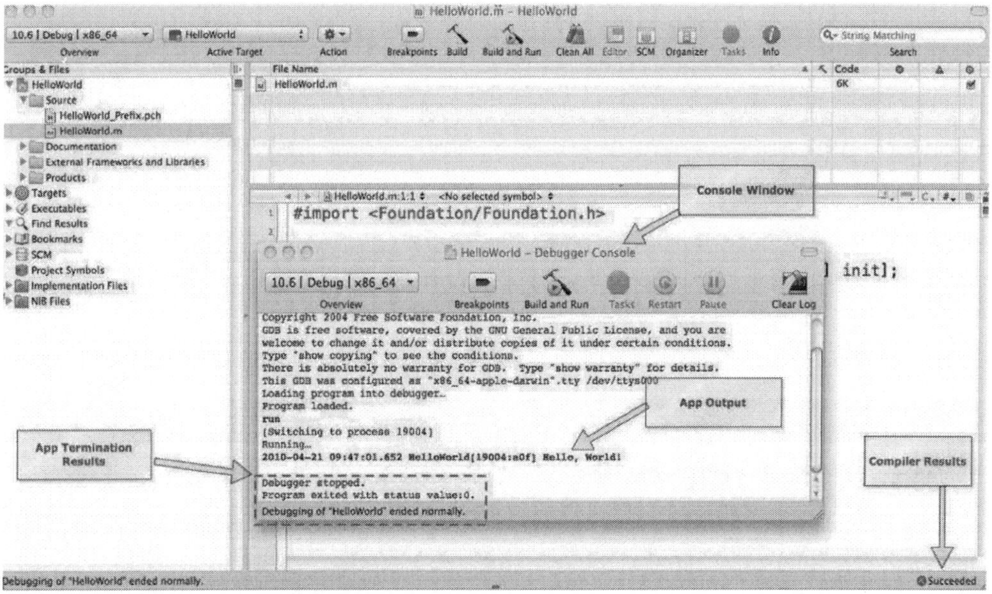

Figure 2–22. *Our app executing in the Debugger Console.*

Let's modify our application to do what we did with our astronauts:

1. Navigate to the HelloWorld.m file.

2. Change lines 7 and 8 to be as shown in Figure 2–23.

3. We are going to intentionally misplace a semicolon at the end line 8. This will cause a compiler error.

4. Click the **Build and Run** button.

You can see that something went wrong when we try to compile and run our app. We have a compiler error, a red pointer, and the notices in the Xcode IDE denote this. See Figure 2–23.

When we write Objective-C code, everything is important—even semicolons, capitalization, and parentheses. The collection of rules that enable our compiler to compile our code to an executable app is called **syntax**.

NSLog is a function that will print out the contents of its parameters to the console.

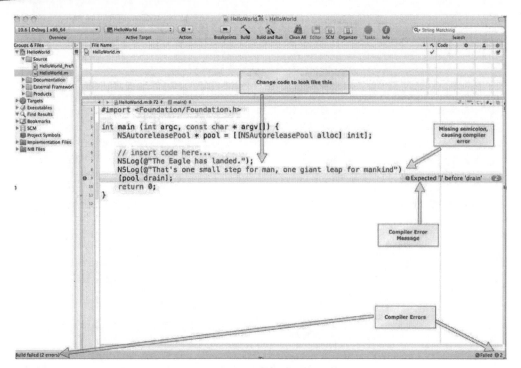

Figure 2–23. *Our app with a syntax error caught by our Objective-C compiler*

Now, let's fix our app by adding the semicolon at the end of line 8. Building and running the app will enable us to see the output to the debug console. See Figure 2–24.

Feel free to play around and change the text that is printed out. Have fun!

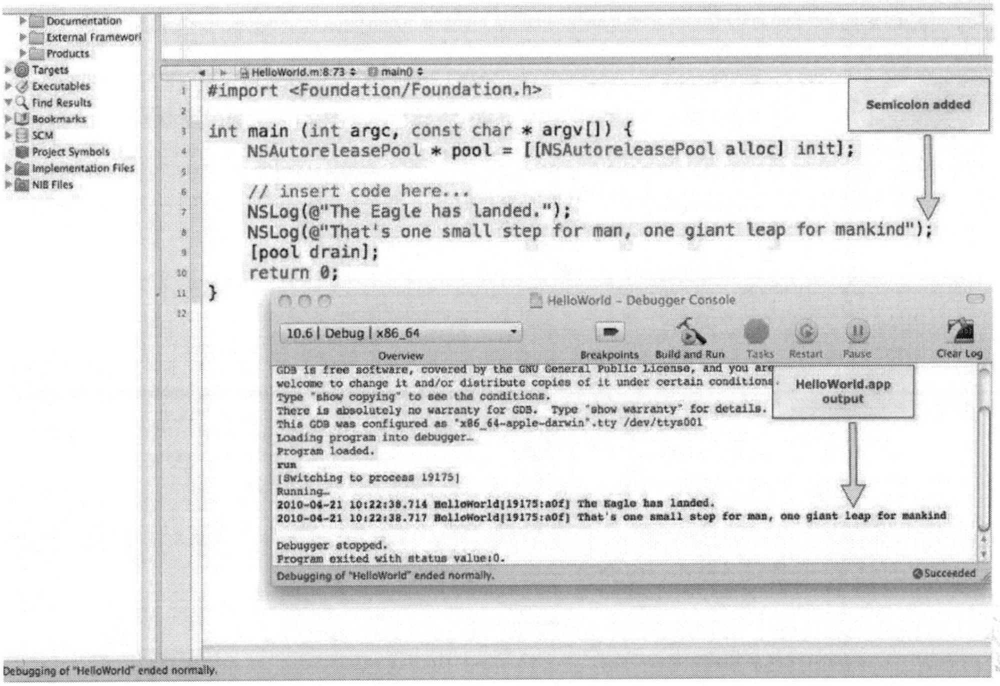

Figure 2–24. *Our app compiled with no compiler errors and completion executed successfully with the output we wanted.*

Summary

In this chapter, we have built our first Alice app. We also installed Xcode and compiled, debugged, and ran our first Objective-C app together. We also covered new OOP terms that are key for us to Objective-C.

The terms that you should understand follow:

- Classes
- Objects
- Methods
- Parameters
- Instances
- Instantiation

Exercises

- Extend your toTheMoonAlice.a2w Alice app. Place another object of your choosing in the world and have the object say something to the two astronauts when they are finished speaking.

- Extend your Objective-C HelloWorld.app by adding a third line of code that prints to the console any text of your choosing.

Chapter 3

It's All About the Data

As you probably know, data is stored as zeros and ones in your computer's memory. However, zeros and ones are not very useful to developers or app users, so we need to know how our program uses data and how data is stored on our computer.

In this chapter, we will look at how data is stored on computers and how we can manipulate that data. Then we'll write a fun Alice app illustrating data storage, and then write the same Alice app in Objective-C. So let's get started!

Numbering Systems Used in Programming

Computers work with information differently than do humans. This section covers the various ways information is stored, tallied, and manipulated by devices such as your Mac, iPhone, and iPad.

Bits

A **bit** is defined as the basic unit of information used by computers to store and manipulate data. A bit has a value of either **0** or **1**. When computers were first introduced, transistors and microprocessors didn't exist. Data was manipulated and stored by vacuum tubes being turned on or off. If the vacuum tube was on, the value of the bit was 1, and if the vacuum tube was off, the value was zero. The amount of data a computer was able to store and manipulate was directly related to how many vacuum tubes the computer had.

The first recognized computer was called the ENIAC. It took up more than 136 square meters and had 18,000 vacuum tubes. It was about as powerful as your handheld calculator.

Today, computers use transistors to store and manipulate data. The power of a computer processor depends on how many transistors are placed on its chip or CPU. Like the vacuum tube, transistors have an off or on state. When the transistor is off, its value is 0. If the transistor is on, its value is 1. At the time of this writing, the A4 processor that comes on all iPhone 3GS, iPhone 4, and iPads has up to 149 million transistors. See Figure 3–1.

Figure 3–1. *Apple's proprietary A4 processor*

Moore's Law

The number of transistors on your iPhone's or iPad's processor is directly related to your device's processing speed, memory capacity, and the sensors (accelerometer, gyroscope) available on the device. The more transistors, the more powerful your device is.

In 1965, the cofounder of Intel, Gordon E. Moore, described the trend of transistors in a processor. He observed that the number of transistors in a processor doubled every 18 months from 1958 to 1965, and would likely continue "for at least 18 months." The observation became famously known as "Moore's Law" and has proven accurate for more than 55 years. See Figure 3–2.

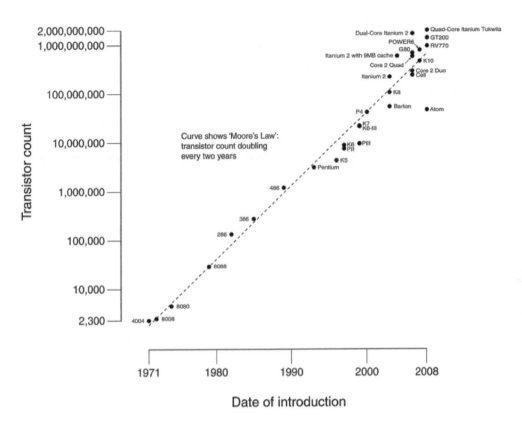

Figure 3–2. *Moore's Law*

> **NOTE:** There is a downside to Moore's Law, and you have probably felt it in your pocket book. The problem with rapidly increasing processing capability is that it renders technology obsolete quickly. So when your iPhone's two-year cell phone contract is up, the new iPhones on the market will be twice as powerful as the iPhone you had when you signed up. How convenient for everyone!

Bytes

A byte is another unit used to describe information storage on computers. A **byte** is composed of 8 bits and is a convenient power of 2. Whereas a bit can represent up to two different values, a byte can represent up to 2^8 or 256 different values. A byte can contain values from 0–255.

> **NOTE:** In Chapter 12, we discuss in more detail Base-2, Base-10, and Base-16 number systems. However, it is necessary to have an introduction to these systems in this chapter to understand data types.

The **binary** number system represents numerical symbols, 0 and 1. To illustrate how the number **71** would be represented in binary, we will use a simple table of 8 bits (1 byte) with each bit represented as a power of 2. To convert the byte value **01000111** to decimal, simply add the on bits. See Table 3–1.

Table 3–1. *The number 71 represented as a byte*

Power to 2	2^7	2^6	2^5	2^4	2^3	2^2	2^1	2^0
Possible value for "**on**" bit	128	64	32	16	8	4	2	1
Actual bit	0	1	0	0	0	1	1	1

To represent the number **22** in binary, turn on the bits that add up to 22 or **00010110**. See Table 3–2.

Table 3–2. *The number 22 represented as a byte*

Power to 2	2^7	2^6	2^5	2^4	2^3	2^2	2^1	2^0
Possible value for "**on**" bit	128	64	32	16	8	4	2	1
Actual bit	0	0	0	1	0	1	1	0

To represent the number **255** in binary, turn on the bits that add up to 255 or **11111111**. See Table 3–3.

Table 3–3. *The number 255 represented as a byte*

Power to 2	2^7	2^6	2^5	2^4	2^3	2^2	2^1	2^0
Possible value for "**on**" bit	128	64	32	16	8	4	2	1
Actual bit	1	1	1	1	1	1	1	1

To represent the number **0** in binary, turn on the bits that add up to 0 or **00000000**. See Table 3–4.

Table 3–4. *The number 0 represented as a byte*

Power to 2	2^7	2^6	2^5	2^4	2^3	2^2	2^1	2^0
Possible value for "**on**" bit	128	64	32	16	8	4	2	1
Actual bit	0	0	0	0	0	0	0	0

Hexadecimal

Often it will be necessary to represent characters in another format that is recognized by computers, a hexadecimal. You will encounter hexadecimal numbers when you are debugging your apps. **Hexadecimal** is a base-16 number system. It uses 16 distinct symbols, 0–9 to represent values zero to nine, and A, B, C, D, E, and F to represent values 10 to 15. For example, the hexadecimal number 2AF3 is equal, in decimal, to $(2 \times 16^3) + (10 \times 162) + (15 \times 161) + (3 \times 160)$, or 10,995. Figure 3–3 represents the ASCII table of characters. Because 1 byte can represent 256 characters, this works great for Western characters. For example, hexadecimal 20 represents a space. Hexadecimal 7D represents a ")".

Dec	Hx	Oct	Char		Dec	Hx	Oct	Html	Chr	Dec	Hx	Oct	Html	Chr	Dec	Hx	Oct	Html	Chr
0	0	000	NUL	(null)	32	20	040	 	Space	64	40	100	@	@	96	60	140	`	`
1	1	001	SOH	(start of heading)	33	21	041	!	!	65	41	101	A	A	97	61	141	a	a
2	2	002	STX	(start of text)	34	22	042	"	"	66	42	102	B	B	98	62	142	b	b
3	3	003	ETX	(end of text)	35	23	043	#	#	67	43	103	C	C	99	63	143	c	c
4	4	004	EOT	(end of transmission)	36	24	044	$	$	68	44	104	D	D	100	64	144	d	d
5	5	005	ENQ	(enquiry)	37	25	045	%	%	69	45	105	E	E	101	65	145	e	e
6	6	006	ACK	(acknowledge)	38	26	046	&	&	70	46	106	F	F	102	66	146	f	f
7	7	007	BEL	(bell)	39	27	047	'	'	71	47	107	G	G	103	67	147	g	g
8	8	010	BS	(backspace)	40	28	050	(	(	72	48	110	H	H	104	68	150	h	h
9	9	011	TAB	(horizontal tab)	41	29	051	)	)	73	49	111	I	I	105	69	151	i	i
10	A	012	LF	(NL line feed, new line)	42	2A	052	*	*	74	4A	112	J	J	106	6A	152	j	j
11	B	013	VT	(vertical tab)	43	2B	053	+	+	75	4B	113	K	K	107	6B	153	k	k
12	C	014	FF	(NP form feed, new page)	44	2C	054	,	,	76	4C	114	L	L	108	6C	154	l	l
13	D	015	CR	(carriage return)	45	2D	055	-	-	77	4D	115	M	M	109	6D	155	m	m
14	E	016	SO	(shift out)	46	2E	056	.	.	78	4E	116	N	N	110	6E	156	n	n
15	F	017	SI	(shift in)	47	2F	057	/	/	79	4F	117	O	O	111	6F	157	o	o
16	10	020	DLE	(data link escape)	48	30	060	0	0	80	50	120	P	P	112	70	160	p	p
17	11	021	DC1	(device control 1)	49	31	061	1	1	81	51	121	Q	Q	113	71	161	q	q
18	12	022	DC2	(device control 2)	50	32	062	2	2	82	52	122	R	R	114	72	162	r	r
19	13	023	DC3	(device control 3)	51	33	063	3	3	83	53	123	S	S	115	73	163	s	s
20	14	024	DC4	(device control 4)	52	34	064	4	4	84	54	124	T	T	116	74	164	t	t
21	15	025	NAK	(negative acknowledge)	53	35	065	5	5	85	55	125	U	U	117	75	165	u	u
22	16	026	SYN	(synchronous idle)	54	36	066	6	6	86	56	126	V	V	118	76	166	v	v
23	17	027	ETB	(end of trans. block)	55	37	067	7	7	87	57	127	W	W	119	77	167	w	w
24	18	030	CAN	(cancel)	56	38	070	8	8	88	58	130	X	X	120	78	170	x	x
25	19	031	EM	(end of medium)	57	39	071	9	9	89	59	131	Y	Y	121	79	171	y	y
26	1A	032	SUB	(substitute)	58	3A	072	:	:	90	5A	132	Z	Z	122	7A	172	z	z
27	1B	033	ESC	(escape)	59	3B	073	;	;	91	5B	133	[	[	123	7B	173	{	{
28	1C	034	FS	(file separator)	60	3C	074	<	<	92	5C	134	\	\	124	7C	174	|		
29	1D	035	GS	(group separator)	61	3D	075	=	=	93	5D	135	]	]	125	7D	175	}	}
30	1E	036	RS	(record separator)	62	3E	076	>	>	94	5E	136	^	^	126	7E	176	~	~
31	1F	037	US	(unit separator)	63	3F	077	?	?	95	5F	137	_	_	127	7F	177	&#127;	DEL

Source: www.LookupTables.com

128	Ç	144	É	161	í	177	▒	193	┴	209	╤	225	ß	241	±
129	ü	145	æ	162	ó	178	▓	194	┬	210	╥	226	Γ	242	≥
130	é	146	Æ	163	ú	179	│	195	├	211	╙	227	π	243	≤
131	â	147	ô	164	ñ	180	┤	196	─	212	╘	228	Σ	244	⌠
132	ä	148	ö	165	Ñ	181	╡	197	┼	213	╒	229	σ	245	⌡
133	à	149	ò	166	ª	182	╢	198	╞	214	╓	230	µ	246	÷
134	å	150	û	167	º	183	╖	199	╟	215	╫	231	τ	247	≈
135	ç	151	ù	168	¿	184	╕	200	╚	216	╪	232	Φ	248	°
136	ê	152	ÿ	169	⌐	185	╣	201	╔	217	┘	233	Θ	249	∙
137	ë	153	Ö	170	¬	186	║	202	╩	218	┌	234	Ω	250	·
138	è	154	Ü	171	½	187	╗	203	╦	219	█	235	δ	251	√
139	ï	156	£	172	¼	188	╝	204	╠	220	▄	236	∞	252	ⁿ
140	î	157	¥	173	¡	189	╜	205	═	221	▌	237	φ	253	²
141	ì	158	₧	174	«	190	╛	206	╬	222	▐	238	ε	254	■
142	Ä	159	ƒ	175	»	191	┐	207	╧	223	▀	239	∩	255	
143	Å	160	á	176	░	192	└	208	╨	224	α	240	≡		

Source: www.LookupTables.com

Figure 3–3. *ASCII Character*

Unicode

Representing characters with a byte worked great for computers until about the 1990s, when the personal computer became widely adopted in non-Western countries where languages have more than 256 characters. Instead of a one-byte character set, Unicode can have up to a 4 bytes character set.

In order to facilitate faster adoption, the first 256 code points are indicial to the ASCII character table. Unicode can have different character encodings. The most common encoding used for Western text is called UTF-8. As an iPhone developer, you will probably use this character encodings the most.

Data Types

Now that we've discussed how computers manipulate data, we need to cover a very important concept called **data types**. Humans can generally just look at data and the context in which it is being used to determine what type of data it is and how it will be used. Computers need to be told how to do this. The programmer needs to tell the computer the type of data that it is being given. For example

```
2 + 2 = 4
```

The computer needs to know that you want to add two numbers together. In this example they are integers. You might first believe that adding these numbers is obvious to even the most casual observer, let alone a sophisticated computer. However, it is common for users of iPhone apps to store data as a series of characters, not a calculation. For example, a text message might read

```
"Everyone knows that 2 + 2 = 4"
```

In this case we are using our previous example in a series of characters called a **string**. A **data type** is simply the declaration to our program that defines the data we want to store. A **variable** is used to store our data and is declared with an associated data type. All data is stored in a variable, and the variable has to have a variable type. For example, in Objective-C the following is variable declarations with their associated data types:

```
int x = 10;
int y = 2;
int z = 0;
char prefix = 'c';
NSString *submarineName  = @"USS Nevada SSBN-733";
```

Data types cannot be mixed with one another. You cannot do the following:

```
z = x + submarineName;
```

Mixing data types will cause either compiler warnings or compiler errors, and your app will not run.

Most data that you will use in your programs can be classified in three different types: Booleans, numbers and objects. We will discuss how to work with numbers and object data types in the remainder of this chapter. In Chapter 4, we will talk more about Boolean data types when we write apps with decision-making.

> **NOTE:** Localizing your app is the process of writing your app so users can buy and use it in their native language. This process is too advanced for this book, but it is a simple one to complete when you plan from the beginning. Localizing your app greatly expands the total number of potential customers and revenue for your app without your having to rewrite it for each language. Be sure to localize your app. It is not hard to do and can easily double or triple the number of people who buy it.

Using Variable and Data Types with Alice

Now that we have learned about data types, let's write an Alice app that that adds two numbers, prints out the value to the console, and then has a character object tell us the program is done.

1. Open Alice and select File ➤ New World.

2. Select the Grass template and click Open. See Figure 3–4.

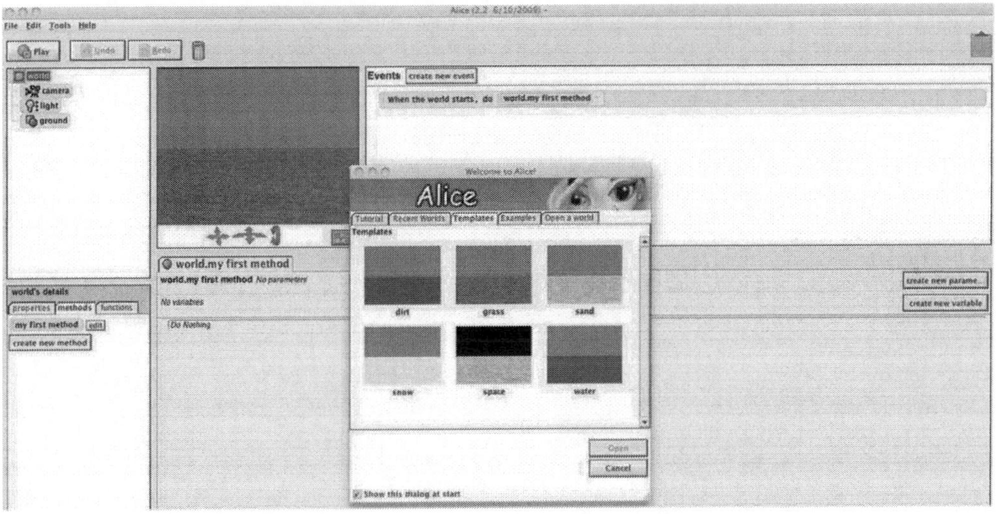

Figure 3–4. *Choosing the Grass template*

Next we need to make our variables and select that data types.

3. Click on "**create new variable**" at the top right of your editor. Name your first variable "**firstNumber**" and define the variable as shown Figure 3–5 The variable's data type is a number. It is initialized with the value of 2 and is shown in the header section.

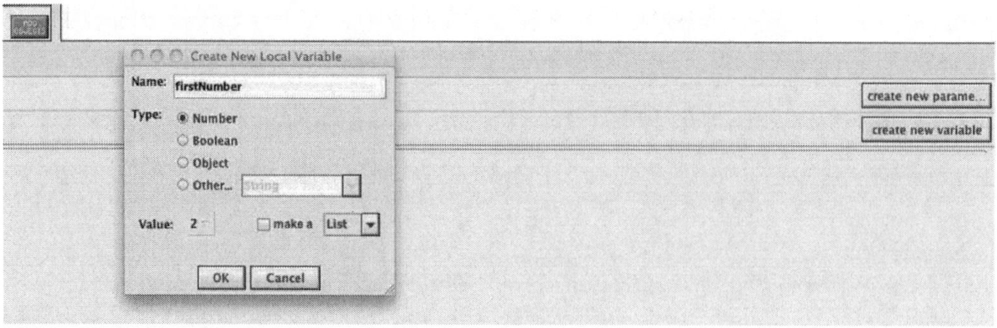

Figure 3–5. *Creating a new local variable*

It is always good programming practice to initialize our variables when they are declared.

4. Create another variable called "**secondNumber**" as shown in Figure 3–6. The variable's data type is a number, is initialized with the value of 3, and is shown in the header section.

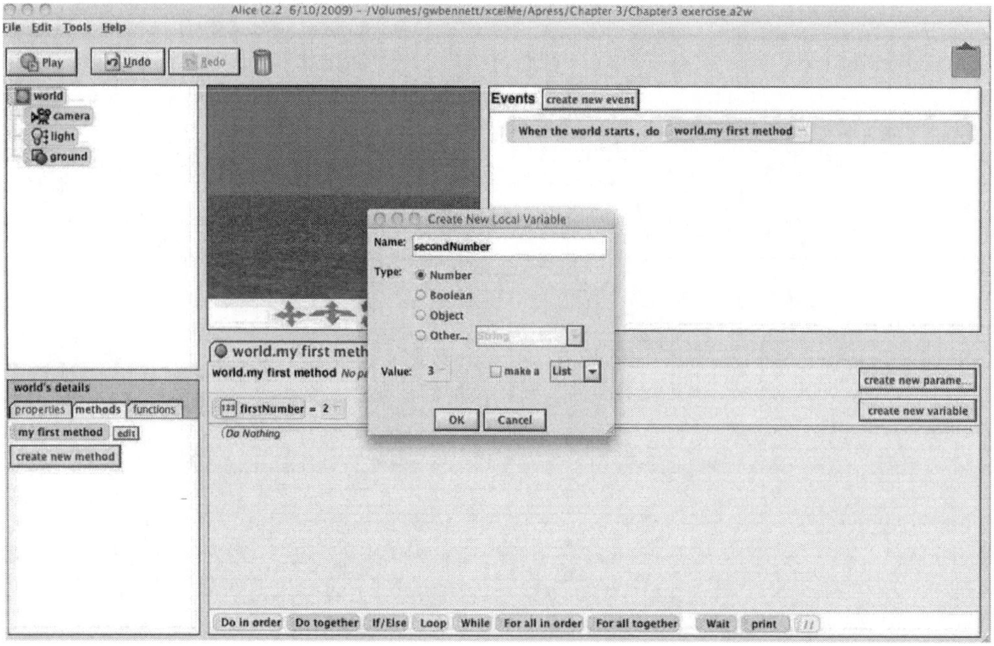

Figure 3–6. *Creating a second local variable*

5. Drag your variables from the header section to the program section, and increment each variable by 1. See Figure 3–7.

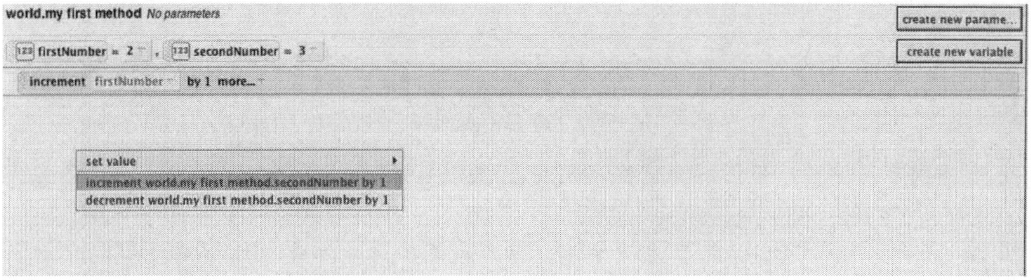

Figure 3–7. *Increment each variable by 1.*

Create a variable to hold the sum. Select Create new variable" and call your variable totalSum. See Figure 3–8.

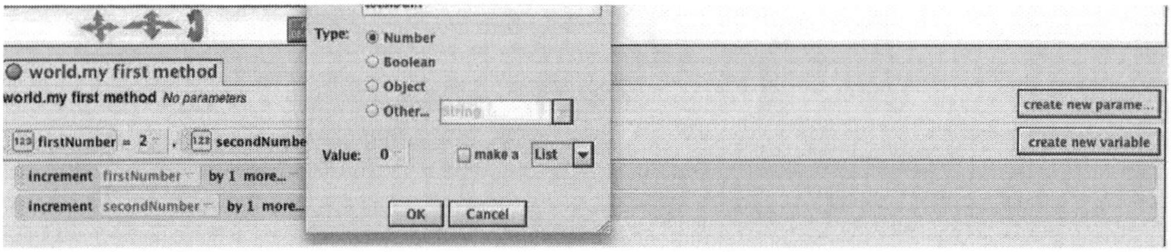

Figure 3–8. *Creating the variable totalSum*

6. Add your two variables together. Drag the totalSum variable from the header section to the program section and set the value to math expressions as shown in Figure 3–9. The math expression will then populate the list box with the instance variables in your object and possible math expressions.

7. Select firstNumber +.

8. Select secondNumber.

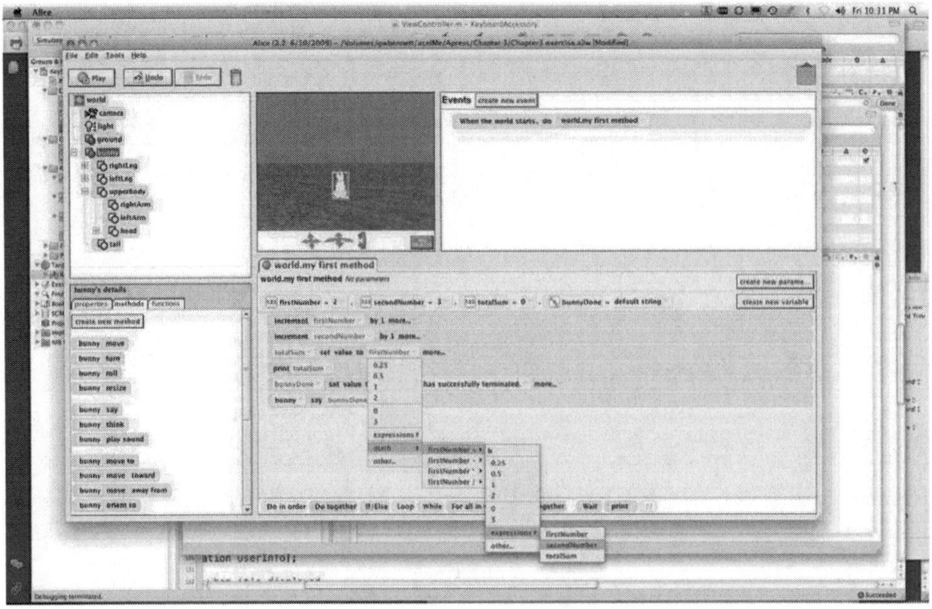

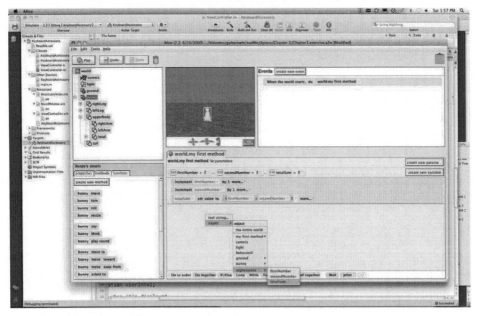

Figure 3–9. *Setting the value to math expressions*

9. Print out the totalSum to the console. Drag the print tile from the bottom of the editor. Select totalSum as a parameter. See Figure 3–10.

Figure 3–10. *Selecting totalSum*

10. Add an object to our World. Click on Add Objects and then add any object of your choosing. We have selected a bunny. See Figure 3–11.

Figure 3–11. *Adding a bunny to our world*

We need to declare a variable that will contain a data type of type **String**. The variable will hold the string, "The program has terminated successfully."

11. Click on the "create new variable" button and create the bunnyDone variable of type String. See Figure 3–12.

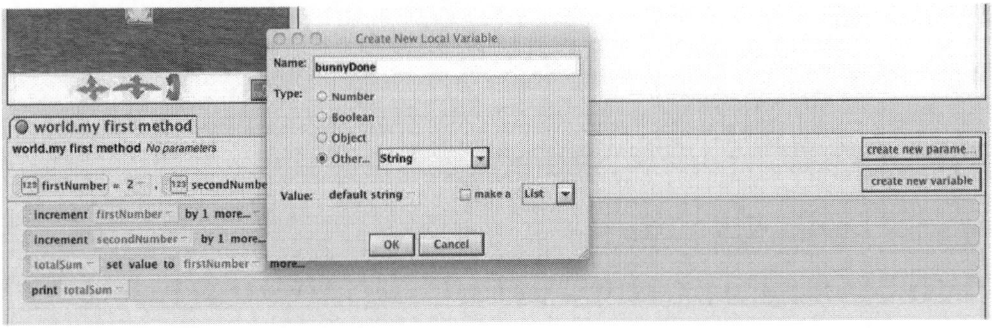

Figure 3–12. *Creating the bunnyDone variable*

We want to assign a string to our bunnyDone variable.

12. Drag the bunnyDone variable to the last line of our editor. Enter "The program has terminated successfully" as the last parameter. See Figure 3–13.

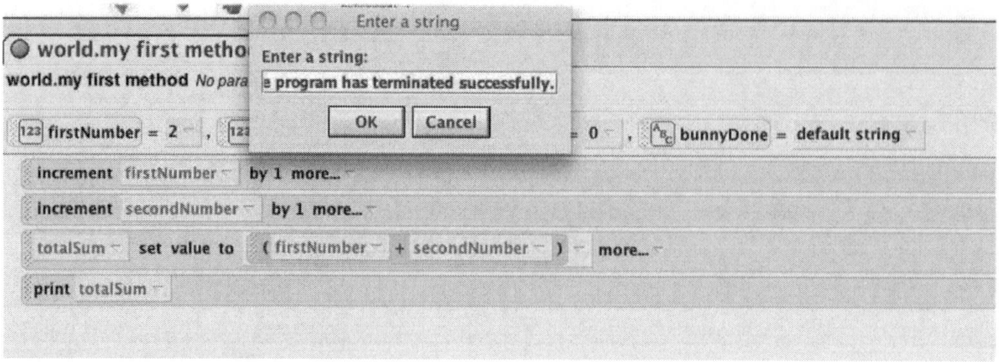

Figure 3–13. *Entering the final parameter*

Now we want the bunny to announce that our app successfully completed running.

13. Make sure you selected the Object in the object tree that you added to the to your world. Drag the "bunny say" tile from the bunny methods to your editor and select the variable bunnyDone as its parameter. See Figure 3–14.

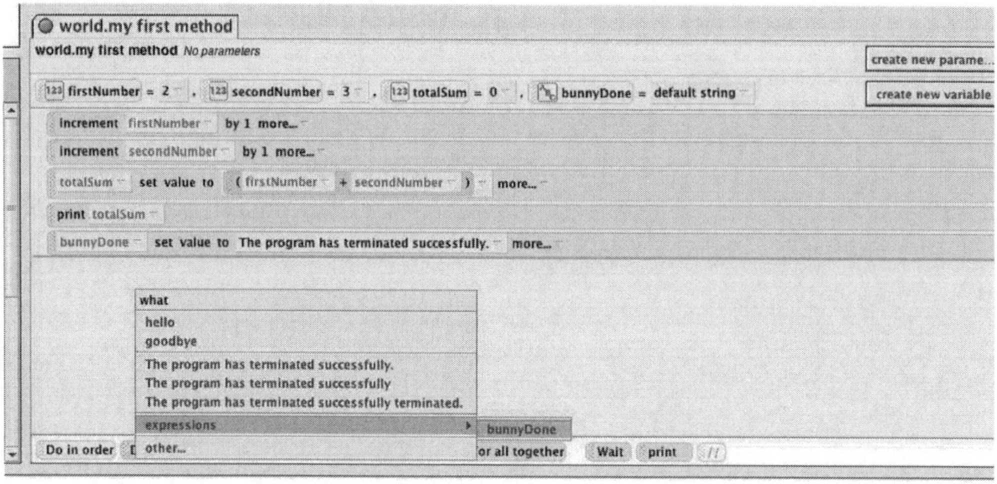

Figure 3–14. *Selecting bunnyDone as parameter*

If we ran our app now, we would notice the bunny's message would disappear quickly.

14. Drag the "wait" function from the bottom of your editor to the last line of your code. The wait function takes one parameter, which is the number of seconds to pause the program. We've selected a three-second wait in our app.

Now we are ready to play the app! You editor section should look like Figure 3–15.

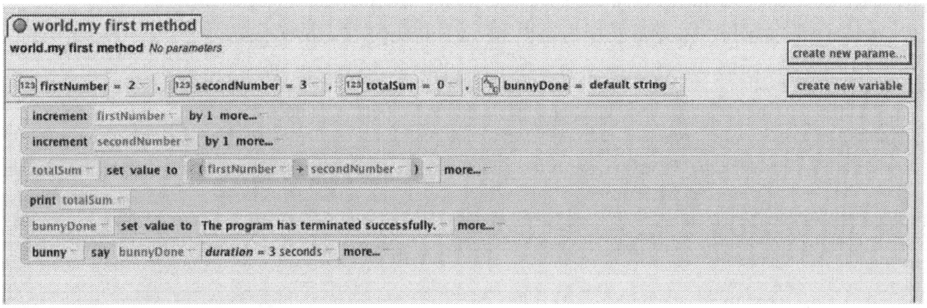

Figure 3–15. *The editor section*

15. Press the play button and, if you've done everything correctly, your app should look like Figure 3–16 when it runs. The value of the variable totalSum is displayed to the console, and your bunny is announcing that your app ran successfully.

Figure 3–16. *The app has run successfully!*

Data Types and Objective-C

Now that we have covered the principles of data types and have written an Alice app to help show how these principles apply, let's write an Objective-C app that accomplishes what we just did in Alice.

In Objective-C we have similar data types as we did with Alice. Some of the most frequently used data types for storing numbers are integers, doubles, floats, and longs. Table 3–5 lists many of the basic data types. Many of these will be covered in later chapters.

Table 3–5. *Objective-C basic data types*

Type	Examples	NSLog chars
char	'a', '0','\n'	%c
int	42, -42, 550 0xCCE0, 099	%i, %d, %x, %o
unsigned int	20u, 101U, 0xFEu	%u, %x, %o
long int	13,-2010, 0xfefeL	%ld, %lx, %lo
unsigned long int	12UL, 100ul, 0xffeeUL	%lu, %lx, %lo
long long int	0xe5e5e5LL, 501ll	%lld, %llx, %llo
unsigned long long int	11ull, 0xffeeULL	%llu, %llx, %llo
float	12.30f, 3.2e-5f, 0x2.2p09	%f, %e, %g, %a
double	3.1415, 3.1e-5l	%f, %e, %g, %a
long double	3.1415, 3.1e-5l	%Lf, %Le, %Lg, %a
id	Nil	%p

Our Objective-C app will add two integers, display their sum to the console. The app will also display the text "The program has successfully terminated." This will be fun and easy, so let's get started.

> **NOTE:** In June 2010 Apple changed the way it names the versions of its operating systems for the mobile devices. Instead of iPhone 3.1 SDK or iPhone 3.2 SDK (iPad), Apple changed its latest version and naming convention to iOS 4. Additionally, some of the popular Apple insider sites are reporting that Apple is considering similar naming conventions for its Mac OS X operating system for the desktop and laptops. We mention this so you are not confused with the older and newer naming conventions that you may come across as you read development sites and books.

1. As iOS developers, Xcode is where we make our living, so open up Xcode and create a new project. To do so, select **File ➤ New project** and select the options shown in Figure 3–17.

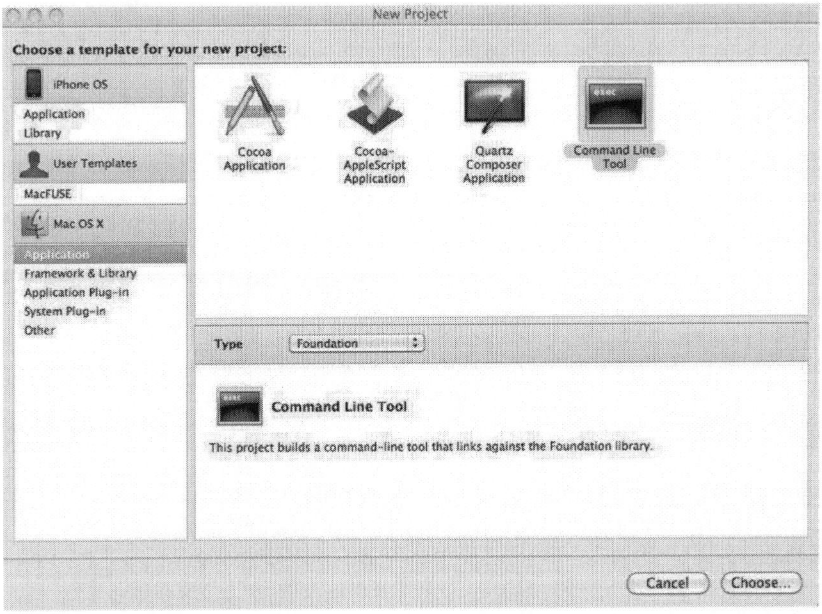

Figure 3–17. *Opening a new project*

NOTE: One of the most common issues new students have when creating a command line app is finding the project in their version of Xcode. Figure 3–17 shows Xcode Version 3.2 on Snow Leopard (10.6). Your version of Xcode may be newer or older, and menus and selections options may be different. So, look around in the **File ➤ New project** settings for the equivalent options. If you have difficulty finding these options, visit our forum for this book at forum.xcelme.com and go to this chapter. We will be happy to answer your questions.

When created, your Xcode project should look like Figure 3–18.

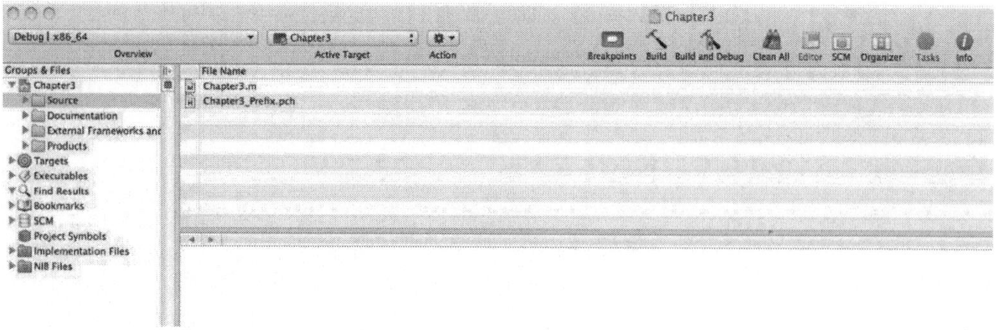

Figure 3–18. *Your XCode project*

2. After you create the project, you need to **open** your source code file in your editor. We named the project **Chapter3**, so open the Source group, and we can access the Chapter3.m source file. Open the Chapter3.m source file.

If you haven't seen "//" used in computer programming before, it enables the programmer to comment his or her code. Comments are not compiled by our applications and are used as notes for the programmer or, more important, programmers who follow the original developer. Comments help both the original developer and follow-up developer understand how the app was developed.

Sometimes it is necessary for comments to span several lines or just part of a line. This can be accomplished with the **/* and the */.** All the text between the **/*** and the ***/** are treated as comments and are not compiled.

First we need to declare and initialize our variables **firstNumber** and **secondNumber**. It is good practice to always initialize variables when they are declared, or soon afterwards.

Increment the variables **firstNumber** and **secondNumber** by 1. We'll print the sum of **firstNumber** and **secondNumber**.

3. Finally, we will print to the console, "The program has successfully terminated." See Figure 3–19.

NSLog is a function that can take one or more parameters. The first parameter is generally the string that is to be printed to the console. The @ symbol in front of the string tells the compiler that this is an Objective-C type string and not a C++ string. The @ symbol is typically used in front of all your strings for iPhone apps. If you don't use the @ symbol, you will probably get a compiler error.

%d tells the compiler that an integer will be printed and to substitute the value of the integer for the %d. See Table 3–6 for other NSLog formatting specifiers. Finally, our second parameter is the integer to be printed.

NSLog is a very helpful function used by developers to test their codes execution.

```
#import <Foundation/Foundation.h>


int main (int argc, const char * argv[]) {
    NSAutoreleasePool * pool = [[NSAutoreleasePool alloc] init];

    // insert code here...
    //declare and initialize variables
    int firstNumber = 2;
    int secondNumber = 3;
    int totalSum = 0;
    firstNumber = firstNumber + 1;
    secondNumber = secondNumber + 1;
    totalSum = firstNumber + secondNumber;
    NSLog(@"%d",totalSum);
    NSLog(@"The program has terminated successfully.");
    [pool drain];
    return 0;
}
```

Figure 3–19. *Printing to the console*

Figure 3–20 shows the completed executed output of our application.

4. To compile and run your application, click on the "Build and Run" option for your toolbar. We can see values that we printed out the NSLog sting along with the notice at the end by the debugger that the apps execution completed successfully.

NOTE: If your editor doesn't have the same menus or gutter that you see in the previous screenshots, you can turn these settings on in the Xcode preferences. You can open the Xcode Preferences by clicking on Xcode menu in the menu bar and then selecting Preferences. You can also customize the toolbar by right-clicking on the toolbar itself and selecting "Customize Toolbars and Menus...".

```
○ ○ ○                        Chapter3 – Debugger Console

Debug | x86_64          ▾        ▬         ⚒         ●         ⓒ         ⵚ                🖼
              Overview                Breakpoints  Build and Run  Tasks  Restart   Pause           Clear Log

[Session started at 2010-06-26 18:19:28 -0700.]
GNU gdb 6.3.50-20050815 (Apple version gdb-1469) (Wed May  5 04:36:56 UTC 2010)
Copyright 2004 Free Software Foundation, Inc.
GDB is free software, covered by the GNU General Public License, and you are
welcome to change it and/or distribute copies of it under certain conditions.
Type "show copying" to see the conditions.
There is absolutely no warranty for GDB.  Type "show warranty" for details.
This GDB was configured as "x86_64-apple-darwin".tty /dev/ttys000
Loading program into debugger…
Program loaded.
run
[Switching to process 91310]
Running…
2010-06-26 18:19:29.626 Chapter3[91310:a0f] 7
2010-06-26 18:19:29.629 Chapter3[91310:a0f] The program has terminated successfully.

Debugger stopped.
Program exited with status value:0.




Debugging of "Chapter3" ended normally.                                      Ⓢ Succeeded
```

Figure 3–20. *Console log displaying the results of our Objective-C app*

Identifying Problems

Believe it or not, your program may not run the way you thought you told it to. The process of hunting down problems with you app is called **debugging**. In order to track down bugs in our apps, we can set breakpoints and inspect our variables to see the contents. To do this, simply click in the left column of our code called the gutter, where the gutter is to set a breakpoint. See Figure 3–21. A breakpoint will stop our application from executing at that line and enable us to inspect our variables.

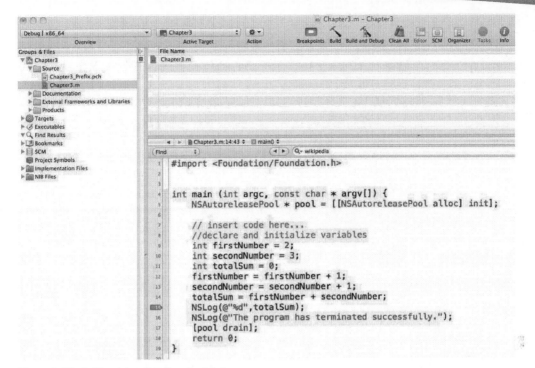

Figure 3–21. *Setting debugging "breakpoints"*

A blue pointer in the gutter of your editor denotes a breakpoint. When you run your application and your app hits a line of code that contains a breakpoint, your app will halt and display a blue line across the line of code with a breakpoint. See Figure 3–22.

Additionally, you can inspect each variable by hovering over it with your mouse.

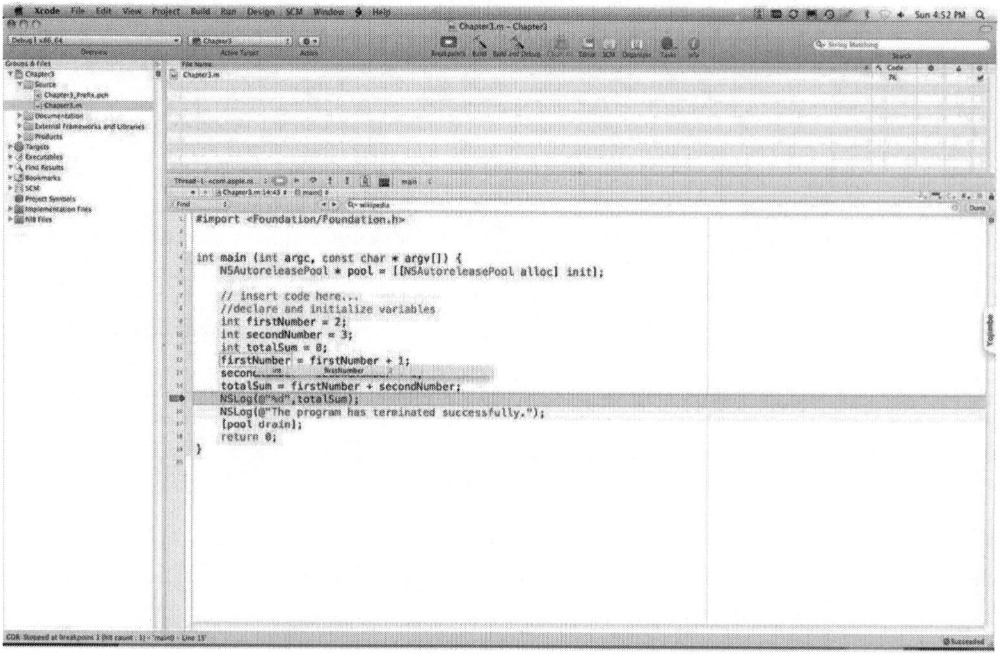

Figure 3–22. *Breakpoint detected!*

We will talk more about debugging your apps in Chapter 12.

Summary

In this chapter you learned about how data is used by our apps. You saw how to initialize variables and how to assigned data to them. We explained that when variables are declared they have a data type associated with them, and that only data of the same type can be assigned to variables.

Finally, we showed you how to use variables in your first Alice app, and finished by using variables with an Objective-C app.

Exercises

■ Write an Objective-C console app (Command-Line Tool) that multiples two integers together and displays the result to the console.

■ Write an Objective-C console app that squares a float. Display the resulting float in the console.

■ Write an Objective-C console app subtracts two floats with the result being stored in an integer. *Note that rounding does not occur.

Chapter 4

Making Decisions About…and Planning Program Flow

One of the cool things about being an iPhone/iPad and Mac developer is we get to tell the device exactly what we want it to do and the device will do it. The device will do it over and over again without getting tired. That's because iPhone/iPads and Macs don't care how hard they worked yesterday, and they don't let feelings get in the way. These devices don't need hugs.

There is a downside to being developer: we have to think of all possible outcomes in our apps. Many students love having this kind of control, and like focusing on the many details of their apps. However, it can be frustrating having to handle so many details. As we mentioned in the introduction to this book, there is a price to pay for developing apps, and that price is time. The more time you spend developing and debugging, the better you will get with all the details and the better your apps will run. Everyone has to pay this price to a successful developer.

Computers are black and white; there are no shades of gray. Our devices give results, and many of the results are based on true and false conditions.

In this chapter we will learn about computer logic and controlling the flow of our apps. The processing of information and arriving at results is at the heart of all apps. Our apps needs to process data based on values and conditions. In order to do this, we need to understand how computers perform logical operations and execute code based on the information our apps have acquired.

Boolean Logic

Boolean logic is a system for logical operations. Boolean logic uses binary operators like AND, OR, and the unary operator NOT to determine if your conditions are met. Binary operators take two operands. Unary operators take one operand. AND and OR are binary operator and NOT is a unary operator.

We just introduced a couple of new terms that can sound confusing. However, you probably use Boolean logic every day. Let's look a couple of examples of Boolean logic with the binary operators AND and OR in a conversation parents sometimes have with their teenage children.

"You can go to the movies tonight if your room is clean AND the dishes are put away."

"You can go to the movies tonight if your room is clean OR the dishes are put away."

Boolean operators result in a TRUE or a FALSE. In Chapter 3 we briefly introduced the Boolean data type. A variable that is defined as Boolean, can only contain the values, TRUE and FALSE.

```
BOOL seeMovies = FALSE;
```

In the first example above, the AND operator takes two operands, one on the left and one of the right of the AND. Each operand can be evaluated independently with a TRUE or FALSE.

For the AND operation to yield a TRUE result, both sides of the AND have to be TRUE. In the example, the teenager has to clean his or her room AND have the dishes done. If either one of the conditions is FALSE the result is FALSE and no movies for the teenager.

For an OR operation to yield a TRUE result, only one operand has to be TRUE or both conditions can be TRUE to yield a TRUE result. In the second example, just a clean bedroom would result in the ability to go to the movies.

> **NOTE:** Behind the scenes, your iPhone/iPad/Mac defines a FALSE as a 0 and a TRUE as a 1. To be technically correct, a TRUE is defined as any non-zero value. So a value of 0.1, 1, and 2 would be evaluated as a TRUE when evaluated in a Boolean expression.

A NOT statement is a unary operator. It takes just one operand to yield a Boolean result. For example:

"You can NOT go to the movies."

This example takes one operand. The NOT operator, turns a TRUE operand to FALSE and a FALSE operand to a TRUE. Here the result is a FALSE.

> **NOTE:** Performing a NOT operation is commonly referred to as flipping-the-bit, or negating. Because TRUE is defined as a 1, a FALSE is defined as a 0, and zeros and ones are referred to bits. A NOT operation turns a TRUE to a FALSE and a FALSE to a TRUE, hence flipping-the-bit or negating the result.

AND, OR, and NOT are three very common Boolean operators. Occasionally, you need to use more complex operators. XOR, NAND, and NOR operators are common for iPhone/iPad and Mac developers.

The Boolean operator XOR means *exclusive or*. An easy way to remember how the XOR operator works is the XOR operator will return a TRUE result if only 1 argument is TRUE not both.

NAND and NOR mean NOT AND and NOT OR. After evaluating the AND or the OR arguments and result, simply flip-the-bit of the result.

Truth Tables

Let's use a tool to help us evaluate all the Boolean Operators. A **truth table** is mathematical table used in logic to evaluate Boolean operators. They are helpful when trying to determine all the possibilities of a Boolean operator. Let's look at some common truth tables for AND, OR, NOT, XOR, NAND, and NOR.

In a AND truth table there are four possible combinations of TRUE and FALSE.

- TRUE AND TRUE = TRUE
- TRUE AND FALSE = FALSE
- FALSE AND TRUE = FALSE
- FALSE AND FALSE= FALSE

Placing these combinations in a truth table results in Table 4–1.

Table 4–1. *A AND Truth Table*

A	B	A AND B
TRUE	TRUE	TRUE
TRUE	FALSE	FALSE
FALSE	TRUE	FALSE
FALSE	FALSE	FALSE

AND truth table's only produces a TRUE result if both of its operands are TRUE.

Table 4–2 illustrates an OR truth table and all possible operands.

Table 4–2. *A OR Truth Table*

A	B	A OR B
TRUE	TRUE	TRUE
TRUE	FALSE	TRUE
FALSE	TRUE	TRUE
FALSE	FALSE	FALSE

A OR truth table produces a TRUE result if one or both of its operands are TRUE.

Table 4–3 illustrates a NOT truth table and all possible operands.

Table 4–3. *A NOT Truth Table*

NOT	RESULT
TRUE	FALSE
FALSE	TRUE

A NOT flips-the-bit or negates the original operand's Boolean value.

Table 4–4 illustrates a XOR or exclusive-or truth table and all possible operands.

Table 4–4. *A XOR Truth Table*

A	B	A XOR B
TRUE	TRUE	FALSE
TRUE	FALSE	TRUE
FALSE	TRUE	TRUE
FALSE	FALSE	FALSE

The operator XOR yields TRUE result if only one of the operands is TRUE.

Table 4–5 illustrates a NAND truth table and all possible operands.

Table 4–5. *A NAND Truth Table*

A	B	A NAND B
TRUE	TRUE	FALSE
TRUE	FALSE	TRUE
FALSE	TRUE	TRUE
FALSE	FALSE	TRUE

Table 4–6 illustrates a NOR table and all possible operands.

Table 4–6. *A NOR Truth Table*

A	B	A NOR B
TRUE	TRUE	FALSE
TRUE	FALSE	FALSE
FALSE	TRUE	FALSE
FALSE	FALSE	TRUE

The easiest way to look at the NAND and NOR operator is simply negate the result from the AND and OR truth tables, respectfully.

Comparison Operators

In software development, comparison of different data items is accomplished with **comparison operators**. These operators produce a logical TRUE or FALSE result. Table 4–7 shows the list of comparison operators.

Table 4–7. *Comparison Operators*

>	greater than
<	less than
>=	greater than or equal to
<=	less than or equal to
==	exactly equal to
!=	not equal to

NOTE: If you're constantly forgetting which way the greater than and less than sign goes, use a crutch I learned in grade school: If the greater than and less than sign represent the mouth of an alligator, the alligator always eats the bigger value. It may sound silly, but it works.

Designing Apps

Now that we've introduced Boolean logic and comparison operators, we can start designing our apps. Sometimes is important express all or part of your app to others without having to write the actual code.

Writing out code helps the developer think out loud and brainstorm with other developer's sections of code that are of concern. This helps to analyze the problem and possible solutions before coding begins.

Pseudo-code

Writing out code that is a high-level description of an algorithm we are trying to solve is called **pseudo-code**. Pseudo-code does not contain the necessary programming syntax for coding. However, it does express the algorithm that is necessary to solve the problem at hand.

Pseudo-code can be written by hand on paper or a whiteboard, or typed on a computer.

Using pseudo-code, we can apply what we know about Boolean data types, truth tables, and comparison operators. See Listing 4–1 pseudo-code examples:

Listing 4–1. *Pseudo-code examples using conditional operators in if-then-else code*

```
int x = 5;
int y = 6;
isComplete  =  TRUE;
if ( x < y)
{
    //in this example, x is less than 5
    do stuff;
}
else
{
    do other stuff;
}

if  (isComplete == TRUE)
{
    //in this example, isComplete is equel to TRUE
    do stuff;
}
else
{
    do other stuff;
}
```

```
//another way to check isComplete == TRUE
if (isComplete)
{
     //in this example,  isComplete is TRUE
     do stuff;
}
//Two ways to check if a value is false
if  (isComplete == FALSE)
{
     do stuff;
}
else
{
      //in this example, isComplete is TRUE so the else block will be executed
}
//another way to check isComplete == FALSE
if (!isComplete)
{
     do stuff;
}
else
{
      //in this example,  isComplete is TRUE so the else block will be executed
}
```

Often it is necessary to combine our comparison test. A compound relationship test is one or more simple relationship tests joined by either the && or the || (two pipe characters).

&& and || or spoken as logical-and and logical-or, respectfully. Pseudo-code in Listing 4–2 illustrates logical-and and logical-or.

Listing 4–2. *Using && and || logical operators*

```
int x = 5;
int y = 6;
isComplete  =  TRUE;
//using the logical and
if ( x < y && isComplete == TRUE)
{
     //in this example, x is less than 5 and isComplete == TRUE
     do stuff;
}
if ( x < y || isComplete == FALSE)
{
     //in this example, x is less than 5. Only one operand has to be TRUE for an OR↵
   to result in a TRUE.
     //See Table 4-2 A OR Truth Table
     do stuff;
}
another way to test for TRUE
if ( x < y && isComplete)
{
     //in this example, x is less than 5 and isComplete == TRUE
     do stuff;
}
another way to test for FALSE
```

```
if ( x < y && !isComplete)
{

    do stuff;
}
else
{
    // isComplete == FALSE
    do stuff;
}
```

Design Requirements

As discussed in Chapter 1, the most expensive process in the software development life cycle is writing code. The least expensive process in the software development life cycle is gathering the requirements for your application, yet this process is the most overlooked and least used process in software development.

Design requirements usually begin by asking clients, customers, and or stakeholders how the application should work, what problems it should solve, and how the app should solve the problem.

Requirements can include long or short narrative descriptions of the app, screen mockups, and formulas. It is far easier to open our word processor and change the requirements and screen mockups before coding begins than it is to modify an iPhone/iPad or Mac app. The following is the design requirement for one view of an iPhone mobile banking app.

- **View:** Accounts View

- **Description:** Display the list of accounts the user has. The list of Accounts will be in the following sections; Business Accounts, Personal Accounts and Car Loans, IRA and Home Equity Loans.

- **Cells:** Each cell will contain the account name, last four digits of the account, available balance and present balance.

A picture is worth a thousand words. Screen mockups are helpful to the developers and users to visualize how the views will look when completed. There are many tools that can be used to quickly design mockups; one of these tools is OmniGraffle. See Figure 4–1 for an example of screen mockup used for design requirements using OmniGraffle.

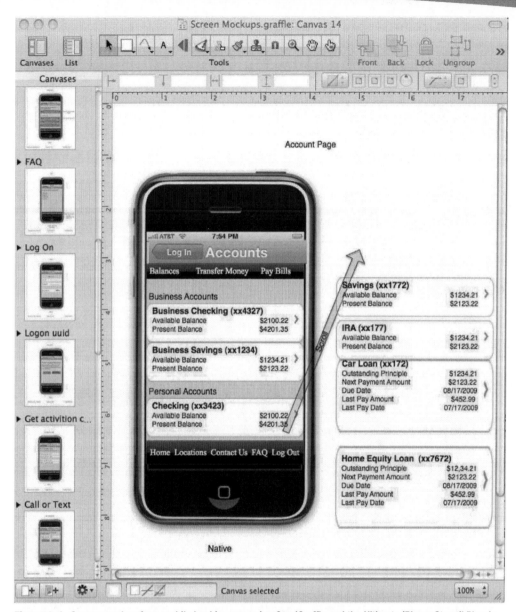

Figure 4–1. *Screen mockup for a mobile banking app using OmniGraffle and the Ultimate iPhone Stencil Plug-in.*

Many developers believe that design requirements take too long and are unnecessary. There is a lot of information presented on the Accounts screen in Figure 4–1. Lots of business rules can exist that determine how information is displayed to the user along with all the error handling when things go bad. Working with all the business stakeholders at the beginning of the development process was critical in getting the app right the first time.

Figure 4–2 is an example of all stakeholders being involved in the app's development. All stakeholders were involved in every view from the beginning, eliminating multiple rewrites and application bugs.

Figure 4–2. *Woodforest Mobile Banking app as it appears on the iTunes Connect app store. Compare with the app requirements Accounts screen in Figure 4–1*

Additionally, Apple recommends that developers spend at least 50% of their development time on the user interface design and development.

Another great tool for laying out your iPhone app's look and feel on paper is Apress's iPhone Sketch Book and Apress's iPad Sketch Book. See Figure 4–3

After design requirements are finalized, we can pseudo-code sections of the app to solve complex development issues. Another tool that developers often use to express code visually is flowcharting.

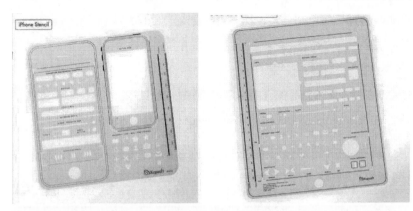

Figure 4–3. *Apress's iPhone Sketch Book Stencil and Apress's iPad Sketch Book Stencil*

Flowcharting

Flowcharting is a common method of diagramming an algorithm. The algorithm is represented as different types of boxes connected by lines and arrows. See Figure 4–4

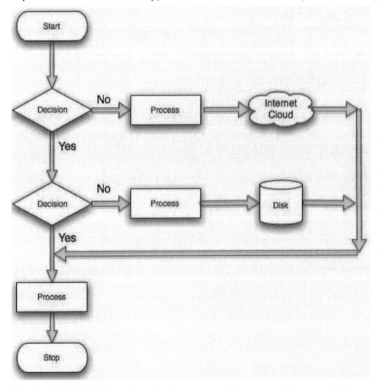

Figure 4–4. *Example flowchart showing common figures and their associated names*

Flowcharts should always have a start and a stop. Branches should never come to an end without a stop. This helps the developer to make sure all branches in their code are accounted for and cleanly stop execution.

Designing and Flowcharting an Example App

We have covered lots of information about decision making and program flow, so its time do what programmers do best, write apps!

The app we have been assigned to write generates a random number between 0 and 100 inclusive and asks the user to guess the number. The user has to keep guessing until the number is guessed. We can use any object from the Alice gallery to ask the user for their guess and we can also chose any world for our object be in. The object will provide a visual queue for each high, low and correct guess. The number that the user guessed is displayed to the console. When the user guesses the correct answer, the user is asked if they want to play again See Figure 4–5.

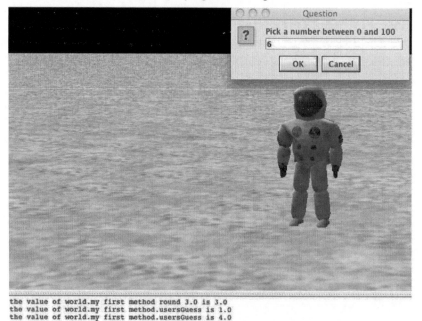

```
the value of world.my first method round 3.0 is 3.0
the value of world.my first method.usersGuess is 1.0
the value of world.my first method.usersGuess is 4.0
```

Figure 4–5. *An astronaut object asking the user to pick a number between 0 and 100*

The App's Design

Using our design requirements, we will make a flowchart for our app. See Figure 4–6.

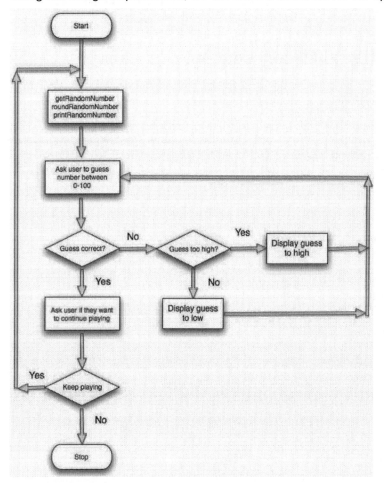

Figure 4–6. *Flowchart for guessing a random number app*

Reviewing Figure 4–6, we notice that as we approach the end of a block of logic in our flowchart, there are arrows that go back to a previous section of our flowchart and repeat that section until some condition is met. This is called **looping**, and enables us to repeat sections of programming logic, without having to rewrite that section of code over, and over until a condition is met.

Using Loops to Repeat Program Statements

A **loop** is a sequence of program statements, which is specified once but can be repeated several times in succession. A loop can repeat a specified number of times (count-controlled) or until some condition (condition-controlled) occurs.

In this section we'll learn about count-controlled loops, condition-controlled loops. We will also learn how to control our loops with Boolean logic.

Count-Controlled Loops

A count-controlled loop is a loop that repeats a specified number of times. In Objective-C and Alice this is a **For Loop**. A for loop has a counter variable. This variable enables the developer to specify the number of times the loop will be executed. See Listing 4–3.

Listing 4–3. *A count-controlled loop*

```
int i;
for (i = 0; i < 10; i++)
{
    //repeat all code in braces 10 times
}
....contine
```

The loop in Listing 4–3 will loop 10 times. The variable i starts at zero and increments at the end of the "}" by one. The incrementing is done by the i++ in the for statement. i++ is equivalent to i = i +1. i is then incremented by 1 to 10 and then checked to see if it is less than 10. This for loop will exit when i = 9 and the "}" is reached.

> **NOTE:** It is common for developers to confuse the number of times they think their loop will repeat. If the loop started at 1 in Listing 4–3, the loop would repeat 9 times instead of 10 times.

In Objective-C, for loops can have their counter variables declared in the for loop declaration itself. See Listing 4–4.

Listing 4–4. *Counter variable is initialized in for loop declaration.*

```
for (int i = 0; i < 10; i++)
{
    //repeat all code in braces 10 times
}
....contine
```

Occasionally, you will need to repeat just one line of code in a for loop. This can be accomplished by not using any {}. The first line of code encountered after the for loop declaration is repeated as specified in the for loop declaration. See Listing 4–5.

Listing 4–5. *Counter variable is initialized in the for loop declaration.*

```
for (int i = 0; i < 10; i++)
    do this line of code 10 times;
....contine
```

Condition-Controlled Loops

Objective-C and Alice have the ability to repeat a loop until some condition changes. We may want to repeat a section of our code until a false condition is reached with one of our variables. This type of loop is called a while loop. A while loop is a control flow statement that repeats based on the given Boolean condition. A while-loop can be thought of as a repeating if statement. See Listing 4–6.

Listing 4–6. *An Objective-C while loop repeating*

```
BOOL isTrue = TRUE;
while (isTrue)
  {
    //do something;
     isTrue = FALSE; // a condition occurs that sometimes sets isTrue to FALSE
  };
....contine
```

The while loop in Listing 4–6 first checks if the variable "isTrue" is TRUE, which it is, so the {loop body} is entered, where the code is executed and eventually some condition is reached which causes isTrue to become FALSE. After completing all the code in the loop body, the condition, (isTrue), is checked again, and the loop is repeated again. This process is repeated until the variable isTrue is set to FALSE.

Infinite Loops

An infinite loop repeats endlessly, either due to the loop not having a condition that causes termination or having a terminating condition that can never be met.

Generally, infinite loops can cause apps to become unresponsive and are a side effect of a bug in the code or logic.

Listing 4–7. *An example of on infinite loop*

```
x = 0;
while (x  != 5)
  {
    do someting;
    x = x + 2;
  };
....contine
```

Listing 4–7 is an example of an infinite loop caused by a terminating condition that can never by met. The variable x will be checked each iteration through the while loop, but will never be equal to 5. The variable x will always be an even number because it was initialized to zero and is incremented by 2 in our loop. This will cause the loop to repeat endlessly. See Listing 4–8.

Listing 4–8. *An example of an infinite loop caused by a terminating condition that can never be met*

```
while (TRUE)
  {
    do someting;
  };
....contine
```

Coding the Example App in Alice

Now that we have our design requirements and flowchart completed, and understand looping, we ready to write our Alice application. See Figure 4–7.

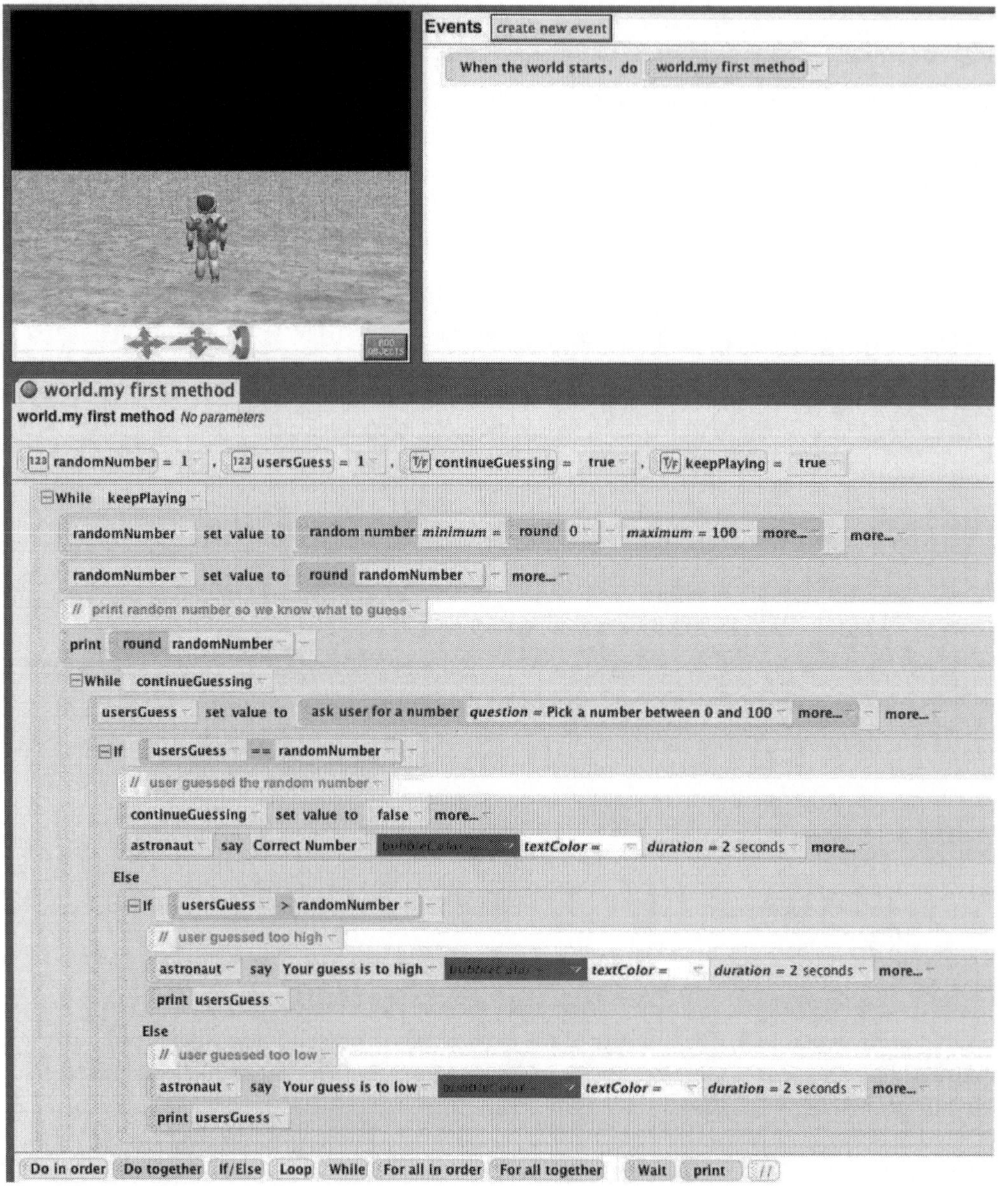

Figure 4–7. *Random number generator app*

It is not possible to list the source code for this Alice program in one screenshot. However, printing out the source code in html, we can all the view the code. See Figure 4–8.

Events

When the world starts
Do: world.my first method

Methods

```
world.my first method ( )
  randomNumber = 1 , usersGuess = 1 , continueGuessing = true , keepPlaying = true
    While keepPlaying
        randomNumber set value to ( random number ( round 0 ) maximum = 100 )
        randomNumber set value to ( round randomNumber )
        // print random number so we know what to guess
        print ( round randomNumber )
        While continueGuessing
            usersGuess set value to ( ask user for a number question = Pick a number between 0 and 100 )
            If ( usersGuess == randomNumber )
                // user guessed the random number
                continueGuessing set value to false
                astronaut say Correct Number             duration = 2 seconds
            Else
                If ( usersGuess > randomNumber )
                    // user guessed too high
                    astronaut say Your guess is to high             duration = 2 seconds
                    print usersGuess
                Else
                    // user guessed too low
                    astronaut say Your guess is to low             duration = 2 seconds
                    print usersGuess
        keepPlaying set value to ( ask user for yes or no question = Play Again. Yes or No? )
    continueGuessing set value to true
```

Figure 4–8. *Random number generator, complete program listing.*

Figure 4–8 shows the entire program listing for our random number generator code.

> **NOTE:** You can download the complete random number generator app at forum.xcelme.com. The code will be under the Chapter 4 topic. There is also a video showing how to drag and drop all the tiles within the While and If code blocks in Alice under this topic.

Coding the Example App in Objective-C

Using our requirements and what we learned with our Alice app, let's write our random number generator in Objective-C.

Our Objective-C app will run from the command line as it asks the user to guess a random number.

1. Open Xcode and start a New Project. Choose Command Line Tool and type **Foundation.** See Figure 4–9.

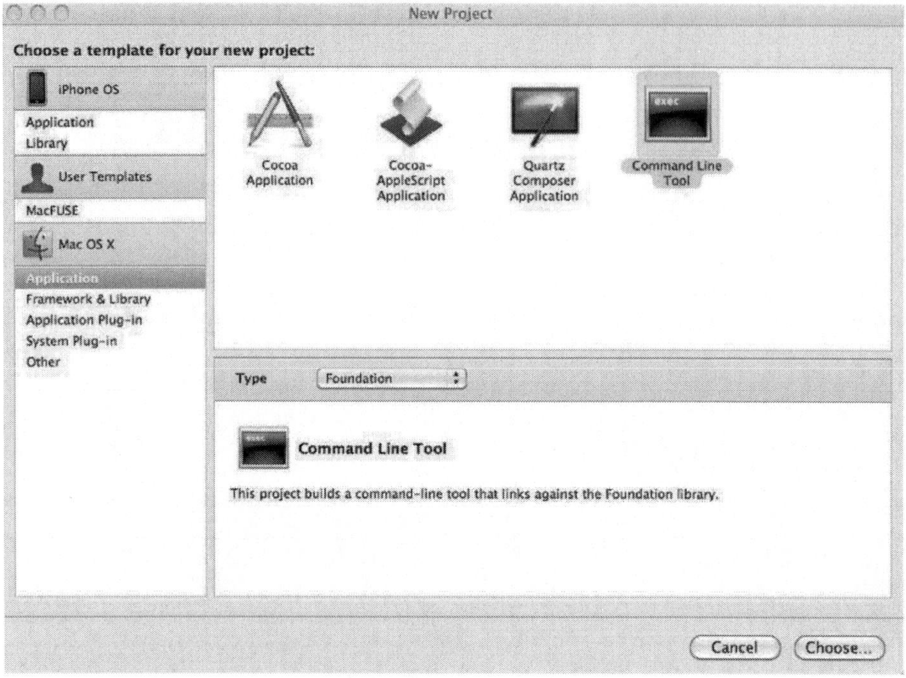

Figure 4–9. *Start a new Command Line Tool project*

2. Let's call our project RandomNumber. See Figure 4–10.

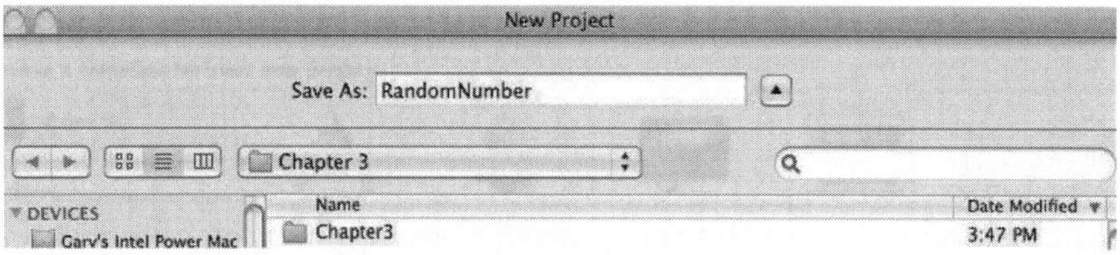

Figure 4–10. *Naming the project RandomNumber*

Now we need to open the implementation file in the Source group. This is where we will write our Objective-C code.

3. Open the RandomNumber.m file. Delete the line of code:

```
NSLog(@"Hello, World!");
```

4. Now we are ready to write our app. Start writing the code under

```
// insert code here…
```

See Figure 4–11.

```
#import <Foundation/Foundation.h>

int main (int argc, const char * argv[]) {
    NSAutoreleasePool * pool = [[NSAutoreleasePool alloc] init];

    // insert code here...

    [pool drain];
    return 0;
}
```

Figure 4–11. *The editor is now ready to us to write our code.*

Following our Alice code, we will write our random number generator app. You will notice that most of the code is very similar to our Alice app. See Listing 4–9.

Listing 4–9. *Source code for the random number generator app.*

```
#import <Foundation/Foundation.h>
int main (int argc, const char * argv[]) {
NSAutoreleasePool * pool = [[NSAutoreleasePool alloc] init];

// insert code here…
int randomNumber = 1;
int userGuess = 1;
BOOL continueGuessing;
BOOL keepPlaying = TRUE;
char yesNo = ' ';

while (keepPlaying)
{
        randomNumber = (random() % 101);
        NSLog(@"The random number to guess is: %d",randomNumber);
        continueGuessing = TRUE;
        while (continueGuessing)
        {
                NSLog (@"Pick a number between 0 and 100.  ");
                scanf ("%i", &userGuess);
                fgetc(stdin);//remove CR/LF i.e extra character
                if (userGuess == randomNumber)
                {
                        continueGuessing = FALSE;
                        NSLog(@"Correct number!");
                }
                //nested if statement
                else if (userGuess > randomNumber) //an else if statement
                {
                        //user guessed too high
                        NSLog(@"Your guess is too high");
                }
```

```
                    else
                    {
                            // no reason to check if userGuess < randomNumber. ↵
            It has to be.
                            NSLog(@"Your guess is too low");
                    }
                    //refactored from our Alice app. This way we only have to↵
            code once.
                            NSLog(@"The user guessed %d",userGuess);
                }
                NSLog (@"Play Again? Y or N");
                yesNo = fgetc(stdin);

                if (yesNo == 'N')
                {
                        keepPlaying = FALSE;
                }

        }
        [pool drain];
         return 0;
        }
```

There is new code that we haven't discussed before in Listing 4–10. The first line of code that is new is:

```
randomNumber = (rand() % 101);
```

This line will produce a random number between 0 and 100. random() is a function that returns a random number. Although this will not generate a truly random number, it will work for this example.

% is called the modulus operator. This operator returns the remainder of its two operands. In this case it's the return value of the rand() divided by 101.

The next line of new code is

```
scanf ("%i", &userGuess);
```

The function scanf reads a value from the keyboard and stores the value in userGuess.

> **NOTE:** The source code for this Objective-C project is available for download forum.xcelme.com. Additionally there is a short video explaining the source code and the project.

Nested If Statements and Else-If Statements

Sometimes it is necessary to **nest if statements**. This means that we need to have if statements nested inside an existing if statement. Additionally, it is sometimes necessary to have a comparison as the first step in the else section of the if statement. This is called an **else-if statement**.

Another line of code that is new to us is `fgetc(stdin);//remove CR/LF i.e extra character`. The function `scanf` can be difficult to work this. In this case `scanf` leaves a remnant in our input buffer that needs to be flushed so we can read a Y or N from the keyboard to determine if the user wants to play again.

Improving the Code Through Refactoring

Often after we get our code working, we examine the code and find more efficient ways to write our code. The process of rewriting our code to make it more efficient, maintainable, and improve readability is called **code refactoring**.

As we were rewriting our code in Objective-C, we noticed that we could eliminate some unnecessary code. Our Alice code had this line repeated in the if-else statement.

```
//refactored from our Alice app. This way we only have to code once.
NSLog(@"The user guessed %d",userGuess);
```

> **NOTE:** As a developer, we have found the best line of code you can write is the line that you don't write. Less code means less to debug and maintain.

Press the Build and Debug icon in our Objective-C project and run our app. See Figure 4–12.

Figure 4–12. *The console output of the Objective-C random number generator app*

Moving Forward Without Alice

We have used Alice to learn object-oriented Programming. It has enabled us to focus on OOP concepts without having to deal with syntax and a compiler. However, it is necessary to become more familiar with the specifics of the Objective-C language. Alice has served us well and we can now focus on using Objective-C and Xcode for the remainder of the book.

Summary

In this chapter we covered a lot of important information on how to control our applications. Program flow and decision making are basic to every iPhone/iPad Mac App. Make sure you completed the Alice and Objective-C examples in this chapters. You might review these examples and believe you understand everything without having to write these apps. This will be a fatal mistake to you becoming a successful iPhone/iPad Mac developer. You must spend time coding these examples.

The terms and in this chapter are very important. You should be able to describe the following:

- AND
- OR
- XOR
- NAND
- NOR
- NOT
- Truth tables
- Negation
- All comparison operators
- Application requirement
- Logical and &&
- Logical OR ||
- Flowchart
- Loop
- Controlled loops
- For Loop
- Condition-controlled loops
- Infinite loops
- While loops
- Nested if statements
- Code refactoring

Exercises

■ Extend the random number generator app to print to the console how many times the user guessed before they guessed the correct random number. Both in Alice and Objective-C.

■ Extend the random number generator app to print to the console how many times the user played the app. Print this value when the user quits the app. Both Alice and Objective-C.

Object Oriented Programming with Objective-C

Over the past 15 years or so, the programming world has been focused on the development paradigm of object oriented programming (OOP). Most modern development environments and languages implement OOP. Put simply, OOP will form the basis of everything you develop today.

You may be asking yourself why we waited until Chapter 5 to present OOP using Objective-C if it is the primary development style of today. The simple answer is that it is not an easy concept for new developers. We will spend this chapter going into detail about the different aspects of OOP and how this will affect your development.

Implementing OOP into your applications correctly will take some front-end planning. But you will save yourself a lot of time throughout the life of your projects. OOP has changed the way development is done. In this chapter, we will look at what OOP is. We will discuss what objects are and how they relate to physical objects we find in our world. We will also look into what classes are and how they relate to objects. We will also discuss steps you will need to take when planning your classes, and some visual tools you can use to accomplish this. When you have read this chapter and are working through the exercises, you will have a better understanding of what OOP is and why it is necessary to you as a developer.

The Object

As you learned in Chapter 2, objects are the basis of OOP. In order to better explain what a programming object is, we will first look at physical objects. A physical object can be anything around you that you can touch or feel. Take, for example, a television. Some characteristics of a television include type (plasma, LCD, or CRT), size (40 inches), brand (Sony, Vizio), weight, cost, and so on. Televisions also have functions. They can be turned on or off. You can change the channel, adjust the volume, and change brightness.

Some of these characteristics and functions are unique to televisions and some are not. For example, a couch in your house would probably not have the same characteristics as a television. You would want different information about a couch, such as material type, seating capability, and color. A couch might have only a few functions, such as converting to a bed.

Now let's talk specifically about programming objects. An object is a specific item. In programming, objects also have characteristics, but they are called attributes. In our example, a TV object would have type, size, and brand attributes, while a Couch object would have attributes such as color, material, and comfort level. Programming objects also have functions, but they are called methods. Methods are the way that other objects can interact with a certain object. For example, with the television, a method would be any of the buttons on the remote control. Each of those buttons represents a way you can interact with your television.

In previous chapters, we have been using the example of the bookstore. A bookstore contains many different objects. It contains book objects that have attributes such as title, author, page count, publisher, and so on. It also contains magazines with attributes such as title, issue, genre, and publisher. A bookstore also has some non-tangible objects such as a sale. A sale object would contain information about the books purchased, the customer, the amount paid, and the payment type. A sale object might also have some methods that calculate tax, print the receipt, or void the sale. A sale object does not represent a tangible object, but it is still an object and is very necessary to creating an effective bookstore.

Because the object is the basis of OOP, it is important to understand objects and how to interact with them. We will spend the rest of the chapter describing objects and some of their characteristics.

What Is a Class

We cannot discuss OOP without discussing what a class is. A class defines which attributes and methods an object will have.

A class is similar to a species in the animal world. A species is not an individual animal, but it does describe many similar characteristics of the animal. In order to understand classes more, let's look at an example of classes in nature. The class of Dogs has many attributes that all dogs have in common. For example, a dog may have a name, an age, an owner, and a favorite activity. If we look at Figure 5–1, you can see the difference between the class and the actual objects that are instances of the class. An object that is of a certain class is called an instance of that class.

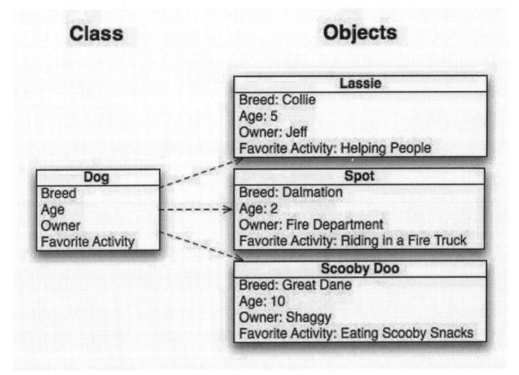

Figure 5–1. *An example of a class and individual objects*

Planning Classes

Planning your classes is one of the most important steps in your development process. While it is possible to go back and add attributes and methods after the fact (and you will definitely need to do this), it is important that you know which classes are going to be used in your application and which basic attributes and methods they will have. Spending some time planning your different classes is very important at the beginning of the process.

Let's look at the bookstore example and some of the classes we will need to create. First, it will be important to create a Bookstore class. A Bookstore class will contain information such as the bookstore name, address, phone number, and logo. By placing this information in a class rather than hard coding it in your application will allow you to easily make changes to this information in the future. Also, if your bookstore becomes a huge success and you decide to open up another one, you will be prepared, because you can create another object of class Bookstore. See Figure 5–2.

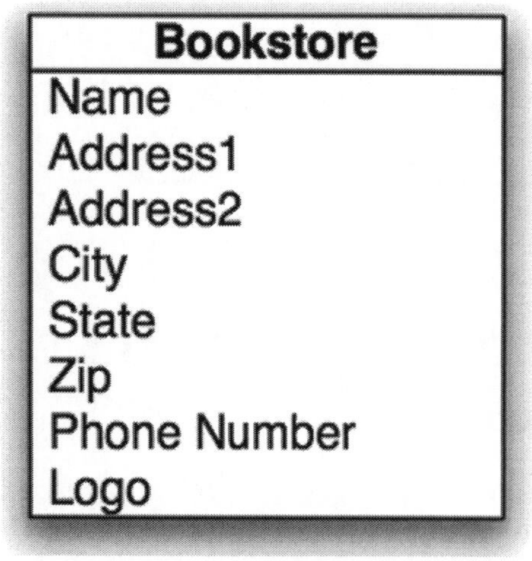

Bookstore

Name
Address1
Address2
City
State
Zip
Phone Number
Logo

Figure 5–2. *The Bookstore class*

We have also planned out the Customer class. Notice how the name has been broken into First Name and Last Name. This is very important to do. There will be times in your project when you may want to use only the first name of a customer, and it is hard to separate the first name from the last if you didn't plan on being able to do so ahead of time. Let's say you want to send a letter to a customer letting them know about an upcoming sale. You do not want your greeting to say, "Dear John Doe." It would look much more personal to say, "Dear John." See Figure 5–3.

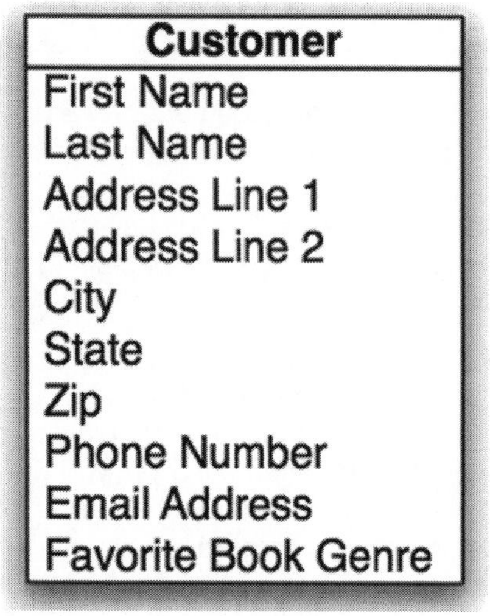

Customer

First Name
Last Name
Address Line 1
Address Line 2
City
State
Zip
Phone Number
Email Address
Favorite Book Genre

Figure 5–3. *The Customer class*

You will also notice how we have broken out the address into its different parts instead of grouping it all together. We separated the Address Line 1, Address Line 2, City, State, and ZIP. This is very important and will be used in your application. Let's go back to the letter you want to send informing your customers of a sale in your store. You might not want to send it to all of the customers that live in different states. By separating the address, you can easily filter out those customers you do not want to include in your mailings.

We have also added the attribute of Favorite Book Genre to the Customer class. We added this to show you how you can keep many different types of information in each class. This field may come in handy if you have a new mystery title coming out and you want to send an e-mail alerting customers who are really interested in mysteries. By storing this type of information, you will be able to specifically target different portions of your customer base.

A Book class is also necessary in order to create our bookstore. We will store information about the book such as author, publisher, genre, page count, and edition number (in case there are multiple editions). The Book class will also have the price for the book. See Figure 5–3.

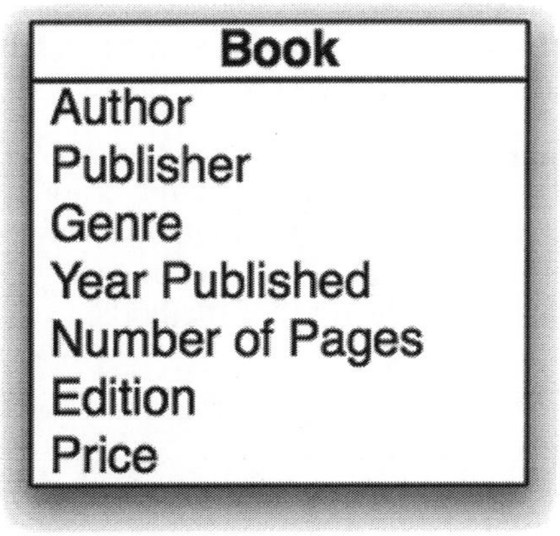

Figure 5–4. *The Book class*

We also added another class called the Sale class. This class in more abstract than the other classes we have discussed, because it does not describe tangible objects. You will notice how we have added a reference to a customer and a book to the Sale class. Because the Sale class will track sales of books, we will need to know which book was sold and to which customer. See Figure 5–5.

Figure 5–5. *The Sale class*

Now that we have planned out the attributes of the classes, we will need to look at some methods that each of the classes will have. We will not add all of the methods now, but the more planning you can do at the beginning, the easier it will be for you down the line. Not all of your classes will have many methods, and some may not have any methods at all. For the time being, we will not add any methods to the Book class or the Bookstore class. We will focus on our other two classes.

For the Customer class, we will add methods to list the purchase history of that client. There may be other methods that you will need to add in the future, but for now, we will add just that one. Your completed Customer class diagram should look like Figure 5–6. You will notice the line near the bottom separates the attributes from the methods.

Customer
First Name
Last Name
Address Line 1
Address Line 2
City
State
Zip
Phone Number
Email Address
Favorite Book Genre
List Purchase History

Figure 5–6. *The completed Customer class*

For the Sales class, we have added three methods. We added the Charge Credit Card, Print Invoice, and Checkout. For the time being, you do not need to know how to implement these methods, but you need to know that you are planning on adding them to your class. See Figure 5–7.

Figure 5–7. *The completed Sale class*

Now that you have finished mapping out the classes and the methods you are going to add to them, you have the beginnings of a unified modeling language (UML) diagram. Basically, this is a diagram used by developers to plan out their classes, attributes, and methods. Starting your development process with creating such a diagram will help you a lot in the long run. An in-depth discussion of UML diagrams is beyond the scope of this book. If you would like more information about this subject, smartdraw.com has a great in-depth overview of them. See Figure 5–7.

www.smartdraw.com/resources/tutorials/uml-diagrams/

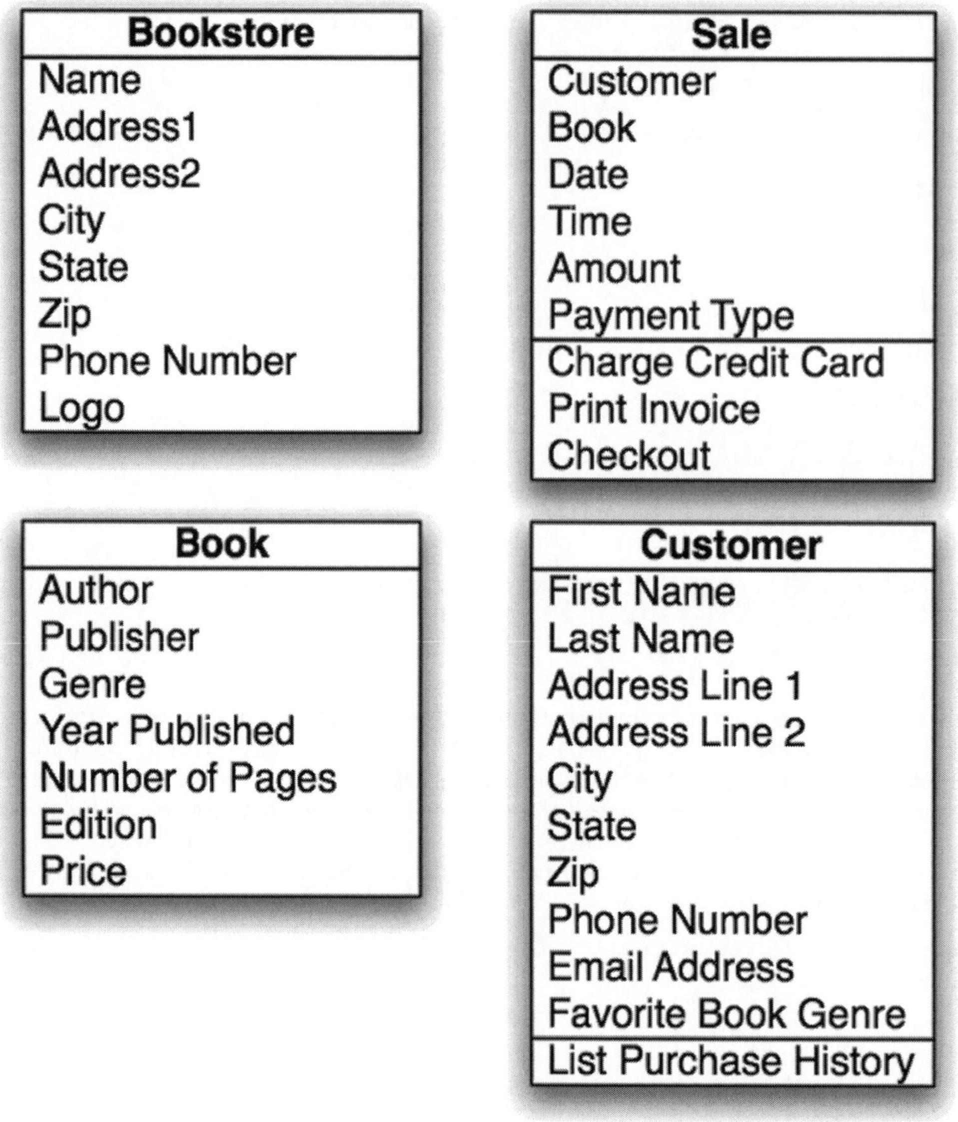

Bookstore
Name
Address1
Address2
City
State
Zip
Phone Number
Logo

Sale
Customer
Book
Date
Time
Amount
Payment Type
Charge Credit Card
Print Invoice
Checkout

Book
Author
Publisher
Genre
Year Published
Number of Pages
Edition
Price

Customer
First Name
Last Name
Address Line 1
Address Line 2
City
State
Zip
Phone Number
Email Address
Favorite Book Genre
List Purchase History

Figure 5–8. *The completed UML diagram for the bookstore*

Now that we understand the objects we are going to be creating, we need to create our first object. In order to do so, please launch Xcode. Click on File ➤ New Project. Select Application under Mac OS X on the left-hand side. One the right-hand side, select Cocoa Application. For now, make sure the Create Document Based Application and Use Core Data for Storage check boxes are unchecked. See Figure 5–9.

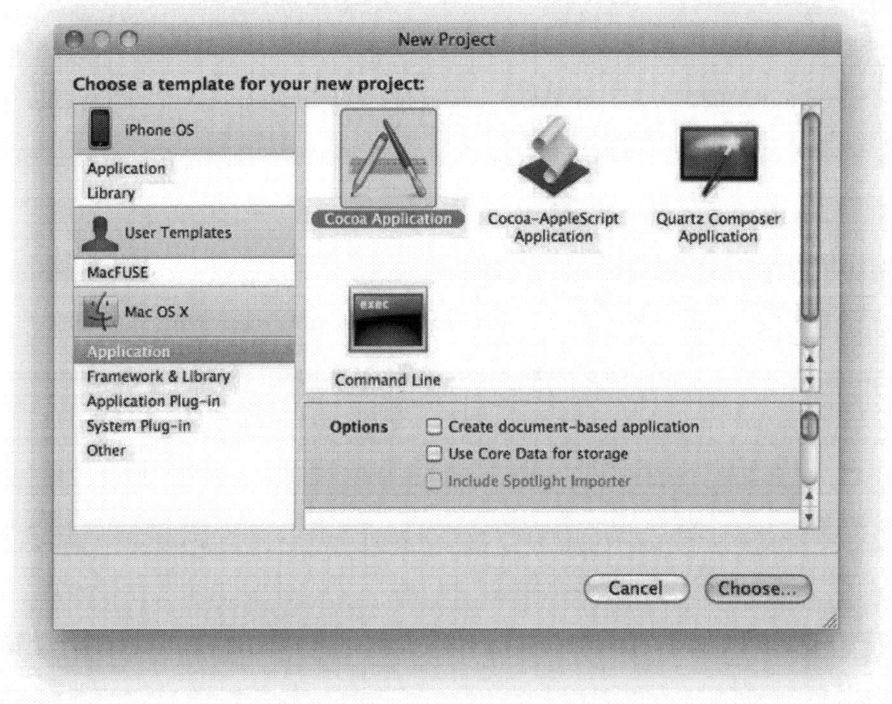

Figure 5–9. *Creating a new project*

Go ahead and save your project. You can use the name "bookstore" or any other project name you want. Select the Classes Folder on the left-hand side of the screen and select File ➤ New File. See Figure 5–10.

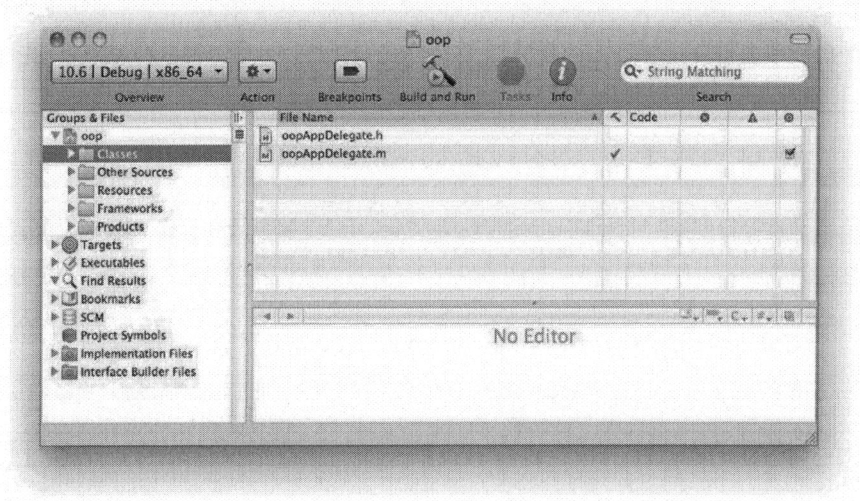

Figure 5–10. *Selecting the Classes folder*

From the pop-up window, select Cocoa Class under the Mac OS X header, and then click on Objective-C Class on the right-hand side. At the bottom of the screen, you will be given the opportunity to choose which class this will be a subclass of. We will not go into detail about that choice now; you can read about inheritance later in this chapter. For now, select SubClass of NSObject. See Figure 5–11.

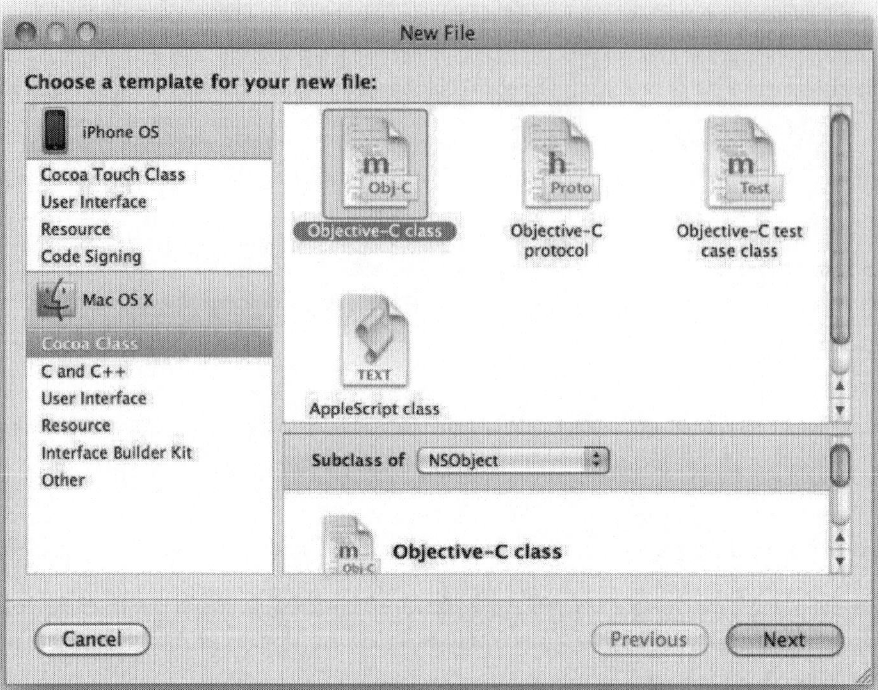

Figure 5–11. *Creating a new Objective-C Class*

You will now be given the opportunity to name your class.

NOTE: For ease of use and for understanding your code, remember that class names should always be capitalized in Objective-C. Object variables should always be lowercase.

Let's create our Customer class. Type in the class name (Customer), then click Finish.

In your Classes folder, you should have two new files. One is called Customer.h and the other is called Customer.m. The .h file is the header file that will contain information about your class. The header file will list all of the attributes and methods in your class, but it will not actually contain the code related to them. The .m file is the implementation file, which is where you write your code.

Double-click on the Customer.h file and you will see the window shown in Figure 5–12. You will notice it does not contain a lot of information currently. The first part, with the double slashes (//) are all comments and are not considered part of the code. We will not go into more detail about the other portions of the header file, except to say that all of the attributes of a class need to be inside the braces ({}) of the @interface portion.

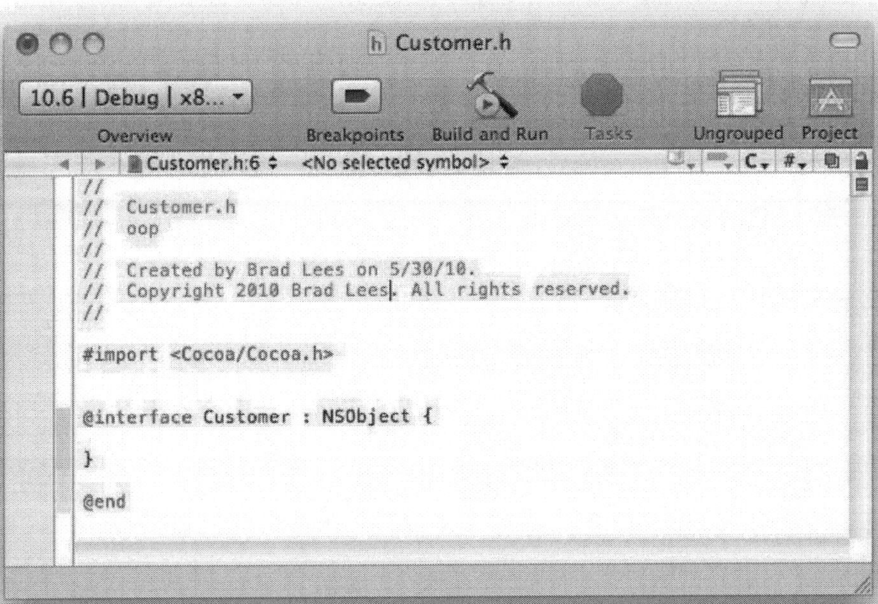

Figure 5–12. *Your finished class*

Now let's add attributes to the header file.

> **TIP:** Attributes should always start with a lowercase letter. There can be no spaces in an attribute name.

For the first attribute, First Name, we will add this line to our file.

```
NSString* firstName;
```

This creates a string object in our class called firstName. Because all of the attributes for the Customer class are strings also, we will just need to repeat the same procedure for the other ones. When all is complete, your @interface portion should look like Figure 5–13.

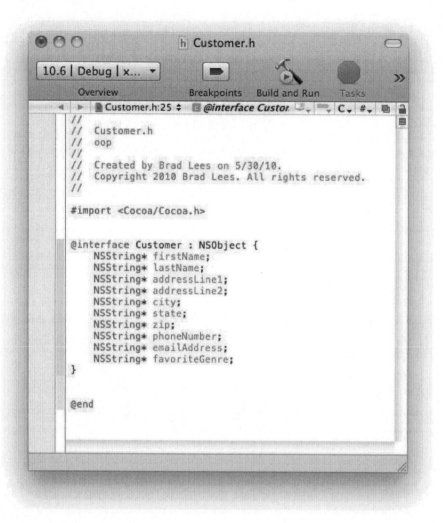

Figure 5–13. *The Customer class interface*

Now that the interface portion is complete, we will need to add our method. Methods need to go outside of the @interface portion, but still inside of the @interface portion of the header file.

> **NOTE:** A string (NSString) is nothing more than a set of characters that we as humans can read.

```
-(NSArray *) listPurchaseHistory;
```

That is all that needs to be done in the header file to create our class. In the next chapter we will go into more detail about the implementation file. See Figure 8-14.

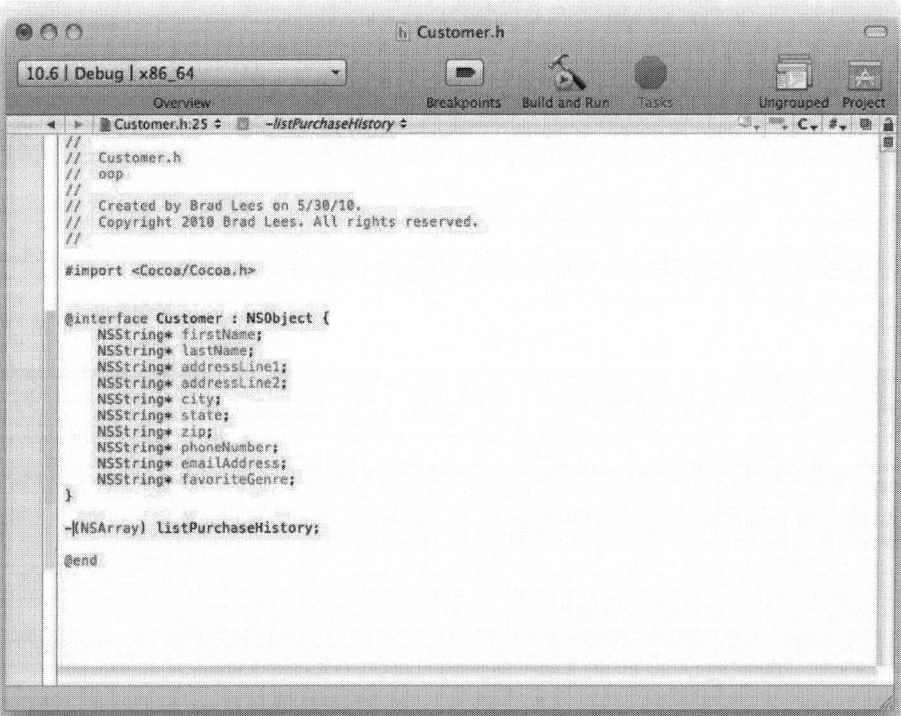

Figure 5–14. *The finished customer class header file*

Inheritance

Another major quality of OOP is inheritance. Inheritance in programming in similar to how you inherit characteristics from your parents. You might have inherited your eye color or hair color from your mother or father. Objects can, in a similar way, inherit attributes and methods from their parent objects. In OOP, a parent object is called a superclass and a child object is called a subclass.

In Objective-C, all classes created by a programmer have a superclass, which is similar to a parent object. The object will inherit characteristics from that parent object. The object is called a subclass of the parent object. In the examples in this chapter, all of our classes are subclasses of the NSObject. In Objective-C, most of the time, your objects will be subclasses of NSObject. We could, however, create a class of printed materials and use subclasses for books, magazines, and newspapers. Printed materials can have many things in common, so we could assign variables to the superclass of printed materials and not have to redundantly assign them to each individual class. By doing this, we further reduce the amount of redundant code that is necessary for you to write and debug. In our example, our class was a subclass of NSObject. In Figure 5–15, you will see a layout for the attributes of a printed material superclass and how that will affect the subclasses of Book, Magazine, and Newspaper. The attributes of the Printed Material class will be inherited by the subclasses so there is no need to definte them explicitly in the class. You will notice that the Book class now has significantly fewer attributes. By using a superclass, you will significantly reduce the amount of redundant code in your programs.

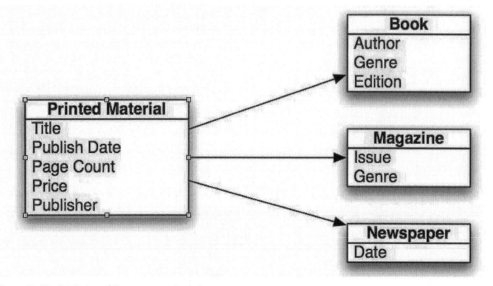

Figure 5–15. *Attributes of the super- and subclasses*

Why Use OOP?

Throughout this chapter we have discussed what OOP is and we have even discussed how to create classes and objects, but I think it is important to discuss why you want to use OOP principles in your development.

If you take a look at the popular programming languages of the day, all of them will use the OOP principles at least to a certain extent. Objective C, C++, Visual Basic, C#, and Java all require the programmer to understand classes and objects to successfully develop in those languages. In order to become a developer in today's world, you will need to understand OOP. But why use it?

Eliminate Redundant Code

By using objects, you will reduce the amount of code you will have to retype. Let's say you create a mechanism to print a receipt and then your company decides to create an admin interface to allow employees to reprint a receipt. If you placed your code to print the receipt in the Sales object, you will not have to rewrite this code again. This not only saves you time, but often will help you eliminate mistakes. If you do not use OOP and there is a change to the invoice (even something as simple as a graphic change), you have to make sure you make the change in your desktop application and the mobile application. If you miss one of them, you run the risk of having the two interfaces behave differently.

Ease of Debugging

By having all of the code relating to a book in one object, you know where to look when there is a problem with the book. This may not sound like such a big deal with a little application, but when your application gets to hundreds of thousands or even millions of lines of code, it will save you a lot of time.

Ease of Replacement

If you place all of your code in an object, then as things change in your application, you can change out objects and give your new object completely different functionality, but it can interact with the rest of the application in the same way as your current object. This is similar to car parts. If you want to replace a muffler on a car, you do not need to get a new car. If you have code related to your invoice scattered all over the place, it makes it much more difficult to change items about an object.

Advanced Topics

We have discussed the basics of OOP throughout this chapter, but there are some other topics that are very important to your understanding.

Interface

As we have discussed in this chapter, the way the other objects interact through each other is with methods. We discussed the header files created when you create a class. This is often called the interface because it tells other objects how they can interact with your objects. Implementing a standard interface throughout your application will allow your code to interact with different objects in similar ways. This will significantly reduce the amount of object specific code you need to write.

Polymorphism

Polymorphism is the ability of an object of one class to appear and be used as an object of another class. This is usually done by creating methods and attributes that are similar to those of another class. A great example of polymorphism that we have been using is the bookstore. In the bookstore, we have three similar classes: Books, Magazines, and Newspapers. If we wanted to have a big sale on all of our inventory, we could go through all of the books and mark them down, then go through all of the magazines and mark them down, and then go through all of the newspapers and mark them down. That would be more work then we would need to do. It would be better to make sure all of the classes have a markdown method, then we could call that on all of the objects without needing know which class they were. This would save a bunch of time and coding.

As you are planning out your classes, look for similarities and methods that might apply to more than one type of class. This will save you time and speed up your application in the long run.

Summary

We've finally reached the end of the chapter! Here is a summary of the things that were covered.

- Object-oriented programming (OOP)
  - We discussed the importance of OOP and the reasons why all modern code should use this methodology.
- Object
  - You learned about objects and how they correspond to real-world objects. We learned that many programming objects relate directly to real-world objects. You also learned about abstract objects that do not correspond to real world objects.
- Class
  - You learned that a class determines the types of data (attributes) and the methods that each object will have. Every object needs to have a class. It is the blueprint for the object.
- Creating a class
  - You learned how to map out the attributes and methods of our classes.
  - We used Xcode to create a class file.
  - We edited the class header file to add our attributes and methods.

Exercises

- Try creating the class files for the rest of the classes we mapped out.
- Map out an Author class. Choose the kind of information you would need to store about an author.
- **For the daring and advanced:**
- Try creating a superclass called PrintedMaterials. Map out the attributes that class might have.
- Create classes for the other types of Printed Materials a store more carry.

Chapter 6

Introducing Objective-C and Xcode

For the most part, all computer languages perform the typical tasks that any computer needs to do—store information, compare information, make decisions about that information, and perform some action based on that decision. Objective-C is a language to make these tasks easier to accomplish and understand. The real trick with Objective-C (actually the trick with any C language) is understanding the symbols and keywords used to accomplish those tasks. This chapter introduces you Objective-C and Xcode—from Objective-C's humble beginnings as an extension to the C language to using Xcode (a tool to build programs using Objective-C) to build programs. By the end of this chapter, you will understand what Objective-C is and know how to write a simple application using Xcode.

A Brief History of Objective-C

Objective-C is really a combination of two languages: the C language and a lesser-known language called Smalltalk. Back in the 1970s, several very bright engineers from Bell Labs created a language they named **C** that made it easy to port their pet project, the UNIX operating system, from one machine to another. Prior to C, people had to write programs in assembly languages. The problem with assembly languages is that each is specific to its machine, so moving software from one machine to another was nearly impossible. The C language, created by Brian Kernighan and Dennis Ritchie, solved this problem by providing a language that wrote out the assembly language for whatever machine it supported, a kind of Rosetta Stone for early computer languages. Because of its portability, C quickly became the *de facto* language for many types of computers, early PCs especially.

Fast-forward to the early 1980s, and the C language is on its way to becoming one of the most popular languages of the decade. Right around this time, an engineer from a company called Stepstone was mixing the C language with another up-and-coming language called Smalltalk. The C Language is typically referred to as a *procedural language*, that is, a language that uses procedures to divide up processing steps. Smalltalk, on the other hand, was something entirely different. It was an *object-oriented programming language*. Instead of processing things procedurally, it used programming objects to get its work done. This new superset of the C language became known as "C with Objects" or more commonly, **Objective-C**.

In 1985, Brad Cox sold the Objective-C language and trademark to NeXT Computer, Inc. NeXT was the brainchild of Steve Jobs, who had been fired from his own company, Apple Computer, that very same year. NeXT used the Objective-C language to build the NeXTSTEP operating system and its suite of development tools. In fact, the Objective-C language gave NeXT a competitive advantage with all of its software. Programmers using NeXTSTEP and Objective-C could write more-functional programs faster than those writing in the traditional C language. While the hardware part of NeXT computers never really took off, the operating system and tools did. Quite interestingly, NeXT was purchased by Apple Computer in late 1996 with the intention of replacing its aging operating system, which had been in existence since the first Macintosh was developed in 1984. Four years after the acquisition, what had been NeXTSTEP reemerged as Mac OS X—with Objective-C still at the heart of the system.

Understanding C Language Basics

Even though Objective-C integrates a great object-oriented language, at the heart of Objective-C is C. Here is the most basic "Hello World" program written in the C language:

```
int main(void)
{
        if (printf("Hello World") == 0)
        {
                return 0;
        }
        else
        {
                return 1;
        }
}
```

Let's dissect this a bit. Every program must start somewhere, right? Well, for Objective-C and C, `main` is the name of the procedure (which is often called a **function** in C) that is called first.

```
int main(void)
```

It must be called "main", not "Main," "MAIN," or anything else. C and Objective-C are *case-sensitive* languages meaning that `main` and `Main` are entirely different names.

Functions (and `main` is a function) all share the following syntax when they are declared:

```
return-type functionName ( argument-list )
```

Our first function, `main`, has the following:

- **A return type of** `int`: `int` is just shorthand for "integer." An **integer** is a 32-bit value that has a range from –2,147,483,648 to 2,147,483,647. That's a pretty large range of values! So, the function, `main`, must return an integer value to the function that called it.

> **NOTE:** A **type** is a kind of data. Integer, character, and float are all different data types. In Objective-C, an object is its own unique type.

- **A function name of** `main`: As mentioned previously, `main` is the starting point of any C or Objective-C program. If we were writing a different function, it could be named pretty much anything, as long as it starts with a letter.

- **An argument list of** `void`: `void` is a special type; it represents, in this case, the fact that there are no arguments.

The next line contains the character {. This is the opening brace symbol and is used to represent the beginning of series of steps, which is commonly referred to as a **block** of code. Every language has something like this, but in other languages, the opening of the block may either be implied or called `BEGIN`. In any case, the opening brace means that we are defining a block.

The third line:

```
if (printf("Hello World") != -1)
```

actually has two parts. First, is the `if` keyword is a special command in the C and Objective-C languages that performs a test on something. To know what the `if` is testing, the next part is important:

```
printf("Hello World")
```

This is a standard C function that *prints* formatted information to the screen. Now, the `printf` function *returns* a value after it completes its job. Basically, the result from the `printf` is whether the function actually worked or not. If `printf` returns a value greater than 0, the procedure worked; otherwise, it didn't. The `printf` function is being passed a single **argument**, that is, the string "Hello World". A **string** is nothing more that a series of characters grouped together.

Therefore, `printf` is called and returns a value, and the `if` statement compares that value with another.

The second part of the statement is the **not-equal sign** (`!=`):

```
!= -1)
```

In C and Objective-C, an exclamation point is a **logical not** operator, so `!=` means "not equal." In this case, the `if` statement is comparing the return value from the `printf` procedure with the integer constant of –1.

The forth, fifth, and sixth lines are as follows:

```
{
        return 0;
}
```

This section starts off with another brace symbol, which means that another block is starting. In this case, the first block that occurs after the `if` keyword represents the things for the program to do if the result of the `if` test is `true`. If the `printf` function call returns 0, the test for 0 will be true. If we replace the `printf` function with a return value of 0, `if (0 ==` 0) is a true statement. Last, the closing brace (}) represents the end of this block.

However, if the test is *not* true, this block is completely ignored. Also notice that the line ends with a semicolon (;). This character is used in C and Objective-C to indicate that the end of a command. Why isn't there one on the `if` statement? Well, the `if` statement is not finished being defined; the `return` statement represents the end of the `true` part of the `if` statement.

To sum it up, in the function `main`, if the `printf` statement returns a value of 0, the block after the `if` is used and this function will return a value of 0. In the C Language, a returned integer value of 0 typically represents a good thing. No news is good news.

Here's the last part of the program:

```
else
{
        return 1;
}
```

The `else` keyword is optionally used along with any `if` keyword. The block that appears right after the `else` keyword represents the things to do if the test in the `if` statement is *not* true. If the return value from `printf` is something other than 0, the `else` block will be executed.

Okay, that's enough C language for now. Although the C Language is at the heart of Objective-C and very important, the "objective" part of Objective-C is used much more prevalently.

Putting the "Objective" into Objective-C

The majority of what makes Objective-C, well, objective, is its basis in Smalltalk. Smalltalk is a 100 percent object oriented language, and Objective-C borrows heavily from Smalltalk concepts and syntax. Here are few of the high-level concepts borrowed from Smalltalk. Don't worry if some these terms seem unfamiliar; they will be discussed in later chapters (Chapter 8 covers the basics).

- Pretty much everything is an **object**.

- Objects receive **messages**. In this context, the object is sometimes known as the **receiver**, since it is receiving the message.

- Objects contain **instance** variables.

- Objects and instance variables have a defined **scope**.

- Classes hide an object's **implementation**.

So how do these concepts translate to Objective-C? Well, for starters, an object in Objective-C is defined using two different sections: @interface and @implementation. The @interface section defines what messages the object can respond to as well as any instance variables the object will be using. The @implementation section contains the actual code to the various messages in the @interface section.

Why is there a split between the interface and implementation? Well, an Objective-C object is defined only once within a program. However, it might be used in may different areas of that program. Where the object is used, the program simply reads in, or **imports**, the interface; it would be inefficient if the code to that object needed to be replicated every time it was used.

> **NOTE:** It is common convention to have an object's interface stored in a .h file and the implementation stored in a .m file. Both files are named after the object. So, if a Library object is to be defined, its interface would be in Library.h and its implementation would be in Library.m (remember that names are case-sensitive).

Let's look at a simple example of the complete definition of an Objective-C object, called HelloWorld.

Here's the interface file (HelloWorld.h):

```
1   #import <Foundation/Foundation.h>
2
3   @interface HelloWorld : NSObject
4   {
5   }
6
7   - (void)printGreeting;
8
9   @end
```

And this is the implementation file (HelloWorld.m):

```
10  #import "HelloWold.h"
11
12  @implementation HelloWorld
13
14  -(void)printGreeting
15  {
16      NSLog(@"Hello World!");
17  }
18
19  @end
```

In the preceding example, an object, HelloWorld, is being defined. This object only has one message defined—printGreeting. What do all of these strange symbols mean? Using the line numbers as a reference, we can review this code line by line.

Line 1 contains a compiler directive, #import <Foundation/Foundation.h>. In order for this little program to know about certain other objects (i.e., the NSObject on line 3), we need to have the compiler read other interface files. In this case, the Foundation.h file defines the objects and interfaces to the **Foundation framework**. This framework contains the definition of most of the non–user-interface base classes of the iPhone and Mac OS X systems. What is important here is that we have a definition to the NSObject object. On line 3 is the actual start of our object with the line @interface HelloWorld : NSObject. HelloWorld is the object, but what does : NSObject mean? Well, the colon (:) after our object's name indicates that we plan to derive additional functionality from another class. In this case, NSObject is that class. HelloWorld is now a *subclass* of NSObject.

> **NOTE:** Why the name NSObject and not just Object? Well, recall that Mac OS X actually started out as a port from the NeXTSTEP system? "NS" is an abbreviation for NeXTSTEP and is used in many of the base objects in Mac OS X and iPhone OS— NSObject, NSString, NSDictionary, and so on.

Lines 4 and 5 simply contain the { and } characters. This block is used to define instance variables that are used by the object, but the HelloWorld class is simple enough that instance variables are not necessary. Later, in Chapter 9, there will be examples where instance variables are defined and used.

Line 7 contains a message definition for this object: - (void)printGreeting. When you're defining a message, that line must start with either a + or - character. In the case of the HelloWorld object, we are using - to indicate that this message can be used *after* the object is created. A + character is used for messages that can be used *before* the object is created. The remainder of the message, (void) printGreeting, represents the return value of the message. In this case, the value (void) is followed by the actual message name, printGreeting.

In line 9, @end indicates that the definition of the object's interface is complete.

That's the complete description of the interface of the HelloWorld object—not a whole lot here. More complicated objects simply just have more messages and more instance variables.

For the implementation, the source code is stored in a different file, HelloWord.m. For starters, line 10 starts with the statement #import "HelloWorld.h". This simply allows our object to know its own interface. While the separation of the interface and implementation files might seem a little odd at first, this convention is very consistent in Objective-C programming. Whenever an object is to be used, simply include its interface. Also, the import indicates "HelloWorld.h" in quotation marks, not <HelloWorld.h> alone. What's the difference? Quite simply, doing an import of a file in quotation marks (e.g., `"HelloWorld.h"`) indicates that the compiler is to look in the local project to find the file, whereas the import of `<Foundation/Foundation.h>` indicates to the compiler that the file is located in some global area for *all* projects. The easy way to remember is that if you created the file, use the double quotation marks. If not, use the angle brackets (< and >).

Line 12 is the start of the implementation of the object:

```
@implementation HelloWorld
```

Line 14 is the definition of the object's message, `printGreeting`. It looks identical to the message definition in the interface file. The only difference here is that code is being defined that implements the `printGreeting` message.

Lines 15–17 form the block of code that implements the message `printGreeting`. For this simple message, the function `NSLog` is called. This base-level function simple takes in a formatted `NSString` object and outputs the result to the console. The `NSString` class is an Objective-C class that implements behavior of a string of characters. Why have a class for this? For one, it gives the framework a consistent object for representing a string. Plus there is a lot of functionality in `NSString` that can be used to manipulate, compare, and convert the actual data.

> **NOTE:** The term **class** is used to represent, generically, the definition or type of an object. An **object** is what is created from the class. For example, an SUV is *class* of vehicle; a class is a blueprint of sorts. A factory builds SUVs. The results are SUV objects that people drive. You can't drive a *class*, but you can drive an *object* built from a class.

The `NSString` object is specified here in a shorthand method. The `@"Hello World!"` is a way of quickly declaring an `NSString` object. The at sign (@) is the symbol used to indicate that the string specified is an `NSString` object.

Line 19 indicates to the compiler that the definition of the implementation section is finished.

But wait, there is more. Now that we have a new Objective-C class defined, how is it used? Here is another piece of code that uses the newly created class, the main program (`myprogram.m`):

```
20   #import "HelloWold.h"
21
22   int main(void)
23   {
24       HelloWorld* myObject = [[HelloWorld alloc] init];
25       [myObject printGreeting];
26
27       [myObject release];
28       return 0;
29   }
```

In this new file, the program first starts by including the `HelloWorld.h` file, which allows this piece of the application access to the `HelloWorld` object.

You saw a code like line 22 in our previous C example. Remember, every C Language and Objective-C program must have a `main` function.

Line 24 is a complicated one. It defines and **instantiates** the `HelloWorld` class. You first see the text `HelloWorld* myObject`. This defines a variable named `myObject` of the type `HelloWorld`, which is our new class. The asterisk (*) is used to represent a **pointer to** the object. This notation basically means that we don't want the object here; we just want a way to get to it, or a pointer to where it is. Think of this like a person who gives you a business card. You have the card, not the actual person. But the business card is a way of getting in touch with the person.

> **NOTE:** Instantiation makes a class a real object in the computer's memory. A class by itself is not really usable until there is an instance of it. Using the SUV example, an SUV means nothing until a factory builds one (instantiates the class). Only then can the SUV be used.

The next part of the line is `[[HelloWorld alloc] init]`. This is a **nested** call. The innermost bracketed instructions are executed first, so `[HelloWorld alloc]` is called first. Wait a second; we never defined the message `alloc`, so how is this going to work? Well, when `HelloWorld` was defined, it was defined as a subclass of `NSObject`. Another way to explain this relationship is to cal that `NSObject` is the parent class of `HelloWorld`. When we send the `alloc` message to the `HelloWorld` object, the system knows that `HelloWorld` doesn't know that particular message, so it automatically passes the message to the parent class.

Once `[HelloWorld alloc]` is called, the return value is a pointer to the newly allocated object (**allocation** means that we use part of the computer's memory to store something). But we're not done yet. The remaining part of the nested statement, the `init` message, gets executed next: `[[HelloWorld alloc] init]`. Now, init simply does some base-level initialization of the object. The final return from all of this is a pointer to the new object, which is the `HelloWorld` object.

> **NOTE:** In Objective-C, whenever objects are sent messages, the code must be within square brackets, [and].

Now that we've created a new object, it can be used. Line 25, `[myObject printGreeting]`, puts our object to use. In this piece of code, we use our newly instantiated object by sending it a message `printGreeting`. The program will output the text `HelloWorld!`.

Line 27 sends another message to our object—the `release` message. This message tells the system that this program is finished using the object and to release any system resources associated with it.

Line 28 returns the value 0 to the caller of our `main` function. This indicates a successful execution.

Line 29 ends the code block and the program.

NOTE: Messages can also accept multiple arguments. Consider, for example, `[myCarObject switchRadioBandTo:FM andTuneToFrequncy:104.7];`. The message here would be `switchRadioBandTo:andTuneToFrequency:`. After each colon, the argument values are placed when a message is actually sent. You might also notice that these messages are named in such a way as to make interpreting what they actually do easy to understand. Using helpful message names is an ideal convention to follow when developing classes, because it makes using the classes much more intuitive. Being consistent in naming messages is also key.

Introducing Xcode

Up to this point, we've basically played being the computer in explaining how to build an Objective-C application. Now, we'll use the tools that all iPhone and Mac OS X developers use to develop all kinds of programs. Xcode is supplied free of charge to any Mac user. In fact, Xcode is included with the Snow Leopard (Max OS X 10.6) DVD. If you're not using Snow Leopard, Xcode can be downloaded from Apple's developer site located at `http://developer.apple.com`. You'll first need to sign up for a free base account. Once you're signed up, simply access the Mac Dev Center and download Xcode. At the time of this writing, Xcode 3.2.2 is the most current release.

Starting Up Xcode

Xcode, by default, is installed in the /Developer/Applications folder right from the main hard drive (Macintosh HD if you're using the default hard drive label); it is not installed in the user's home directory.

When you first open Xcode, you'll see the screen in Figure 6–1.

Figure 6–1. *Xcode opening screen*

Figure 6–1 a great screen to always keep visible at the launch of Xcode. Until you are more comfortable with Xcode, keep the **Show this window when Xcode launches** check box checked. This window allows you to select the most recently created projects, access the developer documentation (that's the **Getting started with Xcode** icon), and quickly link to Apple's developer web site. Regardless of which document set is chosen, all have a wealth of information for both beginning and advanced users.

We are going to start a new project, so click the **Create a new Xcode project** icon. Whenever you want to start a new iPhone or Mac OS X application, library, or anything else, use this icon. Once a project has been started and saved, the project will appear in the Recent Projects list on the right-hand portion of the display.

Creating Your First Project

For this first Xcode project, we're going to choose something very simple. Make sure that a Mac OS X application is chosen. Then ensure that **Command Line Tool** is selected, as shown in Figure 6–2.

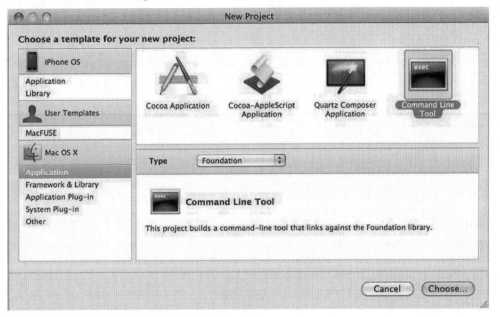

Figure 6–2. *Choosing a new project from a list of templates*

Our first project is going to be a simple application that doesn't require the complexities of a graphical interface. Next, ensure that **Foundation** is chosen in the **Type** drop-down. This option gives the application access to the main foundation framework that contains objects like NSObject, NSString, and so forth. At this point, simply press the Return key or click the **Choose. . .** button at the bottom of this window.

Xcode responds to the new project request by asking where the new project should be placed and what its name should be. It doesn't matter where the project is stored as long as its somewhere within the current user's home directory (because of permission issues). After choosing the location, type a project name of **My First App**. Then, click the **Save** button or simply press the Return key.

Once the new project name and location have been established, Xcode starts creating the necessary base files for the project. Once that is completed, Xcode display the main screen, where we will do all of the editing and debugging, and in our case, viewing of the output from our program (see Figure 6–3). The pane on the left lists all of the files that are associated with our project. The pane on the right is multipurpose but is generally used for editing the source code from the project. When you're first starting a project, it displays all of the main files that make up the project—the framework, the source files, and more.

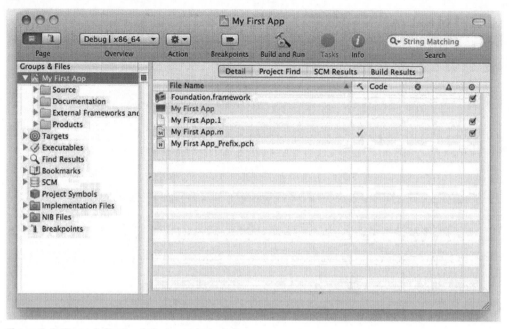

Figure 6–3. *The main Xcode window or project window*

There is quite a bit of information on this page. Note the toolbar of icons at the top of the window. The toolbar is completely customizable, but the default that Xcode provides is perfectly fine.

First, open a list of the project files by clicking the gray triangle right next to the **My First App** icon in the Groups & Files pane. You will see a list of groups displayed as folders. These are not directories on a disk, simply names that group different sets of files. This is extremely helpful, especially with larger projects.

Adding a New Class

The first group is Source. Click its gray arrow to reveal its files and then select the My First App.m source file (see Figure 6–4). Next, press Shift+⌘+E (or select **View ➤ Zoom Editor In**). This reserves the entire right pane for the editor. The editor pane now shows the boilerplate application that Xcode created for us when we first created the project. There is some code shown for what is called an NSAutoreleasePool, which is used to manage object memory. For now, we're going to add in the HelloWorld object discussed earlier. But first, simply delete the line:

```
'NSLog(@"Hello, World!");'
```

We're going to insert our own code here that will, in effect, do the same thing using an Objective-C object that we create. You can also save the file here by using ⌘+S (or **File ➤ Save**).

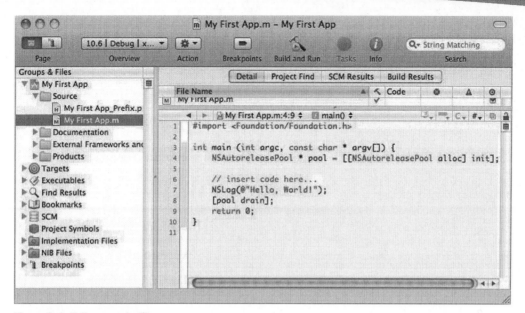

Figure 6–4. *Fully zoomed editor*

Once you've modified the code, your screen should look a lot like what's pictured in Figure 6–4. Next, we're going to add a new file to our project. Start this process by selecting a new file by pressing ⌘+N (or **File ➤ New File. . .**).

This will bring up the New File dialog shown in Figure 6–5. We are going to create a Mac OS X Objective-C class that is a subclass of NSObject. The screen highlights the choices that are needed.

Press Return or click the **Next** button to display the next dialog to name the new Objective-C class (see Figure 6–6). Type **HelloWorld.m** as the file name. Make sure the **Also create "HelloWorld.h"** check box is checked. The location on your screen will be different than the one shown; just leave the location unchanged from its default. Now, simply press the Return key or click the **Finish** button in the dialog.

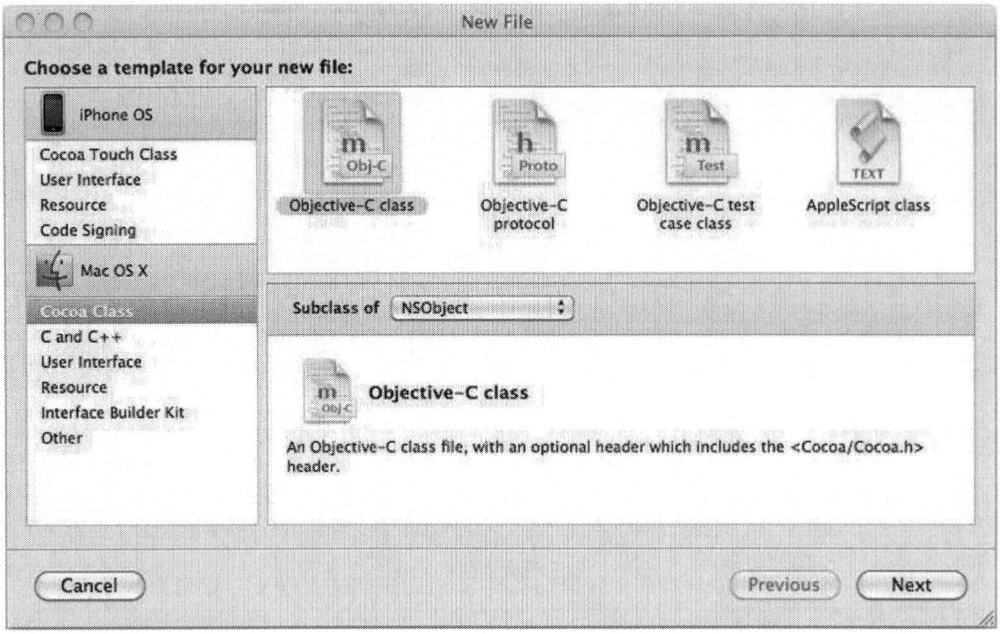

Figure 6–5. *New File dialog*

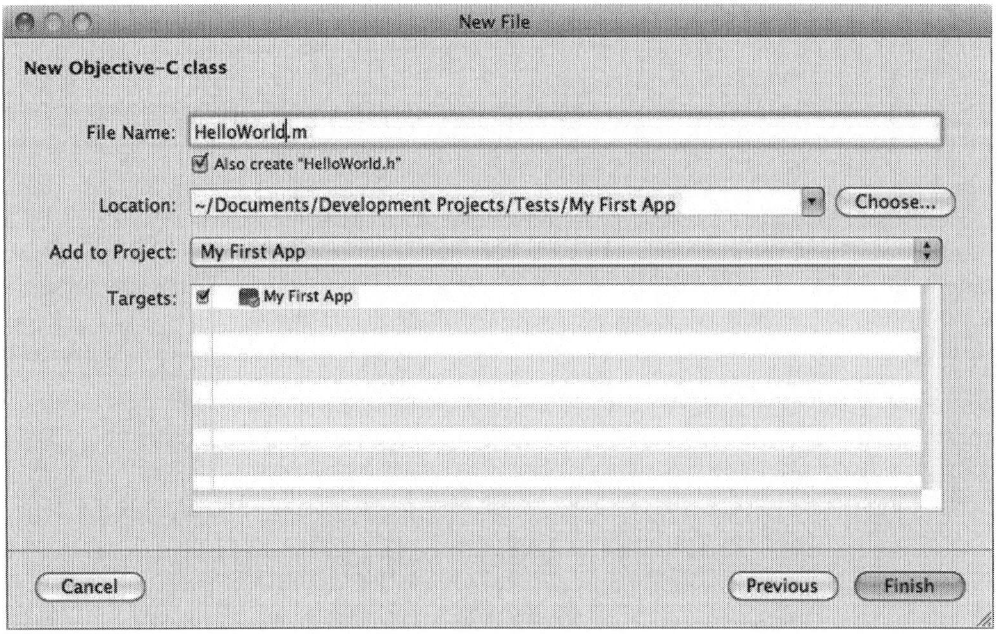

Figure 6–6. *Specifying the file name and location in the New File dialog*

NOTE: The **Add to Project** drop-down should already be set to My First App. This tells Xcode which project to add the new files to. The **Targets** check box and list show which executables these new files will be associated to. This allows Xcode to know about its **dependencies**. This means that Xcode will know that the program that is being built (My First App) needs these files. Now that you now know all this, in most circumstances, it will not be necessary to change anything other than the file name.

Your main screen should look like Figure 6–7. The HelloWorld.h file with the object's @interface section is now in the editor's main window.

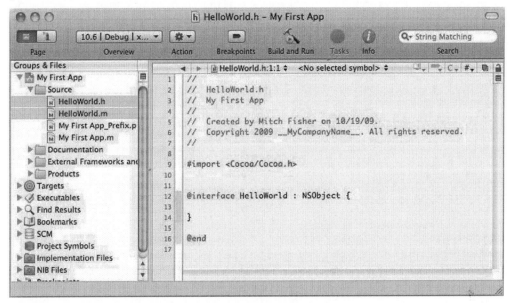

Figure 6–7. *The project with the new object's interface in the editor*

This code should look familiar from the examples earlier. There are a few differences however. First, a lot of text starts with double slash characters (//). Double slashes indicate a comment, so any text on the same line appearing after // is considered a comment. Comments don't do anything but help in explaining what's going on in the code.

Next, the line with @interface has the beginning brace ({) attached to the end of the line. The C and Objective-C languages are both very free form, so the braces don't have to be on separate lines like in our earlier examples. After the ending brace (}) but before @end, add the following line:

```
- (void)printGreeting;
```

This specifies our message that the `HelloWorld` object will respond to. The `@interface` section (please note that this is just the interface section and not the entire file) should now look like this (leave the `#import` statement):

```
@interface HelloWorld : NSObject {


}
- (void)printGreeting;


@end
```

If you want, you can save the file now by pressing ⌘+S (or selecting **File ➤ Save**). If you forget to save, don't worry; the system will save all our changes whenever we build and run of the application.

Next, click the `HelloWorld.m` file in the project. The file should look like the one shown in Figure 6–8.

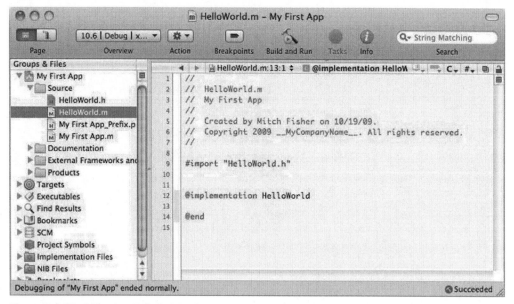

Figure 6–8. *The boilerplate HelloWorld.m file*

Now, we need to add the code to the message we placed in the `@interface` section. In the `@implementation` section, before the `@end`, place the following code:

```
- (void)printGreeting {
    NSLog(@"Hello World!");
}
```

This should also look familiar from our earlier examples. This code makes the printGreeting message actually work. The updated implementation file should look like this:

```
@implementation HelloWorld

- (void)printGreeting {
    NSLog(@"Hello World!");
}

@end
```

Okay, we have created an interface and an implementation file. To use the new class, we need to instantiate the HelloWorld object in the main application. Click the My First App.m file in the Groups & Files pane. Add the following code right *after* the comment // insert code here...:

```
HelloWorld* myObject = [[HelloWorld alloc] init];
[myObject printGreeting];
[myObject release];
```

Again, this code should look very familiar, since it present in the example earlier in this chapter. Next, we need to import the HelloWorld object. Add the following line after import of the Foundation.h file:

```
#import "HelloWorld.h"
```

Now this part of the program can use the HelloWorld object, because it now knows about the object's interface. The My First App.m code should look something like this:

```
#import <Foundation/Foundation.h>
#import "HelloWorld.h"

int main (int argc, const char * argv[]) {
    NSAutoreleasePool * pool = [[NSAutoreleasePool alloc] init];

    // insert code here...
    HelloWorld* myObject = [[HelloWorld alloc] init];
    [myObject printGreeting];
    [myObject release];

    [pool drain];
    return 0;
}
```

This should look very similar to our earlier example. Obviously, the NSAutoreleasePool is something new, and the main function looks a little different.

```
int main (int argc, const char * argv[])
```

While its not important to our little program, the preceding two variables are passed as arguments to main. These arguments hold information about anything passed to this program from the command line. They can be completely ignored for now. In fact, if you simply change the line to look like our example, int main (void), the program will still execute normally.

Building and Running the New Program

Now, it's time to build and run our program. We do so by clicking the **Build and Run** icon in the top toolbar of Xcode. If you haven't saved any of the files, you will be presented with the dialog shown in Figure 6–9 before building can proceed.

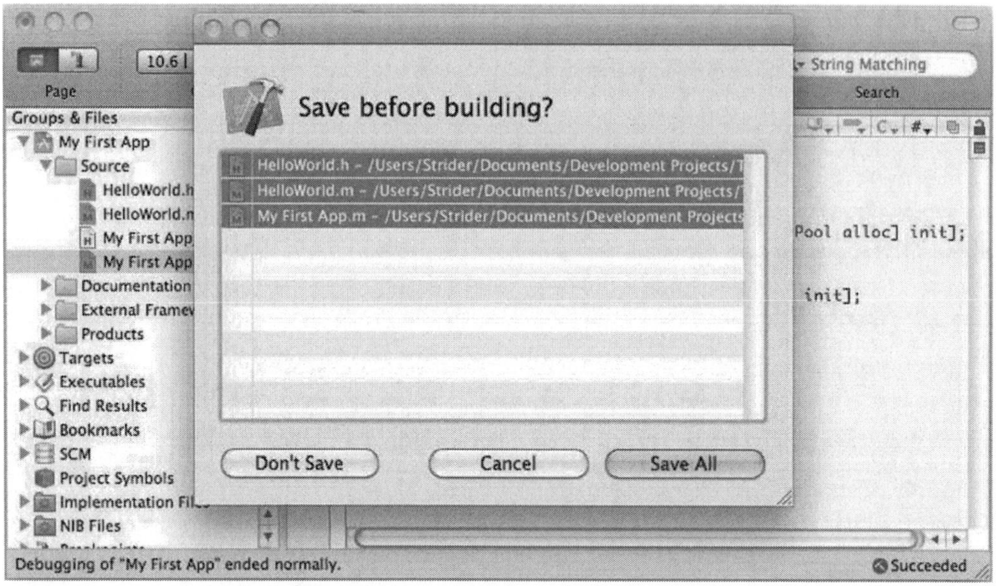

Figure 6–9. *The "Save before building?" dialog is shown only if there are unsaved files. This is one of the few ways to perform a "save all" operation in Xcode.*

Click the **Save All** button, and the build will start. If the steps in this example were followed correctly, you should see something like Figure 6–10. If there were errors, go back and review the code to make sure that the various pieces of code match the examples outlined in this chapter.

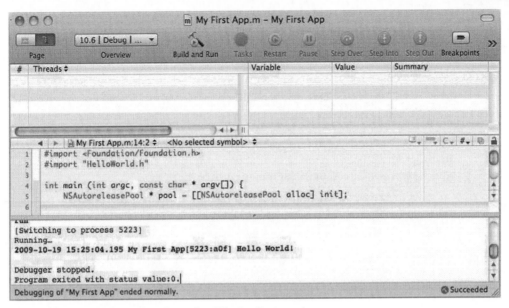

Figure 6–10. *The resulting output of your first Objective-C program!*

This view is the debugging view. The important thing to see here is the output from the HelloWorld object. The bottom pane of the display contains the program's output. The output we are interested is actually in bold, so we can see it easily:

2009-10-19 15:25:04.195 My First App[5223:a0f] Hello World!

The date, time, and other information is just standard NSLog information that is printed before the actual output; NSLog is a system logging function after all. You can get back to the original view by pressing ⌘+0 (that's command + zero), or by selecting the **Project ➤ Project** (yep, you read that right) menu option.

Summary

Well, this chapter covered a lot of information—from the origins of the C and Objective-C languages to actually writing, building, and running your very own program. The examples were very simple, but hopefully, they've whetted your appetite for more complex applications using Objective-C and Xcode. In later chapters, you can expect to learn more about object-oriented programming as well as more about what Objective-C can do. Pat yourself on the back, because you've learned a lot already. Here is a summary of the items presented in this chapter:

- The origins and brief history of the Objective-C language

- A simple C language program, HelloWorld

- An Objective-C version of that same program

- The @interface and @implementation sections of a program

- An introduction to Xcode, including entering and compiling the
  HelloWorld.m source file

Exercises

- Play around with compiling. Change the text "Hello World!" to
  something more interesting; maybe print your name instead.

- Add a new method. Right now, printGreeting is the only method in
  the program. Try adding the new method printTheMeaningOfLife and
  have it print something different than printGreeting.

- Create a third method that calls the printGreeting method and then
  the printTheMeaningOfLife method. Modify main so that this new
  method is called.

Chapter 7

Objective-C Classes, Objects, and Methods

If you haven't already read Chapter 6, please do so before reading this one, because it provides a great introduction to some of the basics of Objective-C. This chapter embellishes that foundation a bit more. Coming out of this chapter, you can expect to have a greater understanding of the Objective-C language and how to use the basics to write simple programs. For Mitch personally, the best way to learn is take small programs and write (or rewrite) them in Objective-C just to see how the language works.

This chapter will cover in more detail what composes an Objective-C class and how to interact with Objective-C objects via methods. We will use a simple radio station class as an example of how an Objective-C class is written. This will hopefully impart an understanding of how an Objective-C class can be used. This chapter also teaches you, by example, how to think out a design for objects that are needed to solve a problem. In this chapter, we'll cover how to create custom objects as well as how to use existing objects provided in the Foundation classes.

If you're coming from a C-like language, you'll find that Objective-C has several similarities. And, as described in Chapter 6, Objective-C's roots are firmly planted in the C Language. This chapter will extend Chapter 6's topics and bake in some of the concepts described in Chapter 8.

Creating an Objective-C Class

Chapter 6 introduced some of the common elements of the Objective-C language, so let's quickly review them:

- `@interface`: This keyword is used to define an interface to new Objective-C class. This is written in an `.h`, or header, file.

- **@implementation**: This keyword is used to define the actual code that implements the methods defined in the interface. This is written in an .m, or Objective-C class, file.

- **Methods**: These are names defined in the @interface section of a class and implemented in the @implementation section in the .m file.

This chapter will go into more detail of the different components of an Objective-C class.

As explained in Chapter 6, an Objective-C class consists of an interface and a corresponding implementation. For now, let's concentrate on the interface. At the most basic level, the interface of a class tells us the name of the class, what class it's derived from, and what messages the class understands. Here is a sample of the first line from a class's interface:

```
@interface RadioStation : NSObject
```

In the preceding example, the class name is RadioStation. The colon (:) after the class name indicates that the class is derived from another class; that is, the RadioStation object **inherits** functionality from the NSObject class. Put another way, in our sample, the RadioStation class is derived from the NSObject class.

> **TIP:** If your object is not inheriting from any other foundation class *always* inherit from NSObject. Without it, your class will be worthless. NSObject provides the base functions that make new objects behave correctly.

Once the class name is defined, the rest of the interface file contains the main guts of the class; see Listing 7–1.

Listing 7–1. *An Interface File,* RadioStation.h

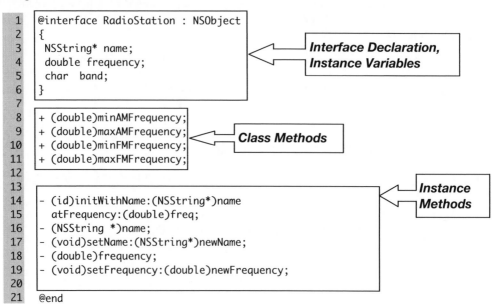

```
1    @interface RadioStation : NSObject
2    {
3      NSString* name;                              Interface Declaration,
4      double frequency;                            Instance Variables
5      char   band;
6    }
7
8    + (double)minAMFrequency;
9    + (double)maxAMFrequency;                    Class Methods
10   + (double)minFMFrequency;
11   + (double)maxFMFrequency;
12
13
14   - (id)initWithName:(NSString*)name           Instance
15     atFrequency:(double)freq;                   Methods
16   - (NSString *)name;
17   - (void)setName:(NSString*)newName;
18   - (double)frequency;
19   - (void)setFrequency:(double)newFrequency;
20
21   @end
```

Declaring Interfaces and Instance Variables

An Objective-C class is defined by its **interface**. Since objects, for the most part, are communicated with using messages, the interface of an object defines what messages the object will respond to. Lines 1–6 start the definition of the class's interface by defining its name (sometimes called the **type**) and the inherited class. Next, there is a block, defined within the braces ({ and }). This block is used to define variables that are used by the *instance* of this class. These are called **instance variables**.

Whenever the RadioStation class is instantiated, the resulting RadioStation object has access to these variables. Furthermore, these variables are only for a specific instance. If there are ten RadioStation objects, each object has its own variables independent from the other objects. This is also referred to as **scope**, in that the object's variables are within the scope of each object.

Sending Messages (Methods)

Every object has methods. In Objective-C, the common concept to interact with an object is sending an object a message:

```
[myStation frequency];
```

The preceding line will send a message to an instance of the RadioStation class named myStation. In our example, myStation is referred to as the **receiver**, since it receives the message. The message is used to select which method will be called within the object. These method names that appear in a message, like the preceding one, are called **selectors**. Since a message selects the method based on the name, for all practical purpose, a message and a method name are synonymous.

If the class does not understand a message, that message is passed to the parent object, in this case, NSObject. If that parent object doesn't understand the message, the message is passed to its parent and so on up the chain until the message is either found or not. This behavior is called **dynamic binding**, which means the method is found at runtime instead of compile time. Dynamic binding allows an Objective-C program to react to changes while the program is running. This is one of the huge advantages Objective-C has over other languages.

Messages can also have parameters passed along with them, for example:

```
[myStation setFrequency: 104.7];
```

The message is setFrequency:. The colon indicates that the message needs a parameter. Messages can have several parameters, as in the following example:

```
myStation = [[RationStation alloc] initWithName:@"KZZP" atFrequency: 104.7];
```

In the preceding example, the message we're interest in is

```
initWithName:atFrequency:
```

In this case, the message consists of two parameters: the station name and its frequency. What's interesting about Objective-C compared to other languages is that the methods basically are named parameters. If this were a C++ or Java program, the call would have been:

```
myObject = New RadioStation("KZZP", 104.7);
```

While a `RadioStation` object's parameters might seem obvious, having named parameters can be a bonus, because they more or less state what the parameters are used for or what they do. Here are some examples:

```
[NSDictionary dictionaryWithContentsOfFile: filename];
[myString characterAtIndex: 1];
[myViewController willRotateToInterfaceOrientation: portrait duration: 60];
```

Using Class Methods

A class doesn't have to be instantiated to be used. In some cases, classes have methods that can actually perform some simple operation and return a value. These methods are called **class methods**. In Listing 7–1, the method names that start with a plus sign (+) are class methods—all class methods must start with a + sign.

Class methods have limitations. One of the biggest is that none of the instance variables can be used. Well, technically Xcode allows instance variables to be coded in a class method. The code will compile with a warning, but accessing or using the instance variable does nothing—just don't do it. Being unable to use instance variables makes sense since we haven't instantiated anything. A class method can have its own local variables within the method itself but can't use any of the variables defined as instance variables.

A call to a class method would look like this:

```
[RadioStation minAMFrequency];
```

Notice that the call is very similar to how a message is passed to an instantiated object. The big difference is that instead of an instance variable, the *class name* itself is used. Class methods are used quite extensively in the Mac OS X and iPhone OS frameworks. They are used mostly for returning some fixed or well-known type of value or to return a new instance of an object. These types of class methods are sometimes referred to as **factory methods**, since, like a factory, they create something new—in this case, a new instance of a class. Here's a factory method example:

```
1.  [NSDate timeIntervalSinceReferenceDate]; // Returns a number
2.  [NSString stringWithFormat:@"%d", 1000]; // Returns a new NSString object
3.  [NSDictionary alloc];         // Returns a new uninitialized NSDictionary
    object.
```

All of the preceding messages are class methods being called.

Line 1 simply returns a value that represents the number of seconds since January 1, 2001, which is the reference date.

Line 2 returns a new `NSString` object that has been formatted and has a value of 1000.

Line 3 is a form that is very commonly used, because it actually allocates a new object. Typically, the line is use not by itself but in a line like this:

```
myDict = [[NSDictionary alloc] init];
```

The preceding call is a **compound call**. The [NSDictionary alloc] class method returns a new NSDictionary object. That object is then sent the init instance method, which is used within a class to initialize itself, such as setting up instance variables. The init function then returns the new object back to the caller.

Where are the class variables? Well, the Objective-C specification doesn't have any class variables *per se*. Some consider static variables that are declared outside of the interface block to be class variables. The problem is that an instance of that class, and even other classes, have access to them as well. For all practical purposes, Objective-C does not have any class variables.

Using Instance Methods

Instance methods (lines 13–19 in Listing 7–1) are methods that are only available once a class has been instantiated, for example:

```
1   RadioStation *myStation;        // This declares a variable to hold the
2   RadioStation Object.
3   myStation = [[RadioStation alloc] init]; // This creates a new object and puts
4   it in my variable.
5   [myStation setFrequency: 104.7];   // This sets the frequency of the myStation
6   object
```

Lines 3 and 4 send a message to the RadioStation object: line 3 calls the method to set the frequency, and line 4 retrieves it. The frequency is stored with the object in the frequency instance variable. Furthermore, instance methods have access to the instance variables defined in the **interface declaration** section of the class. All instance methods must start with a hyphen (-); this easily denotes them from class methods, which use a plus sign.

Working with the Implementation File

Now that you've seen what an interface file looks like, let's take a look at the **implementation file**. First, the interface file had an .h extension, RadioStation.h for example. The implementation file has an .m extension, like RadioStation.m as shown in Listing 7–2.

Another important thing to note is that the interface and implementation files have the same name (excluding the extension). This convention is used universally: while there is nothing preventing an interface and an implementation file from having different names, having different names can cause much confusion, and tools like Xcode won't work as well. For example, the Xcode key sequence Command + up-arrow (⌘ + ↑) moves between implementation and interface file, and it will not work if the two file names are not the same.

Listing 7–2. *Part of Our Implementation File*

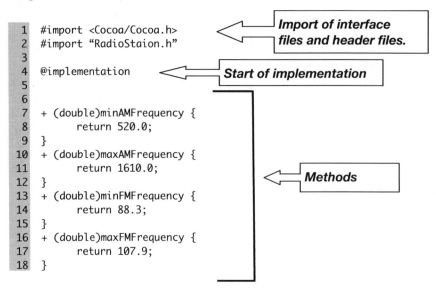

```
1    #import <Cocoa/Cocoa.h>
2    #import "RadioStaion.h"
3
4    @implementation
5
6
7    + (double)minAMFrequency {
8            return 520.0;
9    }
10   + (double)maxAMFrequency {
11           return 1610.0;
12   }
13   + (double)minFMFrequency {
14           return 88.3;
15   }
16   + (double)maxFMFrequency {
17           return 107.9;
18   }
```

Import of interface files and header files.

Start of implementation

Methods

When Xcode creates a class, it creates a very rudimentary stub of an implementation file. Listing 7–2 starts with two #import statements. An #import statement tells the compiler to read in the specified file, because the compiler needs to know about certain predefined things. For example, in our interface file, the RadioStation class is a subclass of NSObject. The NSObject class needs to be defined for the program to compile successfully. In our case, line 1 imports the Cocoa.h file. This file (which imports many other files as well) defines the NSObject class for our program.

Although there is an NSObject.h file that could be imported instead, one of our instance variables defined in the interface file is an NSString class. Therefore, we need to import NSString.h. But because NSString.h is also imported with Cocoa.h, it's a lot easier to just import everything in the Cocoa framework with one #import statement. It takes a just a microsecond longer to compile and doesn't affect the final application's performance; plus, we won't have to worry if we change our RadioStation class to require another class, like NSDctionary.

The second #import statement reads in our interface file for the class. As the compiler goes through our implementation (.m) file, it needs to know what class it is implementing, and the interface file provides all the information that it needs.

NOTE: Look at the #import statements: one uses angle brackets (< >) and the other uses plain double quotation marks (" "). The difference is a file that is in the angle brackets indicate a system-level file and are located using a predefined path that Xcode automatically sets up for our project. Any file that has double quotation marks is searched for in the current project. In our example, the RadioStation.h interface file is part of our project, so we use double quotation marks, whereas the Cocoa.h file is a system file and uses the angle brackets.

Implementing Methods

Listing 7–2 is a very simple example, but it demonstrates what many methods look like in a class. First of all, if we look at the implementation and interface files for one of the class methods, we can see the similarities. The following line is from the interface file:

```
+ (double)minAMFrequency;
```

We can see it is a class method because it starts with a plus sign. The next item (double) is the type of value the method will return, in our case, a double. The next part in the interface file is simply the name of the method, minAMFrequency.

The following line is from the implementation file:

```
+ (double)minAMFrequency {
        return 520.0;

}
```

This line represents an implementation of the method defined in the interface. The word "implementation" indicates that the function is coded here. It looks nearly identical to the interface file but now contains a block with some code in it rather than simply ending with a semicolon.

In our example, our implementation of the minAMFrequency class method simply performs a return of numeric value (a double) of 520.0.

Generally, a class has a definition of a method in an interface file and the actual code of the method in an implementation file.

Now, we will look at the implementation of an **instance method** (see Listing 7–3). The big differences between an instance method and a class method are that instance methods have the option to use the instance variables defined in the interface file; plus, instance methods are only available once the class has been instantiated.

Listing 7–3. *An Implementation of an Instance Method*

```
1   - (id)initWithName:(NSString *)newName atFrequency:(double)newFreq {
2     self = [super init];
3     if (self != nil) {
4       name = newName;
5       frequency = newFrequency;
6     }
7
8     return self;
9   }
```

Listing 7–3 is the implementation of one of the instance methods of our radio station class. It is an initialization method that accepts a new station name and frequency. Many OS X and iPhone OS classes have similar initialization instance methods. Instead of simply initializing the class and then individually setting various values, many class initialization methods allow special initialization or, in our case, multiple values to be passed on initialization.

In our example, line 1 is the interface to our method, and it contains two parameters, the newName and newFrequency variables. To use this method, the caller would simply do the following:

```
RadioStation myStation = [[RadioStation alloc] initWithName:@"WOW FM"
                                         atFrequency: 102.5];
```

This method is also defined to return an id value. An id is a generic object, and all Objective-C objects are of type id, just like the class RadioStation is an object. Now, look at the rest of the implementation.

Line 2 references two special variables that we don't have to define anywhere. The keyword self is used to mean "this instance of this class," so line 2 is assigning "this instance of this class" the value returned from the use of the second special variable: super init. The keyword super is short for "superclass," which can be thought of as "the parent of my class." Any initialization type of a method will typically start with something that looks similar to line 2.

Why is line 2 even necessary? Well, if we have an object that is derived from another object (remember, the class is declared as RadioStation : NSObject), we need to tell the parent object to initialize itself. The parent will do the same by telling its parent to initialize itself and so on up the chain to the topmost object. If another class used ours as a parent, our code would also have to eventually get an init call so RadioStation can be initialized. This is standard convention in the real world of Objective-C. A class needs to tell its parent to initialize when the class is created, and it needs to tell its parent to deallocate itself whenever the class is going away.

Line 3 checks to see if the [super init] call worked or not. If it worked, the value of self will be something other than nil, which is a value that effectively means "not initialized."

Lines 4 and 5 set up the instance variables to the values passed into this method.

Line 8 returns self to the caller. Just like the call to [super init], our initialization function needs to return the new object back to the caller.

Using Our New Class

We've created a simple RadioStation class, but by itself, it doesn't accomplish a whole lot. In this section, we will create the Radio class and have it maintain a list of RadioStation classes. Let's start up Xcode (see Figure 7–1) and create a new project named RadioSimulation.

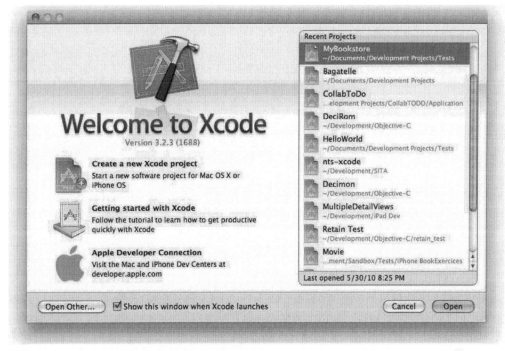

Figure 7–1. *Open Xcode, so you can create a new project.*

Make sure you choose a Mac OS X application, and select the **Command Line Tool** template, as shown in **Figure 7–2.** Also ensure that **Foundation** is chosen for the type.

Figure 7–2. *Selecting a template in the New Project window*

At this point, you should see the screen shown in Figure 7–3.

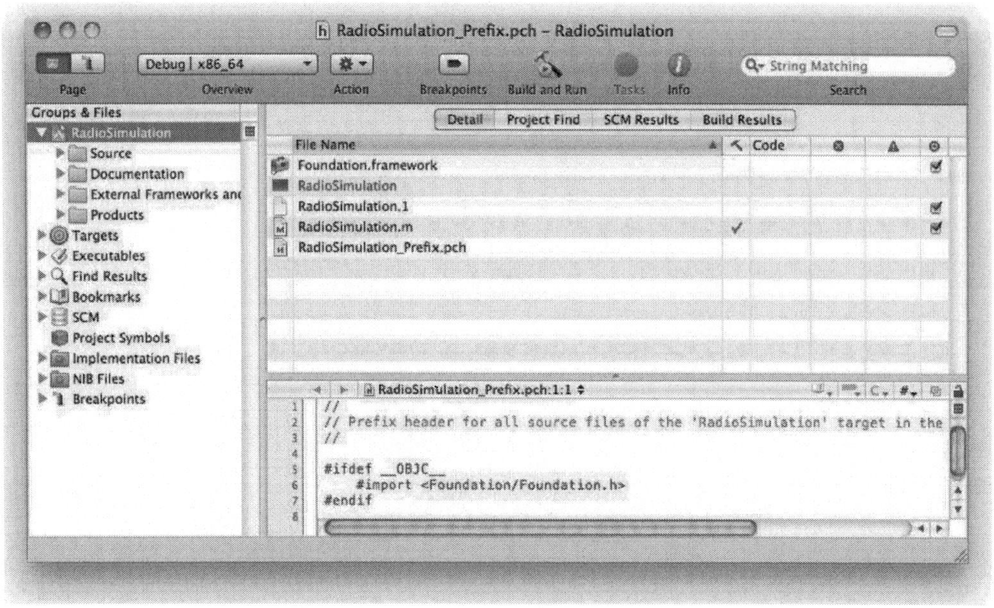

Figure 7–3. *The main Project window*

Now, let's add in our new objects. First, we'll create our RadioStation object. Open the **Source** group in the **Groups & Files** pane, right-click the **Source** group, and select **New File...** as shown in Figure 7–4.

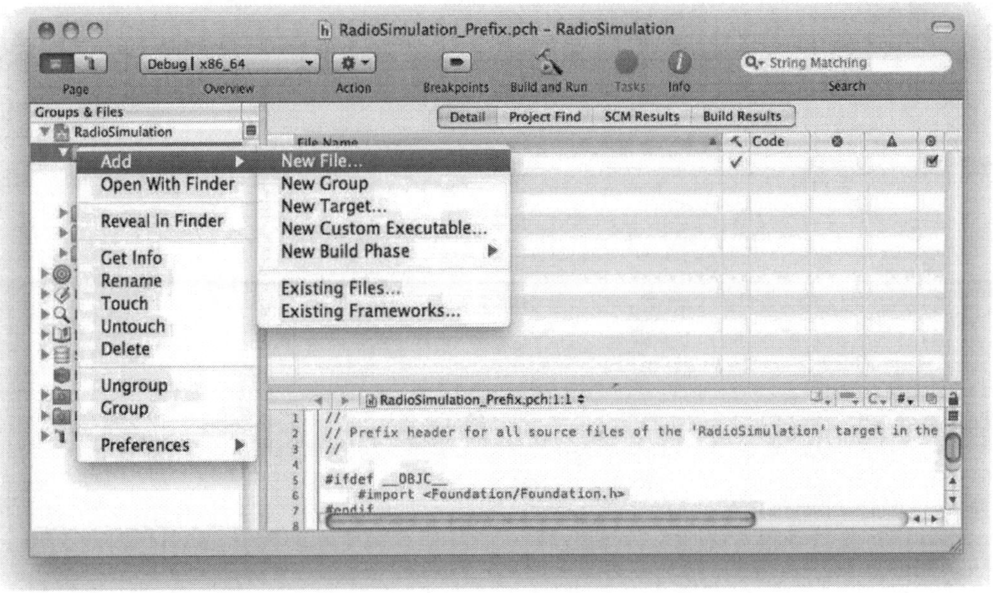

Figure 7–4. *Adding a new file*

The next screen, shown in Figure 7–5, asks for the new file type. Simply choose **Objective-C class** from the Mac OS X group. Make sure that the **Subclass of** drop-down is set to **NSObject**. Then click **Next**.

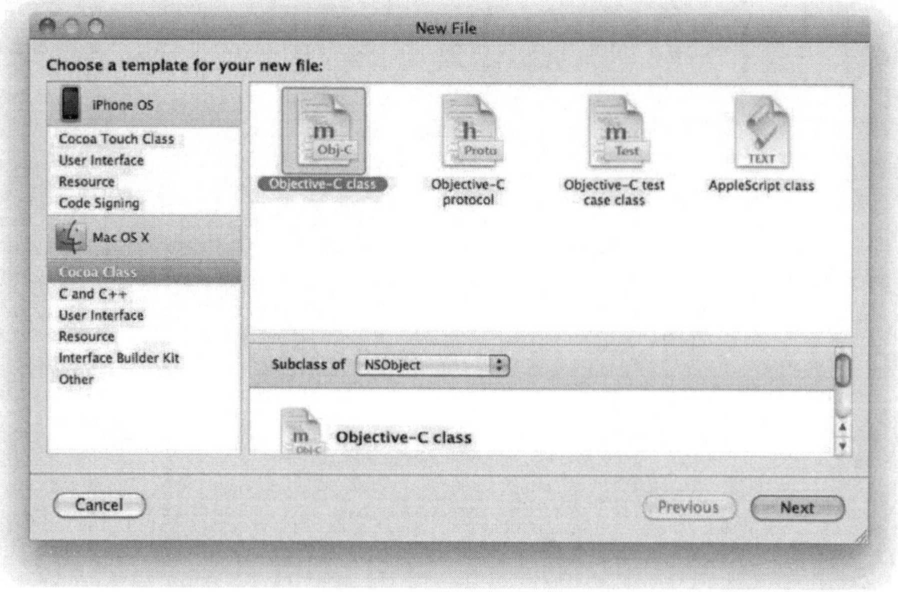

Figure 7–5. *Selecting the new file type*

Now, the dialog shown in Figure 7–6 will be displayed to prompt you for the new file name. Change `untitled.m` to `RadioStation.m`. Make sure that the "R" and "S" are capitalized. While the file and class names technically don't need to be the same, it's the established convention, and thus the way to avoid confusion.

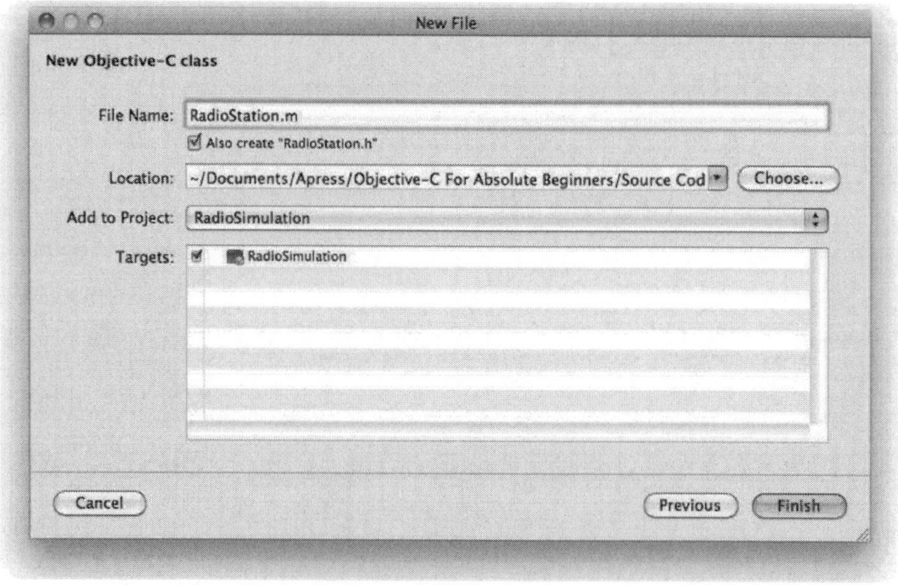

Figure 7–6. *Giving the new file a proper name*

As shown in Figure 7–6 ensure that the **Also create "RadioStation.h"** check box is checked (this box is normally checked by default).

Our project window should now look like Figure 7–7.

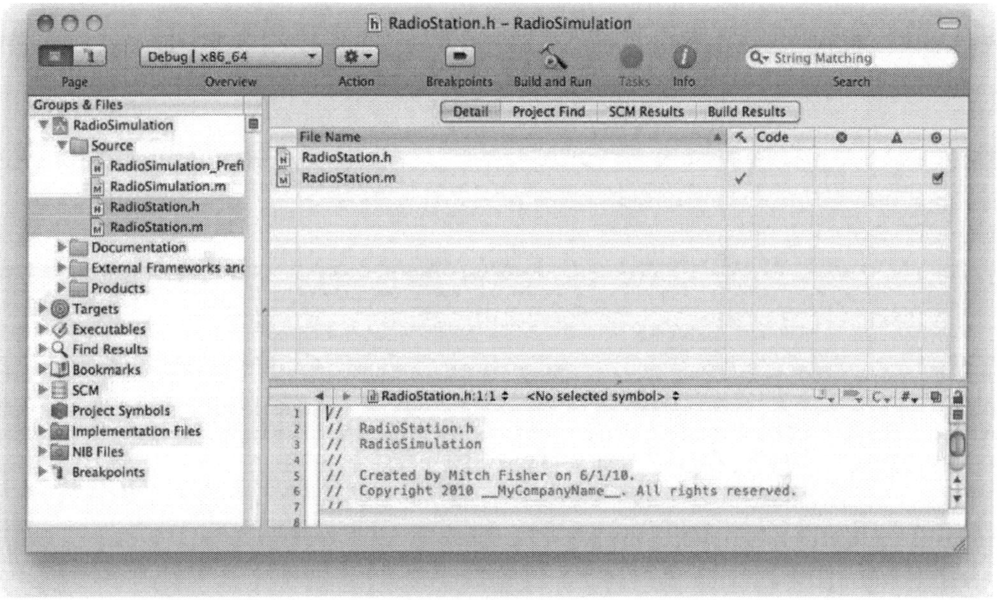

Figure 7–7. *Our newly created file in the project window*

Click the RadioStation.h file, and press ⇧ + ⌘ + E (Shift + Command + E) to expand the source code window. Pressing ⇧ + ⌘ + E a second time will return to the split view. Notice that the stub of our new RadioStation class already present. Now, fill in the empty class to look like Listing 7–1, our RadioStation interface file.

The RadioStation.h file now defines the instance variables, class methods, and instance methods of our new class. Let's move on to the implementation file.

The implementation file we'll use here has been simplified a bit from our example several pages ago but will work perfectly for our radio station simulation. Click the RadioStation.m file, and let's put code to our class as shown in Listing 7–4.

Listing 7–4.

```
#import "RadioStation.h"

@implementation RadioStation

+ (double)minAMFrequency {
        return 520.0;
}

+ (double)maxAMFrequency {
        return 1610.0;
}

+ (double)minFMFrequency {
        return 88.3;
}

+ (double)maxFMFrequency {
        return 107.9;
}

- (id)initWithName:(NSString *)newName atFrequency:(double)newFreq {
 self = [super init];
 if (self != nil) {
  name = [newName retain];
  frequency = newFreq;
 }
 return self;
}

- (NSString *)description {
 return [NSString stringWithFormat:@"Name: %@, Frequency: %.1f", name,
frequency];
}

- (void)dealloc {
 [name release];
 [super dealloc];
}
@end
```

We will come back to a few items in Listing 7–2 and explain them further in a moment. However, with the RadioStation class defined, we can now write the code that will actually use it. From the main project window, click the RadioSimulation.m file. Listing 7–5 shows the default contents of the RadioSimulation.m file, which holds our main function and is where the program starts executing.

Listing 7–5.

```
#import <Foundation/Foundation.h>

int main (int argc, const char * argv[]) {
 NSAutoreleasePool * pool = [[NSAutoreleasePool alloc] init];

 // insert code here...
 NSLog(@"Hello, World!");
 [pool drain];
 return 0;
}
```

Now, add the following highlighted code right after the comment that says:

```
// insert code here...,
```

Delete the text that says "Hello World!", as shown in Listing 7–6.

Listing 7–6.

```
// insert code here...
NSMutableDictionary* stations = [[NSMutableDictionary alloc] init];
RadioStation* newStation;

newStation = [[RadioStation alloc]
      initWithName:@"Star 94 FM" atFrequency:94.1];

[stations setObject:newStation forKey:@"WSTR"];
[newStation release];

NSLog(@"%@", [stations objectForKey:@"WSTR"]);

[stations release];
```

Don't worry if you can't remember the details of NSMutableDictionary from Chapter 6, we'll get to that more in Chapter 10. For now, you just need to know that it's a class provided by Mac OS X and the iPhone OS that offers a mechanism to store objects in a list with a key that can be used to retrieve that object. In our example, we are using the key @"WSTR", because these just happen to be the stations call letters. The key can be anything unique to items in a list, so it just seemed appropriate to use the call letters of the station in our example.

Click the **Build and Debug** button on the Xcode menu bar (see Figure 7–8) to build and run your program.

Figure 7–8. *The Xcode menu bar*

If there are errors, a red stop sign will appear on the offending code lines. Check the program with the source listing, and fix the issues (or just download the project from the Apress web site). If everything goes well and there are no compilation errors, Xcode will switch to the Debug view shown in Figure 7–9. The bold text in the output window should show the name of the station and its corresponding frequency.

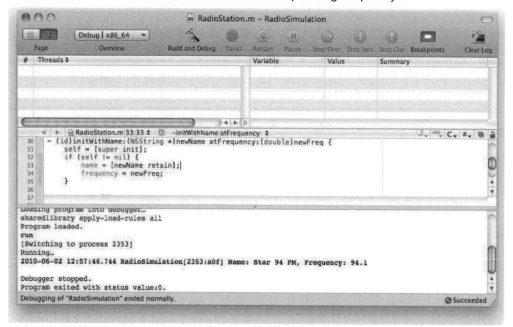

Figure 7–9. *In the Xcode debugging window, the bottom pane is the program's output.*

The important output to notice is what we asked our program to print:

```
RadioSimulation[2353:a0f] Name: Star 94 FM, Frequency: 94.1
```

This line is generated through the description method that was coded in the RationStation.m file. This is the part of the code that needs a little more explanation.

Overriding Default Behavior

Our RadioStation class contains a method called description, and it appears only in the implementation file, not the interface file. We could have defined the method in the interface file, but we left out the method just to demonstrate a few points. First, Objective-C is a dynamic message passing system. You can pass any message to any object. Sometimes, objects will respond; sometimes, their parent will respond, and sometimes, you will get a runtime error because none of the objects knows the message.

In our case, we are overriding a method that exists in the NSObject class. Whenever a program uses a string formatting function like NSLog and %@ is specified, the object is permitted to print information about itself. In this case, the NSLog method calls the object's description method to get that information. If we did not implement a description method, the NSObject class would have eventually handled the message. But the point here is that we are intercepting a message that is sent from the NSLog function and handling it in our class instead of ignoring it. In more advanced programs, overriding messages become more of a standard, although it appears to be an exception here.

If we did not override the description method, the program would still run, but the output would not be what we expected:

```
RadioSimulation[2483:a0f] <RadioStation: 0x100108df0>
```

What is displayed if we don't create our own description method is actually the hexadecimal value that is the pointer of the object (Chapter 12 offers more information on pointers). For now, it's fine to just consider it gibberish!

Taking Class Methods to the Next Level

In our program, we've not at all taken advantage of the class methods for RadioStation, but this chapter does describe what a class method is and how it is used. Use that knowledge to try a few of the exercises mentioned at the end of this chapter. Just play around with this simple working program by adding or changing class or instance methods to get an idea of how they work.

Accessing the Xcode Documentation

We cannot emphasize enough the wealth of information provided in the Xcode **Developer Documentation** dialog. When Xcode is opened, the **Help** menu will appear in the main menu (see Figure 7–10). This is where the Developer Documentation window can be opened.

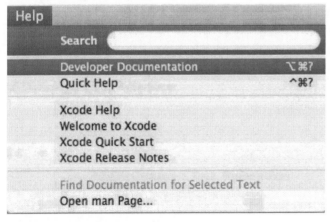

Figure 9-10. *The Xcode help menu*

Once opened, the search window can be used to look up any of the documentation, including NSDictionary class documentation, as shown in Figure 7–11.

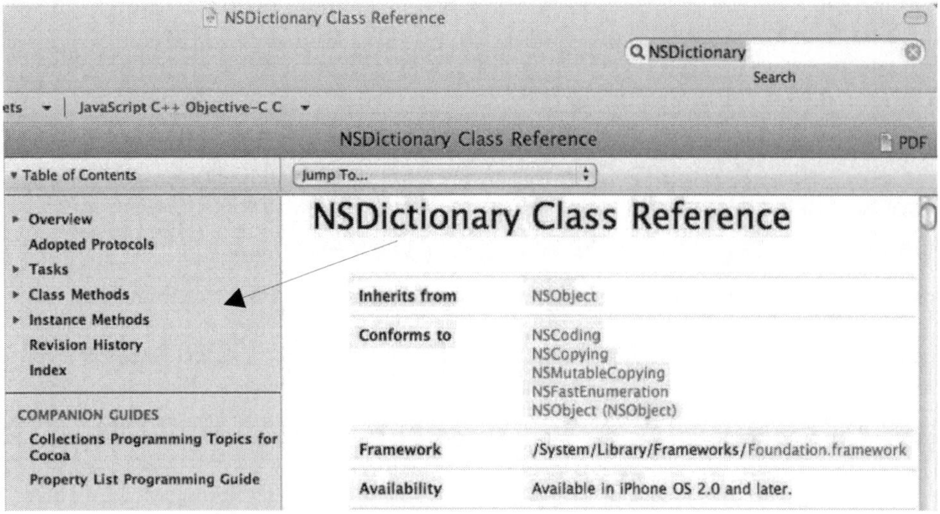

Figure 7–11. *The developers' documentation window*

There are several different things to discover about this class, but in Figure 7–11, the arrow is pointing to two areas that are most important in this chapter. Take the time to look at the **Class Methods** and **Instance Methods** sections to see what the NSDictionary class can do.

Summary

Here we are at the end of another chapter. Once again, congratulate yourself for being able to single handedly stuff your brain with a lot of information. Here is a summary of what was covered in this chapter:

- Objective-C classes review
- Interface files
    - Instance variables
    - Class methods
    - Instance methods
    - Dynamic binding
- Implementation files
    - Defining the methods interface in the interface file and putting code to that interface in the implementation file

- Limitations when using class methods instead of instance methods

  - Initializing the class and making use of the instance variables

- Making use of our new RadioStation object

  - Overriding the description method

Exercises

- Add more radio stations to the Radio dictionary. What happens if a new station is added that has the same dictionary key as an existing one?

- Modify the RadioStation class using the instance variable that will indicate if the station is AM or FM (hint: you'll need to change the initWithName:Frequency: method to accept a new parameter for the radio band).

If you are feeling bold, you can try these exercises too:

- Update the RadioStation class to validate if the frequency set is in the proper range once the AM or FM designation has been set. To make things simple, if the designated frequency is too high for the given band, set the frequency to the maximum of that band. For example, if the band is AM and the frequency is 2000.0, set the frequency to 1620.0.

- Using the Xcode documentation, find a way to iterate through the list of items in the NSMutableDictionary (hint: you need to enumerate the list of objects in the dictionary).

Chapter 8

Programming Basics in Objective-C

Objective-C is a very elegant language. It mixes the efficiency of the C language with the object-oriented goodness of Smalltalk. This combination was introduced in the mid-1980s and is still powering the fantastic applications behind the iPhone and Mac OS X. How does a language that is over 20 years old stay relevant and useful after all of that time? Well, some of its success has to do with the fact that the two languages that make up Objective-C are very well tested and very well designed. Another reason is less obvious; the various frameworks available for the iPhone and Mac OS X make developing full-featured applications much easier. These frameworks benefit from the fact that they have been around for a while, which equates to stability and high functionality. Last, Objective-C is highly dynamic. While we won't be focusing on this in this chapter, the dynamic nature of Objective-C provides a flexibility not found in many compiled languages. With all of these great features, Objective-C and the corresponding frameworks provide an excellent palette from which a masterpiece can be created!

This chapter will introduce some of the more common concepts of Objective-C, such as properties and instance variables, and will touch on memory management. This chapter will also introduce you to a straightforward objective—create a simple project that that consists of a `Book` object and the ability to store many of these objects into a `Bookstore` and then give the bookstore the ability to list the books, add new books, and remove existing books.

This does sound like a lot to accomplish, but Objective-C and the Foundation framework provide a wealth of other objects and methods to help us to accomplish this with ease. Initially, this project will start as a Command Line Tool project. All this means is that we are not going to be doing anything visually complicated at this point. If you're among the eager beavers who just collectively released a sigh of disappointment, there is hope. A later project will take the existing objects that will be created here and hook them into a simple user interface using the iPhone emulator.

Creating a Simple Command Line Tool

First things first, let's start by creating the base application project. We start by opening Xcode and creating a new Command Line Tool project. While a command line tool is not as fun as, say, a simple iPhone application, the purpose of this initial project is to introduce some basic ideas before moving on to something more complicated. In this program, we will create a few simple objects for what is to become our bookstore program: a Book object and the Bookstore object itself. You will learn what an instance variable is and how to get and set the value of one. Last, we'll put our bookstore objects to use, and you'll learn how to make use of objects once we've created them. Fire up Xcode, and start by creating a new project, as shown in Figure 8–1.

Figure 8–1. *Creating the initial project using the Foundation framework*

Click the **Choose** button, and name the project MyBookstore. This will create the boilerplate Bookstore project, as shown in Figure 8–2.

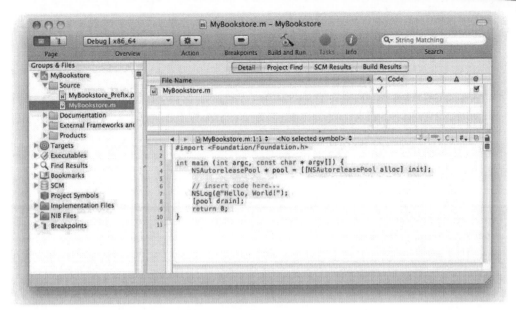

Figure 8–2. *The Source listing of the boilerplate project*

From the project's **Groups & Files** pane, right-click (or control-click) the **Source** group and click **Objective-C class** to add a new class. Make sure that the class is a subclass of NSObject, as shown in Figure 8–3.

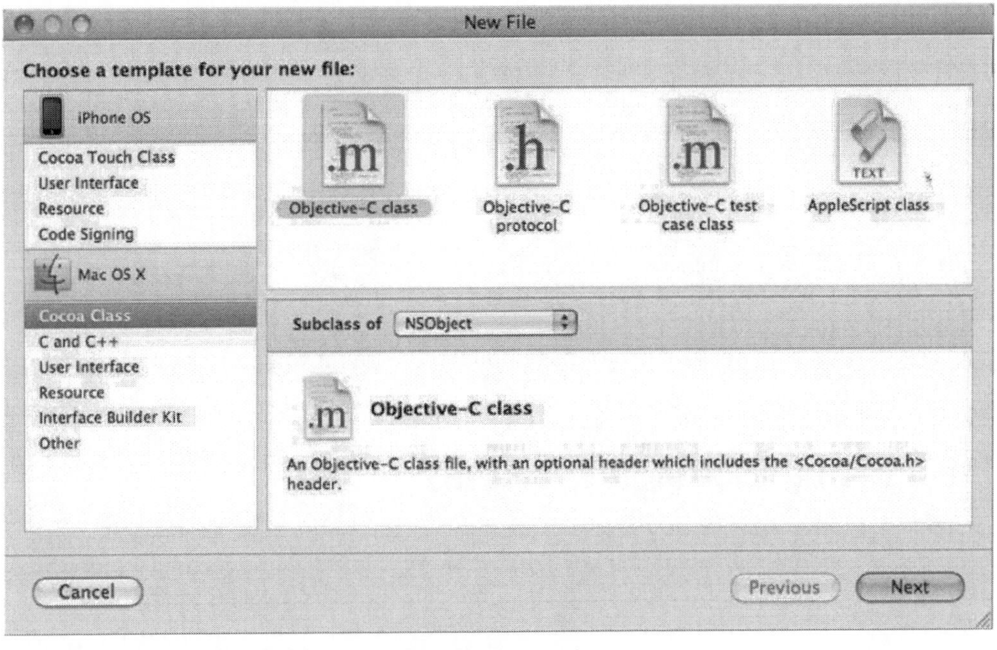

Figure 8–3. *Adding a new Objective-C class to the Bookstore project*

Click the **Next** button, and name this new object Book.m. Make sure that the "B" in Book.m is capitalized, as shown in Figure 8–4. Also make sure that the **Also create "Book.h"** check box is checked (it normally is); this option creates our interface file.

Figure 8–4. *Part of the dialog for creating the new Book object*

Click the **Finish** button to add the new object to the project. At this point, there should be a Book.h and a Book.m file in the **Groups & Files** pane. Clicking the Book.h file should reveal something like the following:

```
1    //
2    //  Book.h
3    //  MyBookstore
4    //
5    //  Created by Mitch Fisher on 10/25/09.
6    //  Copyright 2009 __MyCompanyName__. All rights reserved.
7    //
8
9    #import <Foundation/Foundation.h>
10
11   @interface Book : NSObject {
12
13   }
14
15   @end
16
17
18
```

Lines 1–7 are all just comments about the file. Of course, line 5 will have a different name and date than the one shown here. The real meat of the code is from line 9 onward. We first #import the Foundation header file. This file, for the most part, simply contains the interface declarations of base Foundation framework. Our new object starts at line 11.

Introducing Instance Variables

Our object is simply called Book and is a subclass of NSObject. True, we have an object, but it doesn't *store* anything at this point. In order for this class to be useful, it needs to be able to hold some information, which is done with something called **instance variables**. When an object is used, it has to be instantiated. Once the object is instantiated, it has access to its instance variables. These variables are available to the object as long as the object stays in scope. **Scope** defines the context in which an object exists. In some cases, an object's scope may be the life of the program. In other cases, the scope might be just a function or method. It all depends on where the object is declared and how it's used. Scope will be discussed more in a bit. For now, lets add some instance variables to our Book class to make it more useful.

```
1    //
2    //   Book.h
3    //   MyBookstore
4    //
5    //   Created by Mitch Fisher on 11/1/09.
6    //   Copyright 2009 __MyCompanyName__. All rights reserved.
7    //
8
9    #import <Cocoa/Cocoa.h>
10
11   @interface Book : NSObject {
12        NSString* title;
13        NSString* author;
14        NSString* description;
15   }
16
17   @end
```

This is the same Book object from before, but now, there are three new instance variables placed inside the brackets, lines 12–14. These are all NSString objects, which means that they can hold text information for our Book object. So, the Book object now has a place to store title, author, and description information.

Accessing Instance Variables

Now that we have some instance variables, how can we use them? How are they accessed? As you learned in previous chapters, Objective-C objects respond to messages. Unfortunately, simply declaring an instance variable doesn't necessarily give us access to it. There are two ways to access these variables. One way is, of course, within our Book object. The second way is from outside of the object—that is, another part of the program that uses the Book object.

If we are writing the code for a method within our Book object, accessing an instance variable is quite simple. For example, you could simply write the following:

```
title = @"Test Title";
```

Of course, the preceding line is written within the Book class. Outside of the object, the title instance variable is not visible at all. Of course, outside objects need to be able to access these instance variables as well. To accomplish this, you need to create two types of methods: a getter and a setter. A **getter** is a method that returns the value of something in the object, typically an instance variable like the author variable from the Book object. A **setter** is a method that updates or sets that instance variable. Let's take a look at the traditional getter and setter methods that were common before the introduction of Objective-C 2.0 back in 2007.

> **NOTE:** Technically you can access a public instance variable by using the syntax of `object->variable`. However, with the arrival of properties, this syntax is not necessarily recommended or common.

Using Getter and Setter Methods

Here is the Book object's header (.h) file, which contains the Book's interface definition.

```
1    #import <Cocoa/Cocoa.h>
2
3    @interface Book : NSObject {
4         NSString* title;
5         NSString* author;
6         NSString* description;
7    }
8
9    - (NSString*)title;                    // Getter  method
10   - (void)setTitle(NSString* newString); // Setter Method
```

The two methods declared on lines 9 and 10 are the getter and setter methods respectively. Conventionally, the getter method is named the same as the instance variable. In our example, we are fetching the title of a book object so our getter method is simply `title`. It is defined to return an `NSString` object to the caller.

The setter object is named by convention to `setInstanceVariableName`. So for our example, the setter method is named `setTitle`. Notice that the instance variable name's first character uses an uppercase letter; this is also part of the standard convention.

> **NOTE:** A naming convention called **camel case** (or **CamelCase**) uses an uppercase letter to distinguish different words in a method, variable, or class name. The text is suggestive of a camel, since the uppercase letters tend to form humps. It makes the label easier to read. For example, `stringWithContentsOfURL` is much easier to read than `stringwithcontentsofurl`. The camel case convention is used extensively through the Foundation frameworks for all types of labels (e.g., class and method names).

Now, the word "convention" has been mentioned several times. Objective-C does not require that a method be named anything specific. However, since most applications follow the guidelines we discussed, the convention becomes the *de facto* standard. Knowing this becomes very important when the topic of properties is discussed in a bit.

For now, however, we are going to manually write a getter and a setter method so that they can be better understood.

First, the getter—this is the simplest of the methods to implement:

```
1    - (NSString *)title {
2          return title;
3    }
```

In the preceding example, the method `title` simply returns the local instance variable called `title`. Remember that to access the method, the syntax [object title] is used.

It might seem that the instance variable and the method name might somehow get confused. Because an instance variable is accessed completely differently from a method name, the Objective-C runtime environment doesn't have a problem with instance variable and method names that are the same.

Now, here is the setter:

```
1    - (void)setTitle (NSString* newTitle) {
2          if ([newTitle count] > 0) {
3            title = newTitle;
4          }
5    }
```

This example is a little more complicated than out getter method, although it doesn't have to be. In our setter example, there is a check to see if the `newTitle` has a length greater than 0 before assigning the string. Clearly, our setter code doesn't want the current title to be blank.

The benefit of a setter method is that the object can perform some validation logic on the parameters before accepting the value. If the object were to allow direct access to the instance variable, either this type of validation would have to be everywhere or there would be no validation at all and the object's title could potentially be set to something invalid (like a blank title!).

Now, it is not necessary to *always* create a getter and/or a setter for every instance variable. A good example of this might simply be an object that represents today's date. There is no need to set it, just retrieve it, so there would only be a getter method.

The needs of the object and variables will dictate how the getter and setter methods are built. If a getter gets the value and the setter sets a value, it's going to take a lot of coding to simply write all the getters and setters in an object, especially if there are many instance variables. Fortunately, Objective-C 2.0 introduced a way to reduce this burden with minimal effort on the programmer's part. These features in Objective-C 2.0 are called properties.

NOTE: Objective-C 2.0 was introduced in 2006 and is included in Xcode 3.0 and later.

Introducing Properties

When we created instance variables for the Book object, we manually created the methods that could be used to access these variables. Now that you know how to do this manually, let's look at how to take advantage of something called properties. A **property** is a shorthand way of having the compiler create functions to get and/or set the value of an instance variable. As you learned earlier, instance variables are generally not accessible from outside of the object itself, so having methods to get and set these variables becomes essential.

The following is the **interface** (header) file to the Book object that we created earlier. Let's see what it takes to have the Objective-C compiler create our getters and setters for us.

```
1   //
2   //  Book.h
3   //  MyBookstore
4   //
5   //  Created by Mitch Fisher on 11/1/09.
6   //  Copyright 2009 __MyCompanyName__. All rights reserved.
7   //
8
9   #import <Cocoa/Cocoa.h>
10
11  @interface Book : NSObject {
12          NSString* title;
13          NSString* author;
14          NSString* description;
15  }
16
17  @property (nonatomic,retain) NSString* title;
18  @property (nonatomic,retain) NSString* author;
19  @property (nonatomic,retain) NSString* description;
20
21  @end
```

Lines 17–19 show the property declarations for the instance variables. Properties are not required for all instance variables, just the ones we want to expose to the world. In the example, however, we are creating properties for all of our instance variables.

A property starts with a @property directive. This tells the Objective-C compiler to build us the automatic getter and/or setter. Whether it is a getter and or setter is included in the declaration. Let's dissect this code:

@property[1] (retain)[2] NSString* title[3];

1. This is the property directive.

2. The parenthesis and the comma-separated keyword contained therein
   are completely optional. In our particular case, we are specifying
   retain. This tells the Objective-C compiler to build the setter so that the
   object is automatically retained when an assignment is made. Second,
   a retain directive will automatically send a release message to the
   object before it is replaced with the new value. Many other options can
   be included here; one is readonly, which tells the compiler to only
   create a getter, not a setter, and thereby prevents the instance variable
   from being set external to the object.

3. Last, NSString* title, is the instance variable declaration. It must
   include the type and, of course, the instance variable name.

This defines half of the property. What's that you say, "Only half? What else is
missing?" Well, the second half of the @property is declared in the implementation (.m)
file.

```
1   //
2   //  Book.m
3   //  MyBookstore
4   //
5   //  Created by Mitch Fisher on 11/1/09.
6   //  Copyright 2009 __MyCompanyName__. All rights reserved.
7   //
8
9   #import "Book.h"
10
11  @implementation Book
12  @synthesize title, author, description;
13
14  @end
```

This is the implementation file to the Book object. Line 12 is significant, because it is the
second half of what is required to complete our property. This part is much simpler than
the interface file. All that is necessary is to use the @synthesize keyword and provide a
list of one or more property names. There can be many property names specified on a
@synthesis statement, and there can be many @synthesize lines too. It's all a matter of
personal preference.

Now that we've created three different properties, how are the properties used?

Using Properties

Once a property has been specified in both the interface and implementation files, using
properties are very straightforward and simple. First, the syntax changes a bit. Let's
look at a traditional setter:

```
[myBookObject setTitle:newTitle]; // Traditional setter
```

Here is an example of sending a set message to set some the title to our book object—like we said, pretty straightforward. However, when using properties, things change:

```
myBookObject.title = newTitle; // Setter example
```

Some things are very important to note. For starters, the object access is not within brackets ([ ]). Second, the method is no longer called setTitle; it's just title. Internally, there is still a setTitle method; it's just hidden. Why is this important? Well, if we create our own explicit setTitle method, our new method will be called rather that the compiler-created one. This may or may not be the behavior we specifically want.

For the getter, things look remarkably familiar:

```
NSString* title = myBookObject.title;  // Getter example
```

The getter is also called title. The significance here is that how the object's property is accessed determines whether the getter or setter is called.

One last big difference is that the syntax to access a property now uses a period (.) between the object and the method. This is necessary because the brackets are gone, so the period distinguishes between using a property and sending a message to an object.

Understanding the Importance of Conventions

As mentioned earlier, there is a convention to naming a getter and a setter. While these naming guidelines are not strictly enforced, the value of understanding the convention comes in handy when using properties. Here is our previous example:

```
1   - (void)setTitle (NSString* newTitle) {
2       if ([newTitle count] > 0) {
3          title = newTitle;
4       }
5   }
```

If we create a property like @property title and pair that with the @synthesize keyword, the compiler will generate two methods—one named title as the getter and one called setTitle as the setter. However, if we provide our own setter and name it according to the convention (like the preceding code), the compiler won't generate its own.

```
myBookObject.title = newTitle; // Call the custom setter
```

The preceding code will call our own custom setter instead of the standard one. The same would be true had we written our own getter method. Now, let's continue with the Bookstore application.

Creating the MyBookstore Program

With the understanding of instance variables and properties, we are going to now venture forth to create the actual bookstore program. The idea is simple enough—create a class called Bookstore that will be stocked with Book objects.

From the project's **Groups & Files** pane, right-click (or control-click) the **Source** group and click **Objective-C class**. Make sure that the class is a subclass of NSObject, as shown in Figure 8–5.

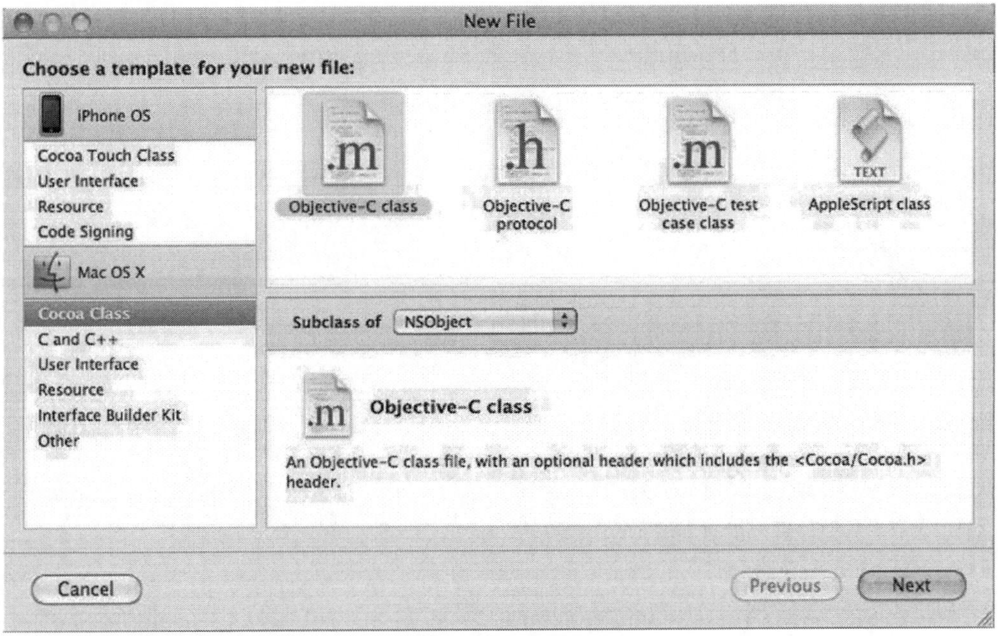

Figure 8–5. *Adding a new Objective-C class to the Bookstore project*

Click the **Next** button and then name this new object Bookstore.m, as shown in Figure 8–6.

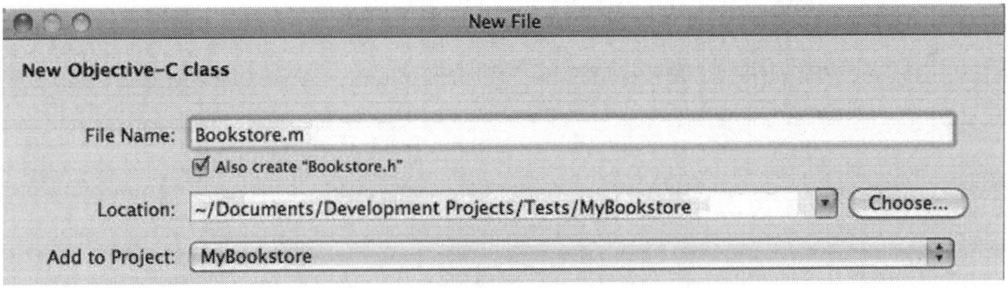

Figure 8–6. *Adding a new Objective-C class to the Bookstore project*

The Xcode window should look something like the one shown in Figure 8–7.

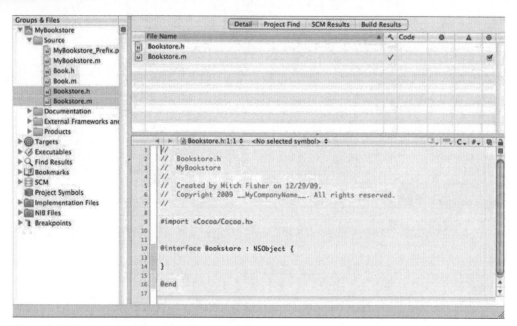

Figure 8–7. *The Bookstore object added into the project*

The Bookstore class that has been added will be used to store all the Book objects. To do this, there needs to be something that allows these Book objects to be stored and retrieved easily. Fortunately, Mac OS X and the iPhone OS have existing classes that will do this; they're called NSDictionary and NSMutableDictionary.

Using the NSMutableDictionary Class

The NSMutableDictionary class is a type of dictionary, based on another class called NSDictionary. Both these classes are used to conveniently and efficiently retrieve information associated with some arbitrary key. In a physical dictionary, the **key** is the word that we're looking for, and the information stored at that key is the definition of the word. So, an NSMutableDictionary and NSDictionary pattern themselves with the real-world thing (or object).

What exactly does this mean? You now know what a dictionary is, so how is the NSMutableDictionary different from an ordinary NSDictionary? The short answer: it's really not that different.

There are two important terms to know about classes to understand the difference: "immutable" and "mutable." With a **mutable** class, the data can be modified; in an **immutable** class, the data is set permanently (the life of the object that is). When dealing with data objects, you must determine how the object data can be modified. For example, an NSString class represents a string value, but it cannot be changed. Once the value is set, that's it. There is another version of that class called the NSMutableString. Because NSMutableString is a mutable class, the data can be modified. In other words, a program can reassign, concatenate, and otherwise alter the data in an NSMutableString.

Let's add the NSMutableDictionary class to our bookstore object. In our implementation file, we are going to add the following items highlighted in bold.

```
1  @interface Bookstore : NSObject {
2      NSDictionary* myBookstore;
3  }
4
5  @property (retain) NSDictionary* myBookstore;
```

On line 2, we are simply declaring the instance variable of the bookstore variable called myBookstore. We also declare the property so that the variable will have an automatic getter and setter method defined for it.

In the property declaration on line 5, there is the code (retain). This option informs the compiler to generate the getter and setter in a specific way. The retain keyword is used so that the setter will use the retain-and-release memory management mechanism when assigning values (see Chapter 12).

Making Our Object Do Something

Now that a skeleton object has been created, it needs to do something. For our simple program, the Bookstore object will do the following:

- Add new Book objects.

- Remove existing Book objects.

- Print the inventory of books in the bookstore to the screen.

These are very basic functions; the Bookstore object can, of course, be expanded to do much more. However, for the purposes of this chapter, this should be enough.

For starters, let's add some new instance methods to our Bookstore class. Here is an excerpt from the interface file, Bookstore.h:

```
1  - (id)init;
2  - (void)printInventory;
3  - (BOOL)addBook:(Book *)newBook;
4  - (BOOL)removeBookWithTitle:(NSString *)whichTitle;
5  - (void)dealloc;
```

We have the init method, which initializes our Bookstore object; this is just standard convention. The remaining method names should be self-explanatory.

Implementing Behavior

Now that we have an interface file, let's write some code that will give the Bookstore class some life.

```
1    #import "Bookstore.h"
2
3    @implementation Bookstore
4    @synthesize myBookstore;
5
6    - (id)init {
7        self = [super init];
8        if (self != nil) {
9            myBookstore = [[NSMutableDictionary alloc] init];
10       }
11       return self;
12   }
```

You see the standard stuff in the beginning here. Our implementation file needs to include its interface on line 1. Without it, our implementation file would have no clue what methods we are defining! Line 4 represents the implementation part of the property for the Bookstore object. The original @property was declared in the interface file, Bookstore.h.

Lines 6–9 initialize our object. For the most part, these lines contain just the standard stuff: initialize your parent and return self. The biggest change here is that we are now initializing the Bookstore instance variable—myBookstore—on line 8. Notice that the bookstore is only initialized if self is valid, that is, when it is not nil. The code is just a precaution but generally a good practice. The reality is that if [super init] returns nil, there are bigger issues at hand.

```
14   - (BOOL)addBook:(Book *)newBook {
15       [myBookstore setObject:newBook forKey:newBook.title];
16       return YES;
17   }
```

This method is what adds a book object into the NSMutableDictionary class, the myBookstore instance variable (line 15). The following message

        setObject:forKey:

is sent to the NSMutableDictionary object to basically add an object to the dictionary. In our case, the object is the book, and the key is the book's title. Why do we need a key? Well, the key allows us to retrieve the book by a unique name. In this case, the key is simply the title of the book.

It's important to note that a dictionary must have *unique* keys. In this example, this means that it is not possible to have two different book objects associated with the same key. If a call to setObject:forKey: is called and that key already exists in the dictionary, the dictionary will remove the old object and *replace* it with the new one.

> **NOTE**: NSDictionary and NSMutableDictionary store information using what is commonly referred to as **key-value pairs**. You can think of it like this:
>
>   Name = Ernest Hemingway
>
> Here, the data, Ernest Hemingway is associated with a label Name. Using a concept like this within something like the NSDictionary allows the program to look up data using a known key like Name. However, keys must be *unique* within a specific dictionary.

When newBook was added to the dictionary, the dictionary automatically sends a retain message to the newBook object. This tells the program that the object is still in use. Now, we have two references to the newBook object: one when the newBook was allocated and a second when it was added to the dictionary.

Since there really needs to be only one reference to the newBook object at this point, we'll need to release this reference in the program eventually. In a later program, you'll see the call to the addBook: method followed by a release of the new object. While the retain-and-release mechanism takes a while to grasp, it's a very flexible and efficient way of managing memory.

The following method is called to remove the book from the dictionary:

```
20    - (BOOL)removeBookWithTitle:(NSString *)whichTitle {
21        [myBookstore removeObjectForKey:whichTitle];
22        return YES;
23    }
```

The NSMutableDictionary class has a simple method for removing an item. Line 21 demonstrates the removeObjectForKey: method. All that is required is the key for the object that is to be removed from the dictionary. Unfortunately, there is no return value from the removeObjectForKey: method, so there is no way to determine if an object was removed or not. A better way implementing this function would be as follows:

```
20    - (BOOL)removeBookWithTitle:(NSString *)whichTitle {
21        if ([myBookstore objectForKey:whichTitle] != nil) {
22            [myBookstore removeObjectForKey:whichTitle];
23            return YES;
24        }
25        return NO;
26    }
```

The big difference in this method is the new line 21. The if statement calls the objectForKey: method. This dictionary method will return the object for the specified or nil if the key was not found in the dictionary. While this code does require some additional processing (the object is looked up twice if it's found), the advantage it has is that it can now return YES if the object was found and removed or NO if the object was not found. This method could then inform the user if the remove operation failed or was successful.

TIP: Notice that we are returning YES or NO and not TRUE or FALSE; this is simply another example of a coding convention. While YES is analogous to TRUE and NO to FALSE in Apple's SDK, the convention is to use YES and NO for clarity. If TRUE and FALSE were substituted, the code would work exactly the same.

```
28    - (void)printInventory {
29          Book *book;
30          for (NSString* key in myBookstore) {
31            book = [myBookstore objectForKey:key];
32            NSLog(@"      Title: %@ ", book.title);
33            NSLog(@"     Author: %@ ", book.author);
34            NSLog(@"Description: %@ ", book.description);
35          }
36    }
```

This last method, as the name implies, prints the inventory of books that are present in the dictionary. There is an interesting difference here from what is present in most other C-type programs. This big difference is line 30. Instead of the standard for loop, there is a **for...in loop** (or **for...in feature**, as its called in the Objective-C manual). This special for loop is specific to Objective-C 2.0 and above. It provides a quick way to iterate through a list of items—in our case, this list is the myBookstore dictionary.

The way that the for...in loop works is quite simple. Line 30 looks like this:

```
for (NSString* key in myBookstore)
```

For *each* item in the myBookstore dictionary, the key NSString will be set to the key of that item. If there are five entries in the dictionary, the for...in feature will loop five times, and each iteration will have a new value for key corresponding to one of the five entries in the dictionary. The process of going through each key in a list or dictionary is called **enumeration**.

NOTE: Documentation for the for...in feature can be found under "Using Fast Enumeration" in the *Objective-C 2.0 Programming Language* manual available directly from Apple's developer site.

Line 31 retrieves the Book object given the key we assign in the for...in loop. The program doesn't check for a nil value here, since we have an actual key from the dictionary and the setObject:forKey: method will not accept nil as an object to associate with a key.

The remaining lines, 32–34, simply output the book's information in a log format to the screen:

```
      Title: Objective-C for Absolute Beginners
     Author: Bennett, Lees and Fisher
Description: iPhone and Mac Programming Made Easy
```

The typical date and time stamp that appears on each line is omitted so that the meaningful output can be shown here (the lines are too long otherwise).

Cleaning Up Our Objects

One of the last methods in the Bookstore implementation file is to clean up everything. While this method isn't called explicitly, it is called internally by the system when cleaning up objects. It's the dealloc method and should be present in every implementation file.

```
38    - (void)dealloc {
39          self.myBookstore = nil;
40          [super dealloc];
41    }
```

Line 40 sets the myBookstore property to nil. One of the great things about properties is that, whenever you assign a value to a property that is defined with the retain option like the following, any existing object stored in the property is sent a release message before the instance variable is reassigned:

```
@property (retain) NSDictionary* myBookstore;
```

Conversely, when a property is assigned, the object being assigned is sent a retain message. So, in our program, setting the property to nil on line 40 is equivalent to the following:

```
[myBookstore release];
```

It doesn't matter if the object is explicitly released or the property is set to nil (or even another object). In both cases, the myBookstore instance variable will be released. The release method you choose is a matter of taste and exposure to the convention. To some people, the fact that the release is *implied* seems to hide too much functionality. The good thing is that either will work. In our case, we are the only user of the myBookstore NSMutableDictionary. Releasing it will cause the NSMutableDictionary to release all of its objects in turn.

Line 41 tells the parent of this class to deallocate itself as well, and so on up the chain of objects. This call to dealloc is equivalent to the call to [super init] whenever the object is first created.

Using the Bookstore and Book Objects

Now that we have created the Bookstore and Book objects and added some methods to do something with the bookstore object, we need a place to actually use the Bookstore object. First, select the MyBookstore.m file from the Xcode project, which is shown in Figure 8–8.

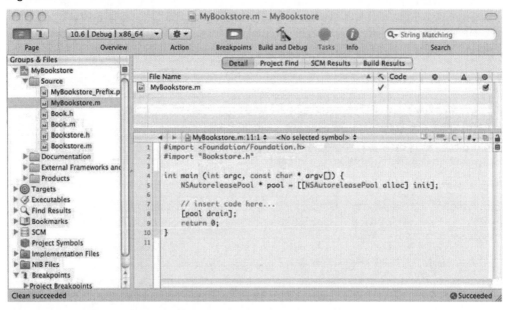

Figure 8–8. *This stub was generated automatically and doesn't do much at all.*

The main function, which is the start of the program, doesn't do too much at this point. To make use of the Bookstore object, we need to change main.

```
1    #import <Foundation/Foundation.h>
2    #import "Bookstore.h"
3
4    int main (int argc, const char * argv[]) {
5        NSAutoreleasePool * pool = [[NSAutoreleasePool alloc] init];
6        Bookstore* theBookNook = [[Bookstore alloc] init];
7        NSString * newTitle = @"A Farwell To Arms";
8        Book *newBook = [[Book alloc]
9                            initWithTitle:newTitle
10                                   author:@"Ernest Hemingway"
11                              description:@"The story of an affair "
12                                          "between an English nurse "
13                                          "and an American soldier "
14                                          "on the Italian front "
15                                          " during World War I."]];
16
17
18        [theBookNook addBook: newBook];
19        [newBook release];
20
21        [theBookNook printInventory];
22        [theBookNook removeBookWithTitle:newTitle];
23        [theBookNook printInventory];
24        [theBookNook release];
25        [pool drain];
         return 0;
```

Here is the new main. Lines 6–18 were added to make use of the Bookstore object. Line 6 declares and allocates the Bookstore object and assigns it to the local variable called theBookNook.

Line 8 calls the addBook: method on the Bookstore object. This method requires one parameter: the Book object to add.

Lines 9–15 allocate a new Book object and assign it a title, author, and description. Notice that there is no intermediate object to store the Book object first. The new object is being passed directly into the addBook: method. If you recall, the addBook: method does an explicit release on the passed in Book object once its added to the dictionary. Because this is the case, we don't need to store it, simply allocate and forget about it; the Bookstore class is now managing the memory of its Book objects.

Line 16 calls the printInventory method. This method will enumerate all the books in the dictionary (our one book) and print each book to the screen using the NSLog function.

Line 17 calls the removeBookWithTitle: method. This should remove the book from the Bookstore. Considering the title we used to remove the book is the same title we used to create the book, there is little chance of this failing.

Just for grins, line 18 calls the printInventory method again. Nothing should print, because the Bookstore is now empty.

Line 19 cleans up the theBookNook Bookstore object by releasing it.

Summary

We've finally reached the end of this chapter! Here is a summary of the things that were covered.

- *Using instance variables*: Instance variables are variables that are defined in the interface file of the class and are accessible once the class has been instantiated.

- *Working with properties*: Properties are shorthand ways of created getters and/or setters. Getters and setters get or set the values of an instance variable.

- *Storing data with* NSMutableDictionary: This Foundation class introduced you to the ability to store data that's accessible by a predefined key.

- *Looping with* for...in: This feature offers a new way to iterate through an enumerated list of items.

- *Building a simple program*: We built a simple Bookstore program that had the ability to add, remove, and print a dictionary of books. In creating the Bookstore program, you learned how to

  - Allocate and use objects.

  - Use the NSLog function to print information to the screen.

Exercises

- Add more books to the bookstore using the original program as a guide.
- Enhance the Book class so it can store another attribute, an ID (or ISBN) number for example.
- Add a new method to the Bookstore class that will provide an interface to find a book (or books) by author or title.
- Fix the addBook: method so that it checks to see if a title is already in the dictionary. If the title already exists, don't add it, and return NO.
- Add a new method to the Bookstore class that will update a specific book.
- Change the printInventory: method so that if there are no books in the dictionary, it will print a message like "The bookstore is empty."

If you're daring, try these more advanced ideas:

- Change the Bookstore object so that, instead of storing individual Book objects, it stores NSArray arrays of books. After all, a good bookstore has more than one of each book, right?
- Modify the printInventory method so that it also displays the quantity-on-hand (using the NSArray count method).

Chapter 9

Comparing Data

In this chapter, we will discuss one of the most basic and frequent operations you will perform as you program: comparing data. In our bookstore example, you may need to compare book titles if your clients are looking for a specific book. You may also need to compare authors if your clients are interested in purchasing books by a specific author. Comparing data is a common tasks for developers. Many of the loops you learned about in the previous chapter will require you to compare data to know when your code should stop looping.

Comparing data in programming is like using a scale. You have one value on one side and another value on the other side. In the middle you have an operator. The operator determines what kind of comparison is being done. Examples of operators are "greater then," "less than," or "equal to."

The values on either side of the scale are usually variables. We learned about the different types of variables in Chapter 3. In general, the comparison functions for different variables will be slightly different. It is imperative to become very familiar with the functions and syntax to compare data, as this will form a basis for your development.

For the purpose of this chapter, we will use an example of a bookstore application. This application will allow users to log in to the application, search for books, and purchase them. We will try to relate the different ways of comparing data to how it would be used in this type of application.

Introducing Boolean Logic

At the heart of any comparison is Boolean logic. With Boolean logic, there can only be one of two answers: yes or no. The following are some good examples of Boolean questions that you will use in your applications:

Is 5 larger than 3?

Does "now" have more than 5 letters?

Is 6/1/2010 later than today?

In order to start using these types of questions in your programs, you will first need to become familiar with the different relational operators available to you in the C and Objective-C languages. We will cover those first. After that, we will look into how different variables can behave with these operators.

Using Relational Operators

Objective-C supports the standard algebraic operators with only one real change: In the Objective-C language, as in most other programming languages, the equal to operator is made by two equal signs (==). Table 9–1 shows the different operators available to you as a developer.

Table 9–1. *Objective-C Operators*

Operator	Description
==	Equal to
>	Greater than
>=	Greater than or equal to
<	Less than
<=	Less than or equal to
!=	Not equal to

> **NOTE:** A single equal sign is used to assign a value to a variable. Two equal signs are needed to compare two values.

Comparing Numbers

One of the difficulties developers have had in the past was dealing with different data types in comparisons. Objective-C helps us out with that. In Objective-C, you can compare any two numeric data types without having to typecast (typecasting is still sometimes needed when dealing with other data types, and we cover it later in this chapter). This allows a developer to write code without worrying about the data types that need to be compared.

In our application, there are many ways in which we will need to compare numbers. For example, let's say that our bookstore offers a discount for people who spend over $30 in a single transaction. We will need to add the total the person is spending and then compare it to $30. If it is larger than $30, we will need to calculate the discount. See the following example.

```
float totalSpent;
int discountThreshhold;
int discountPercent;

discountThreshold=30;
discountPercent=0;
totalSpent=calculateTotalSpent();

if(totalSpent>discountThreshold) {
        discountPercent=10;
}
```

Let's walk through the code. First we declare our variables. As we discussed in Chapter 3, if the number can contain decimals, we should declare it as a float rather than an int. We know that the discountThreshold and the discountPercent will not have a decimal in them, so we can declare them as ints. In this example, we assume we have a function called calculateTotalSpent that will calculate the total spent in this current order. We then simply check to see if the total spent is larger than the discount threshold; if it is, we set the discount percent. Also, notice that it was not necessary to tell the code to convert the data when comparing the different numeric data types. This is all handled by Objective-C.

Another action that requires the comparison of numbers is looping. As discussed in Chapter 4, looping is a core action in development and many loop types require some sort of comparison to know when to stop. Let's take a look at a For loop.

```
int numberOfBooks;
numberOfBooks=50;

for (int y = 1; y <= numberOfBooks; y++) {
    doSomething();
}
```

In this example, we iterate through the total number of books we have in the bookstore. The for statement is where the interesting stuff starts to happen. Let's break it down.

```
int y=1;
```

This portion of the code is declaring y as an int and then assigning it a starting value of 1.

```
y<=numberOfBooks;
```

This portion is telling the computer to check to see if our counting variable y is less then or equal to the total number of books we have in our store. If y becomes larger than the number of books, the loop will no longer run.

```
y++
```

This portion increases y by 1 every time the loop is run.

Creating an Example Xcode App

Now let's create an Xcode application so we can start comparing numeric data.

1. Launch Xcode. From your hard drive, go to Developer ➤ Applications folder. Drag it to the Dock, as we will be using it throughout the rest of this book. See Figure 9–1.

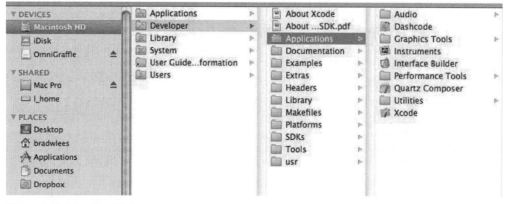

Figure 9–1. *Launching Xcode*

2. Click on Create a New Xcode Project.On the left-hand side of the resulting window, under Mac OS X, select Application. Then select Command Line Tool. In the Type drop-down menu, select Foundation, and then click Choose. See Figure 9–2. You will then be prompted to choose a name for your project. We used Comparison as the name, but you can choose whatever name you want.

Note: Xcode Projects by default are saved in the Documents Folder in your user home.

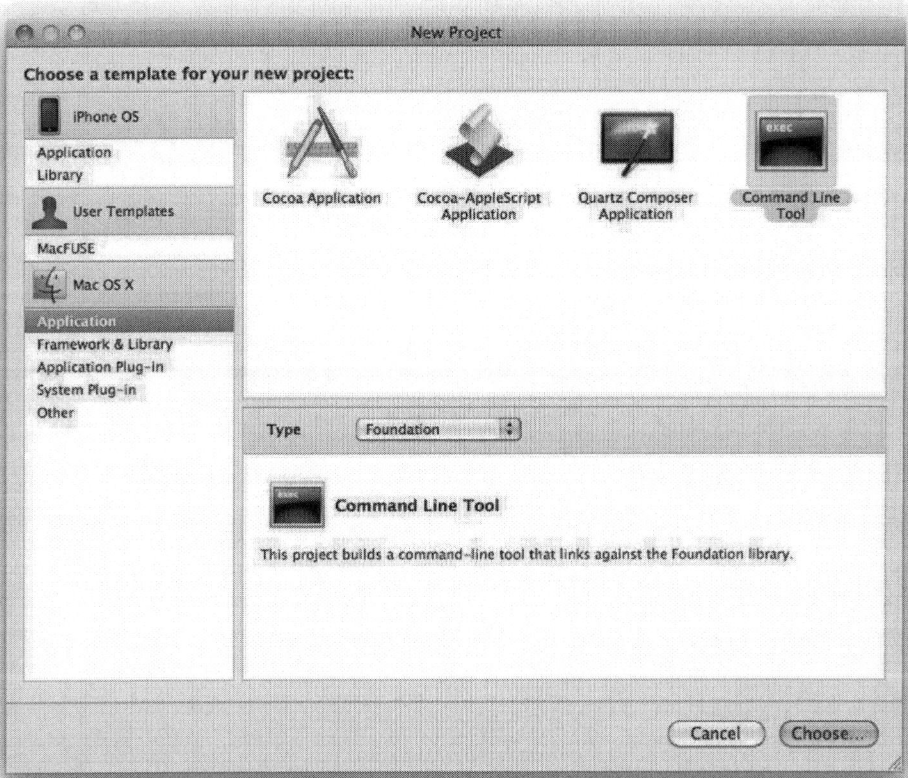

Figure 9–2. *Creating a new project*

Once the new project is created, you will see the standard Xcode Window.

3.   Select the expand arrow next to the Source folder to expand it. You will see two files, Comparison_Prefix.pch and Comparison.m. The actual names will change depending on the name you used when creating the project. For the purpose of these examples, we are only going to be focusing on the Comparison.m file.

4.   Double-click on that file and you will see the following code:

```
#import <Foundation/Foundation.h>

int main (int argc, const char * argv[]) {
    NSAutoreleasePool * pool = [[NSAutoreleasePool alloc] init];

    // insert code here...
    NSLog(@"Hello, World!");
    [pool drain];
    return 0;
}
```

At this point, we are only going to concern ourselves with the line of code that begins with NSLog. It has one basic purpose: to print information to the console. Before we change any of the code, let's run our application to see how it works.

5. Click on the Build and Run button in the menu or select Build and Run from the Build menu.

6. It will appear as if nothing happened. To see the result, click on the menu Run → Console (or press the Shift-Command R buttons). You will be presented with the a window similar to Figure 9–3.

```
[Session started at 2010-05-31 14:00:32 -0700.]
GNU gdb 6.3.50-20050815 (Apple version gdb-1461.2) (Fri Mar  5 04:43:10 UTC 2010)
Copyright 2004 Free Software Foundation, Inc.
GDB is free software, covered by the GNU General Public License, and you are
welcome to change it and/or distribute copies of it under certain conditions.
Type "show copying" to see the conditions.
There is absolutely no warranty for GDB.  Type "show warranty" for details.
This GDB was configured as "x86_64-apple-darwin".tty /dev/ttys000
Loading program into debugger…
Program loaded.
run
[Switching to process 24439]
Running…
2010-05-31 14:00:32.477 Comparison[24439:a0f] Hello, World!

Debugger stopped.
Program exited with status value:0.
```

Figure 9–3. *Debugger console*

Most of the information in this window will mean very little to you. The most important line is the bold section that actually shows the output of your application. The first part of the line shows the date, time, and name of the application. The "Hello, World!" part was generated by the NSLog line we looked at before.

7. Go back to the application and open the comparison.m file.

8. Go to the beginning of the line that begins with NSLog. This is the line that is responsible for printing the "Hello, World!" section. We are going to comment out this line by placing two backslashes (//) in front of the line of code. Commenting out code tells Xcode to ignore it when it builds and runs the application. Code that is commented out will not run.

9. Once you comment out the line of code, you will no longer see the line in bold if you run the program, because the application is no longing outputting any line.

10. In order for the application to output the results of our comparisons, we will have to add one line.

```
NSLog(@"The result is %@", (6>5 ? @"True" : @"False"));
```

11. Place this line into your code. This line is telling your application to print out "The result is." Then it will print "True" if 6 is greater than 5, or "False" if 5 is greater than 6.

Because 6 is greater than 5, it will print out True.

You can change this line to test any of the examples we have put together thus far in this chapter, and all of the examples we will do further on.

Let's try another example.

```
int i=5;
int y=6;
NSLog(@"The result is %@", (y>i ? @"True" : @"False"));
```

In this example, we created an integer and assigned its value to 5. We then created another variable and assigned the value to 6. We then changed the NSLog example to compare the variables *i* and *y* instead of using actual numbers. When you run this example, you will get the following result:

```
[Switching to process 24637]
Running…
2010-05-31 14:44:17.979 Comparison[24637:a0f] The result is True

Debugger stopped.
Program exited with status value:0.
```

Figure 9–4. *NSLog output*

We will now explore other kinds of comparisons, and then we will come back to our application and test some of them.

Using Boolean Expressions

A Boolean expression is the easiest of all comparisons. Boolean expressions are used to determine if a value is true or false. False is defined as 0 and true as non-zero. For example:

```
int j;
j=5;
if(j) {
        some_code();
}
```

This will always evaluate to true, because *j* is equal to 5 and is not 0 or null.

```
int j;
j=0;
if(j) {
        some_code();
}
```

If we change the value of *j*, this will evaluate to false, because *j* is now 0. This can be used with BOOL and number variables.

```
int j;
j=0;
if(!j) {
        some_code();
}
```

Placing an exclamation point in front of a Boolean expression will change it to the opposite. This line now asks "if not *j*," which in this case is true, because *j* is equal to 0.

Let's look at an example related to the bookstore. We have a frequent buyer's club that entitles all members to a 15% discount on all books they purchase. This is easy to check. We simply set the variable clubMember to TRUE or YES if they are a member and FALSE or NO if they are not. The following code will apply only the discount to club members:

```
int discountPercent;
BOOL clubMember;

clubMember=FALSE;
discountPercent=0;
if(clubMember) {
        discountPercent=15;
}
```

Comparing Strings

Strings are a very difficult data type for most C languages. In ANSI C (or standard C), a string is just an array of characters. Objective-C has taken the development of the string even further and made it an object called NSString. As an object, there are many more properties and methods available to us when working with them. Fortunately for us, NSString has many methods for comparing data, which makes our job much easier.

While developing for the Mac and the iPhone, you will be able to use both NSStrings and standard C strings. For the purposes of this book, we will be focusing on comparing the NSString objects. If you have C type strings in your application, they will need to be converted to NSStrings to use to code included in this book. Fortunately, for us, this conversion is very simple.

```
char *myCString;
NSString *myNsstring;

myCString="testing a string";
myNsstring= [NSString stringWithUTF8String: myCString];
```

The first two lines are code you have seen before. They are your variable declarations. You are declaring a standard C string called myCString and a NSString called myNsstring. The third line is just a simple initiation of your standard C string. We are just assigning a value to it.

The last line is where everything happens. You are assigning your NSString object to be equal to creating a new NSString object with the value coming from a UTF8string and passing it the standard C string we created. Once you have all of your standard C strings as NSStrings, we can take advantage of the powerful comparison features provided to us by the class.

Let's look at another example. In it, we will compare passwords to see if we should allow a user to login in.

```
NSString *enteredPassword, *myPassword;

myPassword=@"duck";
enteredPassword=@"Duck";
bool continueLogin=NO;

if([enteredPassword isEqualToString:myPassword]) {
        continueLogin=YES;
}
```

The first line just declares two NSStrings. The next two lines initialize the strings. Remember, before you use any objects they need to be initialized. In your actual code, you will need to get the enteredPassword string from the user. These lines use a shortcut. Notice the @ symbol before the C style string. The @ symbol creates a new NSString from the C style string that follows it.

The next line if the part of the code that actually does the work. We are sending a message to the enteredPassword object asking it if it is equal to the myPassword string. The method always needs to have an NSString passed to it. The example code will always be false, because of the capital on the enteredPassword versus the lowercase on the myPassword.

> **NOTE:** If you need to compare two NSStrings regardless of case, you would simply use the caseInsensitiveCompare method instead of the isEqualToString.

There are many other different comparisons you might have to perform on strings. For example, you may want to check the length of a certain string. This is easily done.

```
NSString *enteredPassword;
NSString *myPassword;
myPassword=@"duck";
enteredPassword=@"Duck";
bool continueLogin=NO;

if([enteredPassword length] > 5) {
        continueLogin=YES;
}
```

This code checks to see if the entered password is longer than 5 characters.

There will be other times when you will have to search within a string for some data. Fortunately, Objective-C makes this very easy to do. NSString provides us with a function called rangeOfString, which allows you to search within a string for another string. The function rangeOfString only takes one argument, which is the string for which you are searching.

```
NSString *searchTitle, *bookTitle;
searchTitle=@"Sea";
bookTitle=@"2000 Leagues Under the Sea";

if([bookTitle rangeOfString:searchTitle].location !=NSNotFound) {
addToResults;
}
```

This code is very similar to other examples we have looked at. This example takes a search term and checks to see if the book title has that search term in it. If it does, it adds it to the results. The can be adapted to allow users to search for specific terms in your book titles, authors, or even descriptions.

> **NOTE:** All string searches are case sensitive by default. If you want to search inside of a string regardless of the case, you can change the above call from
>
> [bookTitle rangeOfString:search_title]
>
> to
>
> [bookTitle rangeOfString:search_title options:NSCaseInsensitiveSearch].

For a complete listing of the methods supported by NSString, see the Apple Documentation at http://developer.apple.com/mac/library/documentation/cocoa/reference/Foundation/Classes/NSString_Class/Reference/NSString.html

Comparing Dates

Dates are a fairly complicated variable type in any language. This is mostly due to the amount of functionality in the date classes. Objective-C used to use the NSCalendarDate class, but recently it has been deprecated for a more up-to-date NSDate. The new NSDate has a lot of nice methods to make comparing dates easy. We will focus on the compare function. The compare function returns an NSComparisonResult, which has three possible values: NSOrderedSame, NSOrderedDescending, NSOrderedAscending.

```
NSDate *today = [NSDate date];

//Sale Date as of 9/4/2010
NSDate *saleDate = [NSDate dateWithString:@"2010-0 9-04 04:00:00 -0700"];

NSComparisonResult result;
bool saleStarted;

result=[today compare:saleDate];

        if(result==NSOrderedAscending) {
```

```
            //Sale Date is in the future
            saleStarted=NO;
    } else if(result==NSOrderedDescending) {
            //Sale Date is in the past
            saleStarted=YES;
    } else {
            //Sale Date and Today are the same
            saleStarted=NO;
    }
```

That seems like a lot of work for comparing some dates. Let's walk through the code and see if we can make sense of it.

```
NSDate *today = [NSDate date];
NSDate *saleDate = [NSDate dateWithString:@"2010-0 9-04 04:00:00 -0700"];
```

Here we declare two different NSDate objects. The first one, named "today," is initialized with the system date. The second one, named "saleDate," is initialized with a date in the future. We will use this date to see if this sale has begun. We will not go into detail about the initialization of NSDates, but they can be initialized using the dateWithString function similar to as we showed above.

```
NSComparisonResult result;
```

The results of using the compare function of an NSDate object is an NSComparisonResult. We have to declare one of these to capture the output from the compare function.

```
result=[today compare:saleDate];
```

This simple line runs the comparison of the two dates. It places the resulting NSComparisonResult into the variable called "result."

```
if(result==NSOrderedAscending) {
//Sale Date is in the future
        saleStarted=NO;
} else if(result=NSOrderedDescending) {
//Sale Date is in the past
        saleStarted=YES;
} else {
//Sale Date and Today are the same
        saleStarted=NO;
}
```

Now we need to find out what value is in the variable result. In order to accomplish this, we perform an "if" statement comparing result to the three different options for the NSComparisonResult. The first line finds out if the sale date is greater than today. This means that the sale date is in the future, and thus the sale has not started. We then set the variable saleStarted to No. The next line finds out whether the sale date is less than today. If it is, then the sale has started and we set the saleStarted variable to Yes. The next line just says Else. This captures all other options. We know, though, that the only other option is NSOrderedSame. This means that the two dates are exactly the same, and thus the sale is just beginning.

There are other ways that you may use to compare an NSDate objects. Each of the methods will be more efficient at certain tasks. We have chosen the compare method because it will handle most of your basic date comparison needs.

NOTE: Remember that an NSDate holds both a date and a time. This can affect your comparisons with dates as it not only compares the date but the time.

Combining Comparisons

Many times something more complex than a single comparison is needed. This is where logical operators come in. Logical operators enable you to check to more than one different requirement. For example, if we have a special discount for people who are members of our book club and who spend over $30. We can write one statement to check that:

```
float totalSpent;
 int discountThreshhold;
int discountPercent;
BOOL clubMember = TRUE;

discountThreshhold=30;
discountPercent=0;
totalSpent=calculateTotalSpent();

if(totalSpent> discountThreshhold&& clubMember) {
        discountPercent=15;
}
```

We have combined two of the examples from above. The new comparison line reads as follows: If totalSpent is greater than discountThreshold and clubMember is true, then we set the discountPercent to 15. In order for this to return True, both of the items need to be true. || can be used instead of && to signify "or." We can change the line above to this:

```
if(totalSpent> discountThreshhold|| clubMember) {
        discountPercent=15;
}
```

Now this reads: If totalSpent is greater than discountThreshold **or** clubMember is true, then set the discount percent. This will return True if either of the options are true.

You can continue to use the logical operations to string as many comparisons together as you need. In some cases, you may need to group comparisons together using parentheses. This can be more complicated and is beyond the scope of this book.

Using the Switch Statement

Up to this point, we've had several example of comparing data by simply using the if statement and/or the if/else statements.

```
if (some_value == SOME_CONSTANT) {
    ...
} else if (some_value == SOME_OTHER_CONSTANT) {
    ...
} else if (some_value == YET_SOME_OTHER_CONSTANT) {
    ...
}
```

If the need to compare a specific ordinal type to several constant values is needed, there is a different way that can simplify the comparison code: the switch statement.

> **NOTE:** An ordinal type is a built-in C data type that can be ordered. Examples are int, long, char, BOOL. These data types are typically referred to as Ordinal Data types.

The switch statement allows for comparison of one or more constant values against the ordinal data type. This is important to understand. The switch statement does not allow for the comparison of the ordinal type to a variable. Here is an example of a proper case statement:

```
char value;
value = 'd';

switch (value) {          // The switch statement followed by a begin brace
case 'a':       // Equivalent to if (value == 'a')
    ...                   // Call functions and put any other statements here
after the case.
    ...
break;                    // This indicates that this is the end of the "case
'a':" statement.
case 'b':
    ...
    ...
break;
case 'c':       // If there is a case without a break, the program continues to
execute.
case 'd':                 //  So, in this case, if value is a 'c' or a 'd', this
code will be executed.
    ...
    ...
break;
default:                  // Default is optional and is only used if there is no
case statement
    ...                   // for 'value'. So, if value was equal to 'x', the default part
of the switch
    ...                   // statement will be executed since there is no "case 'x':"
present.
break;
} // End of the switch statement.
```

The switch statement is a very powerful one that simplifies and streamlines comparisons of an Ordinal type to several possible constants. That said, this is also the limiting factor of the switch statement. It is not possible, for example, to use the switch statement to compare an NSString variable to a series of string constants. This is because an

NSString value is not an Ordinal type. Also, the switch statement must compare an ordinal type to a constant. It is not possible to write:

```
switch (value) {
case variable: //case must be a constant, not a variable.
    ...
break;
```

While it does seem that these are severe limitations to the switch statement, the switch statement is still a very powerful statement that can be used to simplify certain if/else statements.

Grouping Variables Together

Objective-C has given us ways to group our like information together into one single variable. These variables are called **container variables** because they hold other variables. We will examine 4 different container classes that exist in Objective-C and will be used quite frequently in your development.

NSArray

1. Many different programming languages have a container called an array. An array allows you to store multiple variables in an ordered fashion. Retrieving data from an array is usually done by knowing the index of the item you want to retrieve. Objective-C has improved the standard array and given us the NSArray and the NSMutableArray.

2. An NSArray is an ordered list of objects. An NSArray can contain different variable types, but in the beginning you will probably be storing data of the same variable types. Creating an NSArray is a very simple process.

```
NSArray *bookList = [NSArray arrayWithObjects:@"Moby Dick", @"Frankenstein", @"Tom Sawyer", nil];
```

We'll start by creating a new NSArray called booklist. We then set bookList equal to a new NSArray with three string objects, Moby Dick, Frankenstein, and Tom Sawyer. The nil at the end just tells the code that you are done creating the array.

> **NOTE:** nil cannot be added to a container variable. If you want to add a empty object, simple add [NSNull null].

Once you have created your NSArray, you are not able to modify the code in any way. You cannot add an item, you cannot remove an item, and you cannot sort the list. These are major limitations of the NSArray class.

Getting information out of an NSArray is very simple. The most useful way to get information out of an NSArray is using a for loop. The following code is an example to take our bookList and get the information out of the NSArray.

```
NSArray *bookList = [NSArray arrayWithObjects:@"Moby Dick", @"Frankenstein", @"Tom Sawyer", nil];
```

```
int count;
count= bookList.count;
for(int y=0;y<count;y++) {
 NSLog(@"Book Title  is %@", [bookList objectAtIndex:y);
}
```

Let's step through the code. The first line creates the for loop. It also creates a new NSString called book for each object in the bookList array. Notice we use the [booklist objectAtIndex:y] to get the string we stored in the array at the index of y. The next line just prints the contents of each book variable out to the NSLog. The Sample output from this would be:

```
Book Title is Moby Dick
Book Title is Frankenstein
Book Title is Tom Sawyer
```

NOTE: NSArrays begin counting the index starting at 0. For example, the first item is 0, the second item is 1 and so on.

NSMutableArray

An NSMutableArray is very similar to an NSArray. The main difference is that an NSMutableArray allows the contents of the array to be modified. This means that now you can add, remove or sort the contents of the array.

Let's first start by declaring an NSMutableArray.

```
NSMutableArray *bookList = [NSArray arrayWithObjects:@"Moby Dick", @"Frankenstein",
@"Tom Sawyer", nil];
```

This code is very similar to the declaration of a standard NSArray. The only piece of info changed is the variable type. As a bookstore, if we were to get in a new book, we could simply add it to the array.

```
[bookList addObject:@"Huckleberry Finn"];
```

All this code is doing is sending a message to our bookList array to add a new string object with the text of Huckleberry Finn. This object will be added at the end of the array. You can use the method insertObject:atIndex: to place new objects at different places in the array.

For example, if you wanted to insert "Huckleberry Finn" at the beginning of the list, you could use the following code:

```
[bookList insertObject:@"Huckleberry Finn" atIndex:0];
```

Removing an object from an NSMutablearray is an easy process. Using the code we used to iterate through the NSArray, we can change the line to have it remove the items from the array.

```
NSMutableArray *bookList = [NSArray arrayWithObjects:@"Moby Dick", @"Frankenstein",
@"Tom Sawyer", nil];
```

```
int count;
count=bookList.count;
for(int y=0;y<count;y++) {
    [bookList removeObject:[booklist objectAtIndex:y]];
}
```

If you wanted to sort your NSMutableArray, you could use the following line. This will place the items in alphabetical order.

[bookList sortUsingSelector: @selector(caseInsensitiveCompare:)];

NSDictionary

The main difference between an NSArray and an NSDictionary is how the information is stored. When creating an NSArray, you merely list the items in order you want them stored. When creating an NSDictionary, you list the items, but you also have to add a key for each of the items. Retrieving information from an NSArray and NSDictionary is also different. In an NSArray, items are retrieved by their index number. In an NSDictionary, objects are retrieved by their keys.

Let's create an NSDictionary. We are going to create an NSDictionary which is going to contain information about a book. We will then be able to query the dictionary for information such as book author or title.

```
NSDictionary *book;
book = [NSDictionary dictionaryWithObjectsAndKeys:
            @"Herman Melville", @"Author",
            @"Moby Dick", @"Title",
        nil];
```
In this code, we start out by declaring a NSDictionary called book. We then assign objects and keys to each of the items we want in the dictionary. Remember that the nil tells the compiler that we are done with our dictionary.
Retrieving information from an NSDictionary is an easy process. If you wanted to get the Author from the NSDictionary you could use the following code.
[book objectForKey: @"Author"]

NSMutableDictionary

The NSMutableDictionary is similar to the NSDictionary except for the fact that the NSMutableDictionary can be modified. Let's start out by creating an NSMutableDictionary and then we will add another key and object to it.

```
NSMutableDictionary *book;
book = [NSDictionary dictionaryWithObjectsAndKeys:
            @"Herman Melville", @"Author",
            @"Moby Dick", @"Title",
        nil];
```

[book setObject: @"Adventure" forKey: @"Genre"];

The final line adds a new string objects that can be accessed by using the key Genre.

Summary

We've reached the end of the chapter! Here is a summary of the things that were covered.

- Comparisons

    - Comparing data is an integral part of any application.

- Relational operators

    - You learned about the six standard relational operators and how each is used.

- Integers

    - Integers are the easiest pieces of information to compare. You learned how comparing integers will be used in your programs and how to implement it.

- Example

    - You created a sample application where you could test your comparisons and make sure you are correct in our logic.

    - You learned how to change the application to add different types of comparisons.

- Boolean

    - You learned how to check Boolean values.

- Strings

    - You learned how strings behave differently from other pieces of information you have tested. You learned some of the pitfalls of comparing strings.

- Objects

    - You learned how difficult it can be to compare objects and that care must be taken to make sure you are getting the response you desire.

Exercises

- Modify the example application to compare some string information. It can either be in the form of a variable or a literal.

- Create a loop in your application to display a number using the methods you learned in the Boolean portion of the chapter.

- Write an Objective-C app that determines if the following years are leap years: 1800, 1801, 1899, 1900, 2000, 2001, 2003 and 2010. Output should be written to the console in the following format: "The year 2000 is a leap year", or "The year 2001 is not a leap year."

Chapter 10

Creating User Interfaces with Interface Builder

Interface Builder is an application that enables iPhone/iPad and Mac developers to easily create their user interfaces using a powerful graphical user interface. It provides the ability to build user interfaces by simply dragging objects from Interface Builder's library to your app's user interface.

Interface Builder stores your user interface design in one or more resource files, called XIBs. These resource files are set to interface objects and their relationships. Changes that you make with your user interface are automatically synchronized with Xcode.

To build a user interface, you simply drag objects from Interface Builder palette library onto your view. Actions and Outlets are two key components of Interface Builder that help us streamline development processes.

Actions that our objects trigger in our views when events fire are connected to our targets (object methods) in the app's code. **Outlets** (pointers) declared in our object's interface file are connected to specific instance variables. See Figure 10–1.

> **NOTE:** At the time of this writing, Xcode 4 is currently in beta version. We the authors are under a non-disclosure agreement with Apple and can't talk much about the new features. However, as the beta stands now, everything in the book will be applicable when Xcode 4 becomes available to all developers.

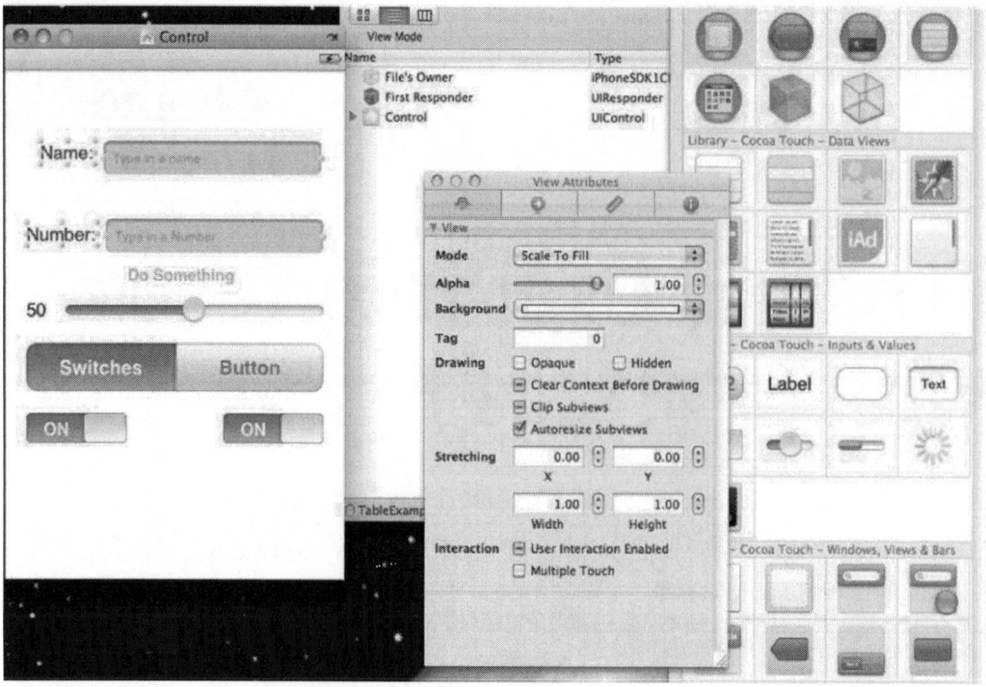

Figure 10–1. *Interface Builder with the 4 main windows displayed*

Understanding Interface Builder

Interface Builder is responsible for the memory management of the objects it creates for iPhone and iPad apps. This relieves the developer of having to keep track of allocating and releasing memory if the developer used Interface Builder to create the object.

Interface Builder saves the user interface file as a bundle that contains the interface objects and relationships used in the application. These bundles have the file extension "NIB." With version 3.0 of Interface Builder, a new XML file format was used and the file extension changed to XIB. However, developers still call these files "NIB" files, when speaking the file name.

Unlike most other graphical user interface applications, NIBs are often referred to as freeze-dried because they contain the archived objects themselves and are ready to run.

The XML file format is used to facility storage with source control systems like Subversion, Perforce, and CVS.

In the next section, we'll discuss an app design pattern call Model-View-Controller. This design pattern enables developers to more easily maintain code and reuse objects over the life of our apps.

The Model-View-Controller

Model-View-Controller (MVC) is the most prevalent design pattern used in iPhone/iPad development, and learning about it will make your life as a developer much easier. MVC is used in software development and is considered an **architectural pattern.**

Architectural patterns describe solutions to software design problems that developers can use in their code. The MVC pattern is not unique to Apple OOP developers; it is being adopted by many makers of IDEs, including those running on Windows and Linux platforms.

Software development is considered an expensive and risky venture for businesses. Frequently, apps take longer than expected to write, come in over budget, and don't work as promised. There was a lot of hype with OOP that companies would realize savings if they adopted its methodology, due to the reusability of objects along with easier maintainability of the code. Initially, this didn't happen.

As engineers looked at why OOP wasn't living up to these expectations, they discovered a key shortcoming with how developers were designing their objects: developers were frequently mixing objects together in such a way that, as the application matured, moved to different platforms, or hardware displays changed, the code became difficult to maintain.

Objects were often designed so that, if any of the following changed, it was difficult to isolate the objects that were impacted:

- Business rules
- User interfaced
- Client-server to Internet-based

Objects can be broken down into three task-related categories:

1. **Models:** Business objects
2. **Views:** User interface objects
3. **Controllers**: Objects that communicate with both the Models and the Views

As objects are categorized in these groups, apps can be developed and maintained easier over time. The following are examples of objects and their associated MVC category for an iPhone banking application:

Model

- Account balances
- User encryption
- Account transfers
- Account login

View

- Account balances table cell
- Account login spinner control

Controller

- Account balance view controller
- Account transfer view controller
- Logon view controller

The easiest way to remember and classify your objects in the MVC paradigm is the following:

Model: Unique business or application rules or code that represents the real world

View: Unique user interface code

Controller: Anything that controls or communicates with the Model or View objects

Figure 10–2 represents the MVC paradigm.

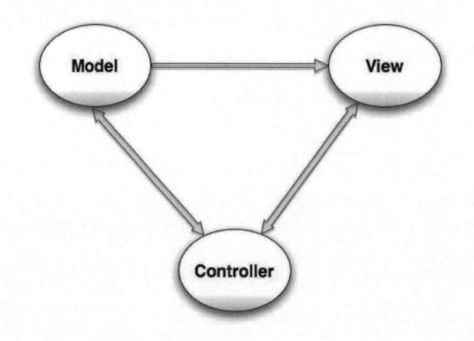

Figure 10–2. *MVC paradigm*

Xcode and Interface Builder do not force developers to use the MVC design pattern. It is up to the developer to organize their objects in such a way to us this design pattern.

Human Interface Guidelines (HIGs)

Before you get all excited and start designing cool user interfaces for your app, you need to learn some rules. Apple has developed one of the most advanced operating systems in the world with iOS 4. Additionally, Apple's products are known for being intuitive and user-friendly. Apple wants users to have the same experience from one app to the next.

In order ensure a consistent user experience, Apple provides developers guidelines on how their apps should look and feel. These guidelines, called the human interface guidelines (HIGs), are available for the Mac, iPhone, and iPad. You can download these docs at `http://developer.apple.com`. See Figure 10–3.

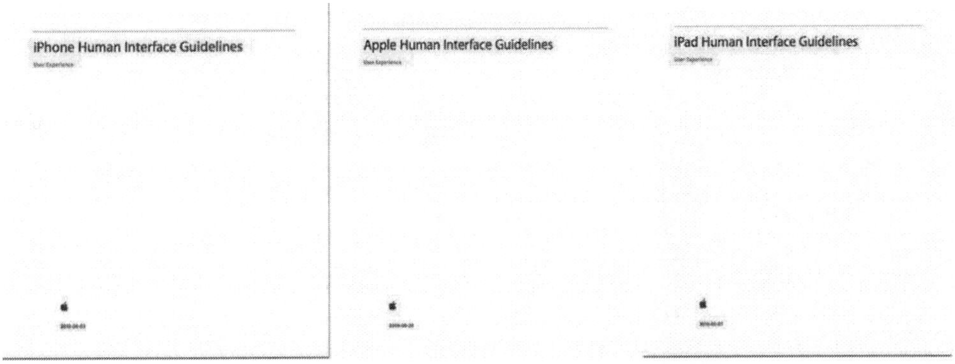

Figure 10–3. *Apple's human interface guidelines (HIGs) for iPhone, iPad, and Macs*

NOTE: Apple's HIGs are more than recommendations or suggestions. Apple takes them very seriously.

The following are the top reasons apps are rejected on Apple's iTunes App store

1. App crashes

2. **Violation of the (HIGs)**

3. Uses Apple Private APIs

4. Doesn't function as advertised on iTunes App Store

You can read, learn, and follow the HIGs before you develop your app, or you can read, learn, and follow the HIG after your app gets rejected by Apple and you have to rewrite all or parts of it. Either way, all iOS developers become familiar with the HIGs.

Many new iOS developers find this out the hard way, but if you the follow the HIGs, your iOS development will be a more pleasurable experience.

Creating an Example iPhone App with Interface Builder

Let's get started by building an iPhone app that generates and displays a random number. See Figure 10–4. This app will be similar to the app we created in Chapter 4, but we'll see how much more interesting the app becomes with an user interface (UI).

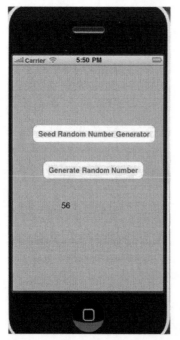

Figure 10–4. *Completed random number generator app*

1. Create a New Project. Make sure you select a View-based Application for the iPhone. See Figure 10–5.

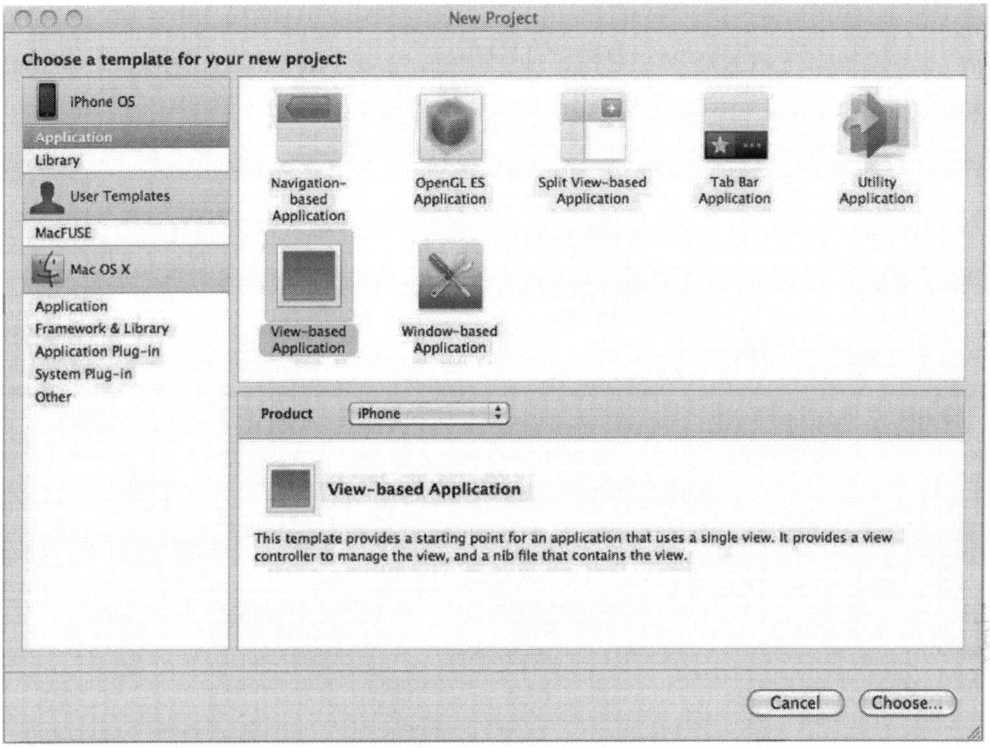

Figure 10–5. *Create an iPhone View-based Application*

2. Name your project **"RandomNumber."** See Figure 10–6.

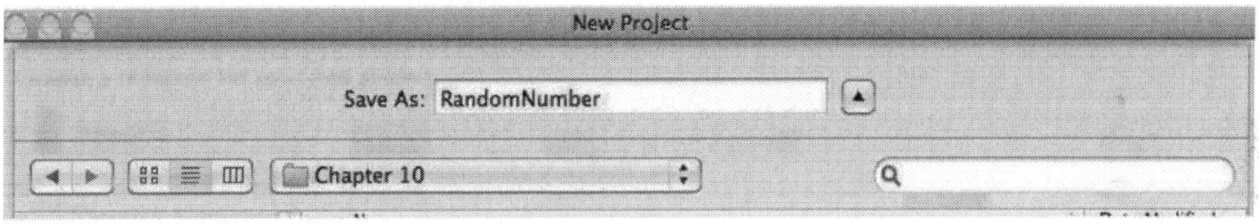

Figure 10–6. *Naming our iPhone project*

3. Expand your groups in the Group & Files pane. See Figure 10–7.

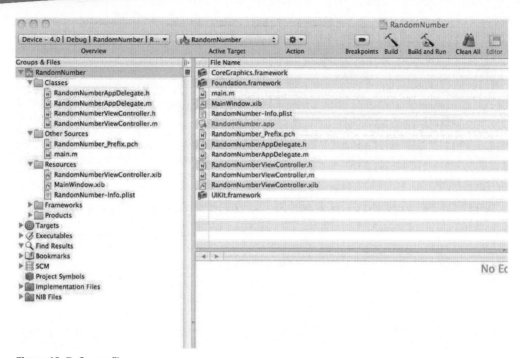

Figure 10–7. *Source files*

Although we only have one controller in this project, it's good programming practice to make your MVC groups at the beginning of your development.

4. Right-click on Classes in the Groups & Files pane, then select Add > New Group. See Figure 10–8.

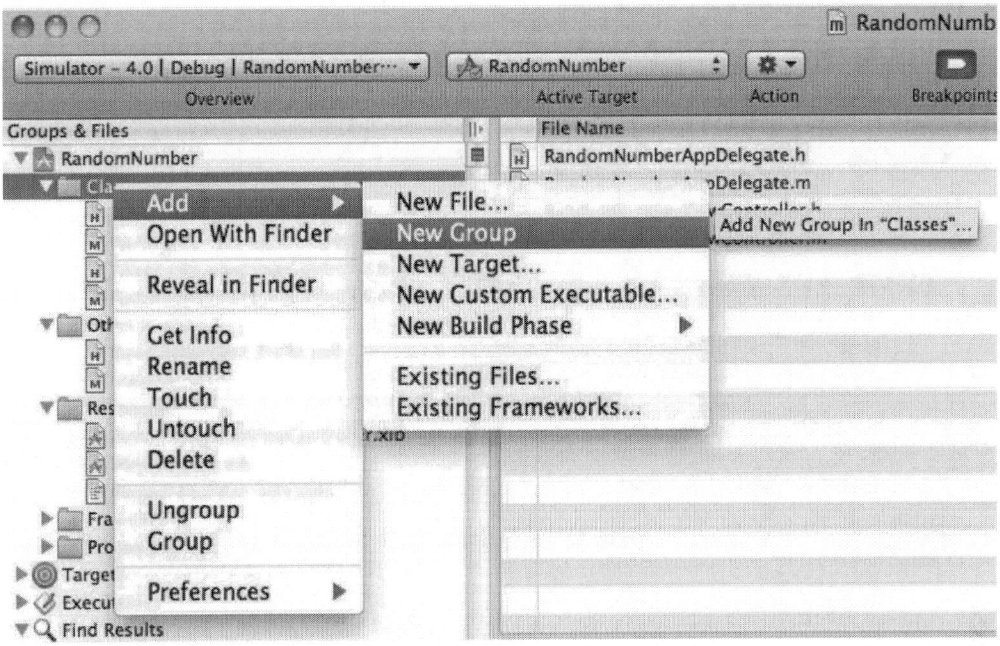

Figure 10–8. *Creating new groups*

5. Create a Models Group, Views Group, and Controllers Group.

6. Drag the RandomNumberViewController.m and .h file the Controllers Group.
   Having these groups reminds you to follow the MVC design pattern as you
   develop your code, so you don't just throw all your code in the controllers. See
   Figure 10–9.

Developers have found it helpful to keep their XIB files with their controllers as their
projects grow. It is not uncommon to have dozens of controllers and XIB files in your
project. Keeping them together helps keep everything organized.

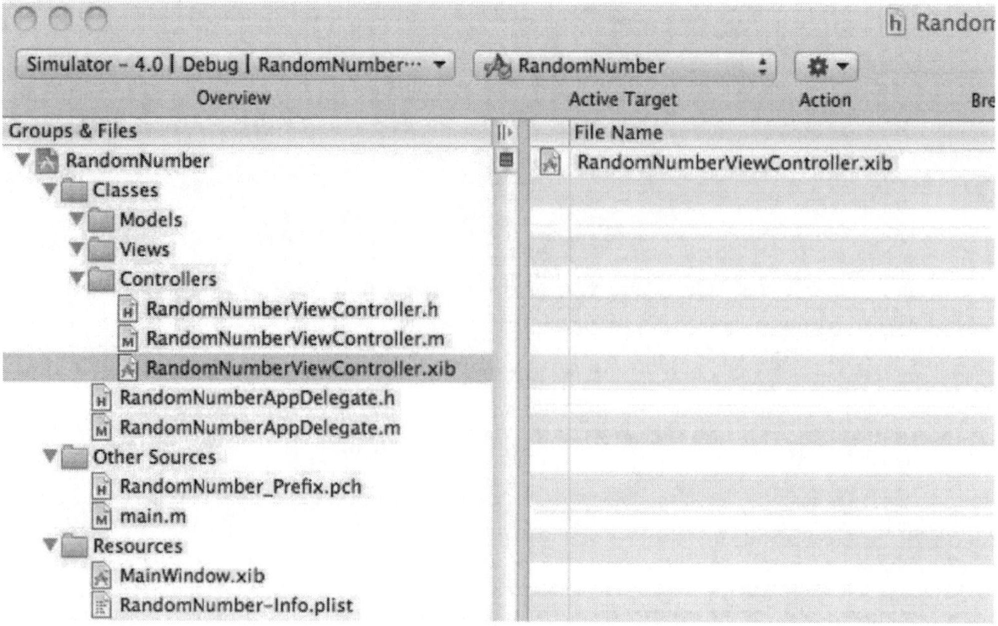

Figure 10–9. *MVC groups with Controller and XIB files organized*

7.   Open the RandomNumberViewController.h file.

8.   Create one instance variable and two methods. The instance variable displays the random number, and methods will seed the random number generator and create a random number. We will also use the @property and @synthesize to create the getter and setter methods for the random number that we will display. See Figure 10–10.

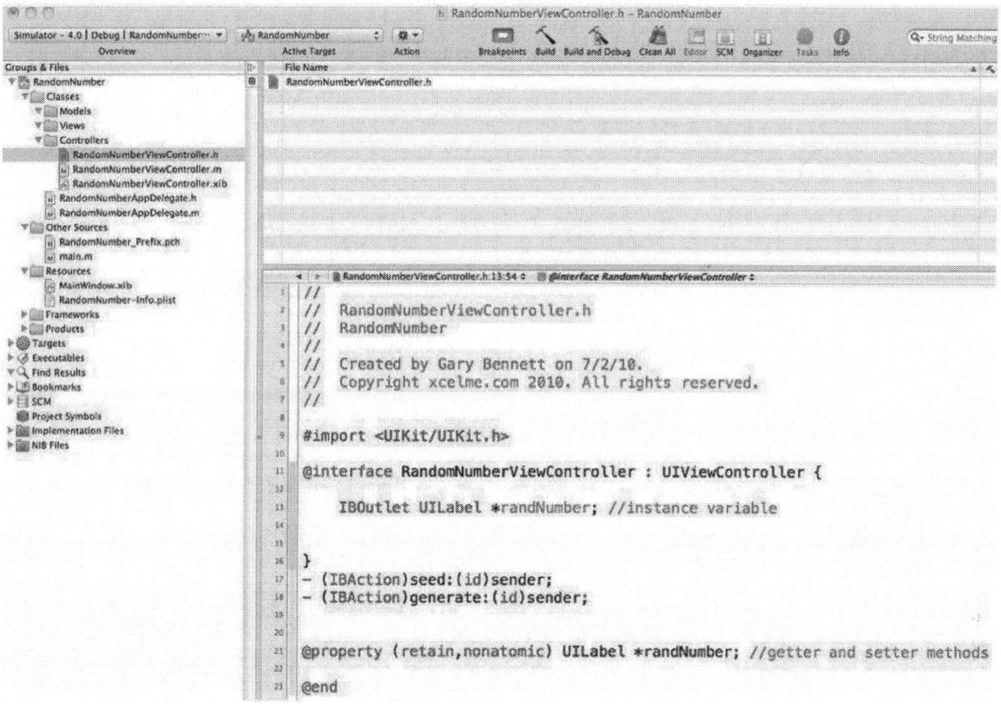

Figure 10–10. *Code listing for RandomNumberViewController.h*

Using Outlets

There is one instance variable declared of type UILabel:.

```
IBOutlet IBOutlet UILabel *randNumber; //instance variable
```

As are reminder, outlets (pointers) are declared in our object's interface file are connected to specific instance variables.

There is also a declaration that is probably new to you. It is called an IBOutlet and is commonly referred to as an outlet. **Outlets** signal your controller that this instance variable is a pointer to another object that is set up in Interface Builder. IBOutlet will enable Interface Builder to see the outlet and enable you to connect the variable to the object in Interface Builder.

Using the analogy of an electrical wall outlet, these instance variables outlets are connected to objects. Using Interface Builder we can connect these instance variables to the appropriate object.

Because Interface Builder will be accessing randNumber outside the object, we need to provide the setter and getter methods for randNumber:

```
@property (retain,nonatomic) IBOutlet UILabel *randNumber; //getter and setter methods
```

We used `retain`, so we will need to release the memory allocated for this instance variable in the Implementation file.

Implementing an Action

We mentioned at the beginning of this chapter that actions, which our objects trigger in our views when events fire, are connected to our targets (object methods) in the app's code.

Our `RandomNumberViewController` object has two methods:

`(IBAction)seed:(id)sender;`

and

`(IBAction)generate:(id)sender;`

Methods can be triggered by user interface objects, also known as events, called **Actions**.

You can now save this header file.

> **NOTE:** If you do not save your header file, you will not see your changes when you go to Interface Builder to connect your outlets and actions. It is common for developers to forget to do this. So when you go to Interface Builder and you don't see an outlet or an action that you declared in your header file, you will know what you forgot to do.

Using Interface Builder

The most common way to launch Interface Builder and begin working on your view is to **double-click** on the XIB file related to the view in the Group & Files pane. In this case it is, RandomNumberViewController.xib. See Figure 10–11.

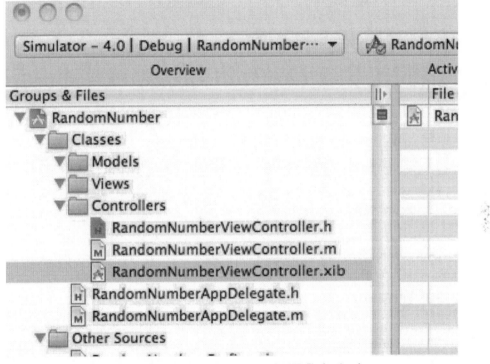

Figure 10–11. *Launch Interface Builder and double-click on the XIB file for the view*

When Interface Builder launches, two windows are displayed: the Document window for the XIB and its view. See Figure 10–12.

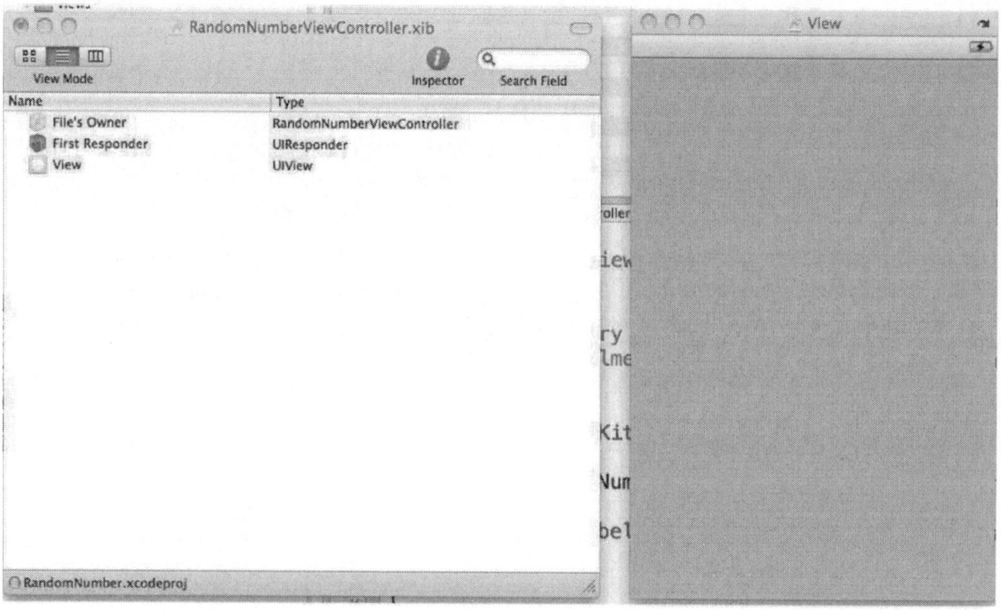

Figure 10–12. *The Document window and its View window*

At the top left of the Document window, you can select the different view modes. In Figure 10–12, the Document window is in Detail mode.

Document Window

The Document window shows all the objects that our view contains. Some examples of these objects are:

- Buttons
- Labels
- Text fields
- Web views
- Map views
- iAd
- Picker views
- Table views

NOTE: If you can't find the Document window in Interface Builder, simply click on Window > Document from the Interface Builder main menu.

Library Window

The Library window is where all the fun happens. It's a smorgasbord of cool objects that you can drag and drop into the View window.

- To open the Library window, click on Tools > Library in the main menu. See Figure 10–13.

Figure 10–13. *The Library window*

The Library window is divided into the following four sections:

- Controllers
- Data views
- Inputs and views
- Windows, views, and bars

Inspector Window

The Inspector window enables you to tweak your control to make your objects behave the way you want. The Inspector window has four tabs across the top. See Figure 10–14.

- View attributes
- View connections
- View size
- View identity

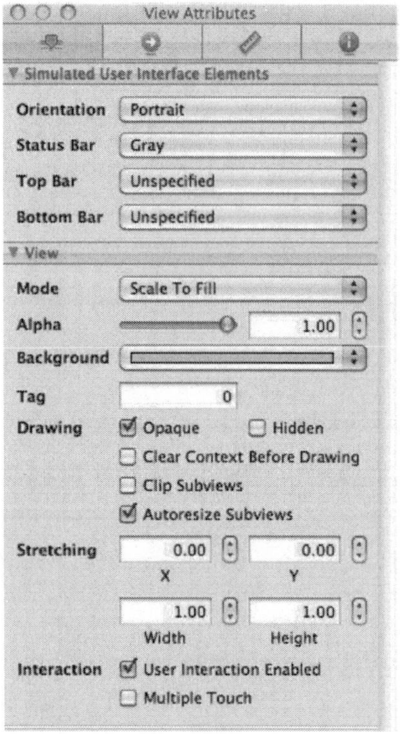

Figure 10–14. *The Inspector window*

To open the Inspector window, click on the blue inspector icon in the top menu of the Document window. Refer to Figure 10–12.

Creating the View

Our random number generator will have three objects in the view: one label and two buttons. The label shows the random number that is generated, one button will generate the seed, and the other button will generate the random number.

1. Drag a Label from the Library window's Inputs & Values section to the View window.

2. Drag two rounded rect buttons from the Library window to the View Window.

3. Click on the top button and label the button **Seed Random Number**.

4. Click on the bottom button and label it **Generate Random Number**. See Figure 10–15.

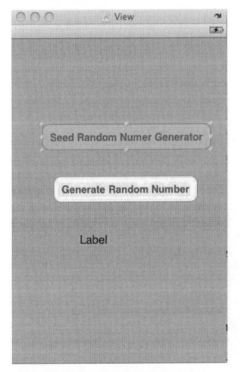

Figure 10–15. *Placing objects in the view*

Connecting the Outlets and Objects

To connect the objects to the outlets and actions, it is best to have the Document and View windows close together.

To Connect the randNumber outlet to the label:

Right-click on the File's Owner icon in the Document window. In the outlet section of the pop-up window, drag from the randNumber open circle icon to the Label icon in the View window, and release. See Figure 10–16.

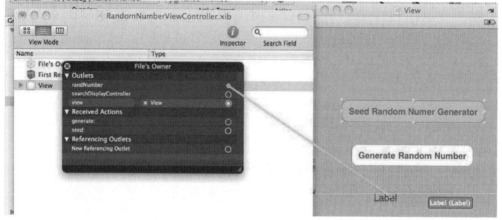

Figure 10–16. *Connect the randNumber outlet to the Label object*

When you release, the pop-up window will populate the randNumber outlet with the objects information. See Figure 10–17.

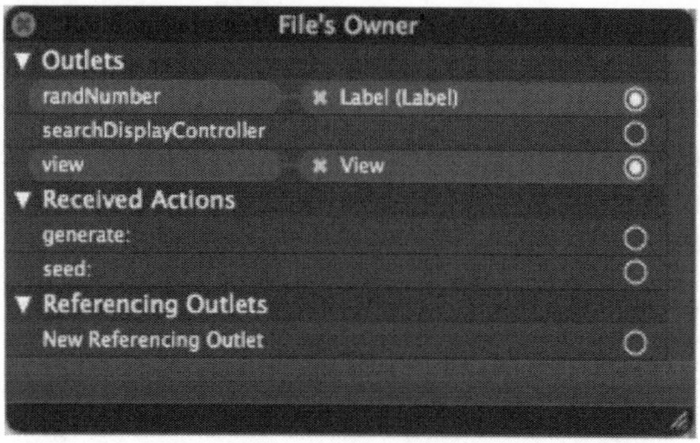

Figure 10–17. *The randNumber outlet is connected to the Label object*

When you are connecting your outlet and actions to the objects in the view, Interface Builder will *not* let you connect the outlet and actions to the wrong type. If you declared an UILabel in your interface file, you will not be able to connect it to a UITextView object.

NOTE: If you made a mistake and want to change your connection, simply click on the X icon next to the object name to delete the connection. Refer to Figure 10–17.

Connecting Actions and Objects

Now you need to connect your actions to your round rect button objects.

Right-click on the File's Owner icon in the Document window.

In the Received Actions section of the pop-up window, drag from the Generate: Open circle icon to the Generate Random Number button in the View window. See Figure 10–18.

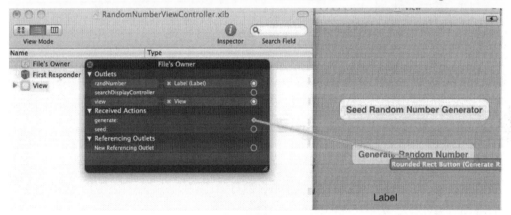

Figure 10–18. *Connecting the Generate: action to the button object*

When you release, another pop-up will display with the events that object can generate. Select Touch Up Inside. See Figure 10–19.

The Touch Up Inside event is fired to your connected method via the controller's action, when the user taps in the button on your iPhone.

Figure 10–19. *All events associated with the round rect button object*

Connect the Seed: action to the Seed Random Number Generator by right-clicking on the File's Owner icon and dragging it from the Seed: open circle icon to the Seed Random Number Generator round rect button. Then select the Touch Up Inside event. See Figure 10–20.

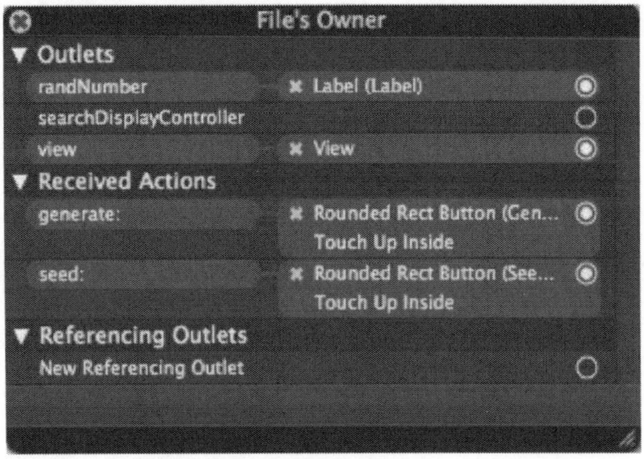

Figure 10–20. *Connecting the Seed: action*

Great, all of our actions and outlets have been connected in Interface Builder. Go ahead and quite Interface Builder now.

> **NOTE:** If you don't save your changes in Interface Builder, they will not be detected by the compiler, and you will not see the changes when you run your app.

Implementation File

All that is left now, is to complete the code for our outlet and actions in the implementation file for the controller.

Open RandomNumberViewController.m and remove all the commented methods in green for readability.

Complete the code in Listing 10–1.

Listing 10–1. *Outlet and actions*

```
#import "RandomNumberViewController.h"

@implementation RandomNumberViewController

@synthesize randNumber;//getter and setter methods (i.e. accessor)


- (void)viewDidUnload {
        // Release any retained subviews of the main view.
        // e.g. self.myOutlet = nil;
        self.randNumber = nil;// set outlets to nil with the view gets unloaded
}
- (IBAction)generate:(id)sender
{
        // Generate a number between 0 and 100 inclusive
        int generated;
        generated = (random() % 101);
        [randNumber setText:[NSString stringWithFormat:@"%i",generated]];
}

- (IBAction)seed:(id)sender
{
        srandom(time(NULL));
        [randNumber setText: @"Generator seeded"];
}

- (void)dealloc {
        [randNumber release];
        [super dealloc];
}


@end
```

There is a method we should examine a bit further: [randNumber setText: The method setText: sets the UILabel value in your view. The connections you established in Interface Builder from your outlet to the Label object does all the work for you.

That is it!

To run your iPhone app in the iPhone simulator, click on Build and Debug and your app should launch in the simulator. See Figure 10–21.

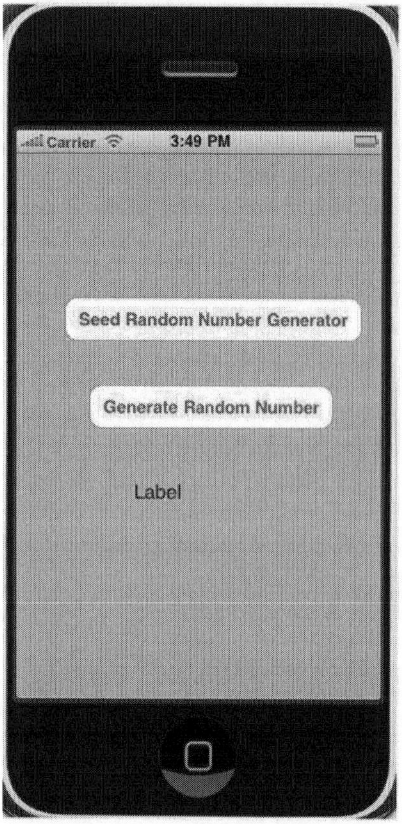

Figure 10–21. *The completed random number generator app running in the iPhone Simulator*

To seed the random function, tap on Seed Random Number Generator and then, to generate the random number, tap on Generate Random Number Generator.

Broken Connections in Interface Builder

If you change or delete an outlet instance variable name or action in your interface file without modified the XIB file, this may cause your application to crash. The compiler may not throw a warning when this occurs.

To detect and fix these problems after you have modified or deleted an action or outlet in the interface file, open the XIB in Interface Builder. It should not have a warning triangle in the bottom right of the Document window. Refer to Figure 10–12.

If an outlet or action has been deleted or modified in the interface file, an orange triangle will appear at the bottom right of the Document window. To see what is causing the error, click on the orange triangle to view the error(s). See Figure 10–22.

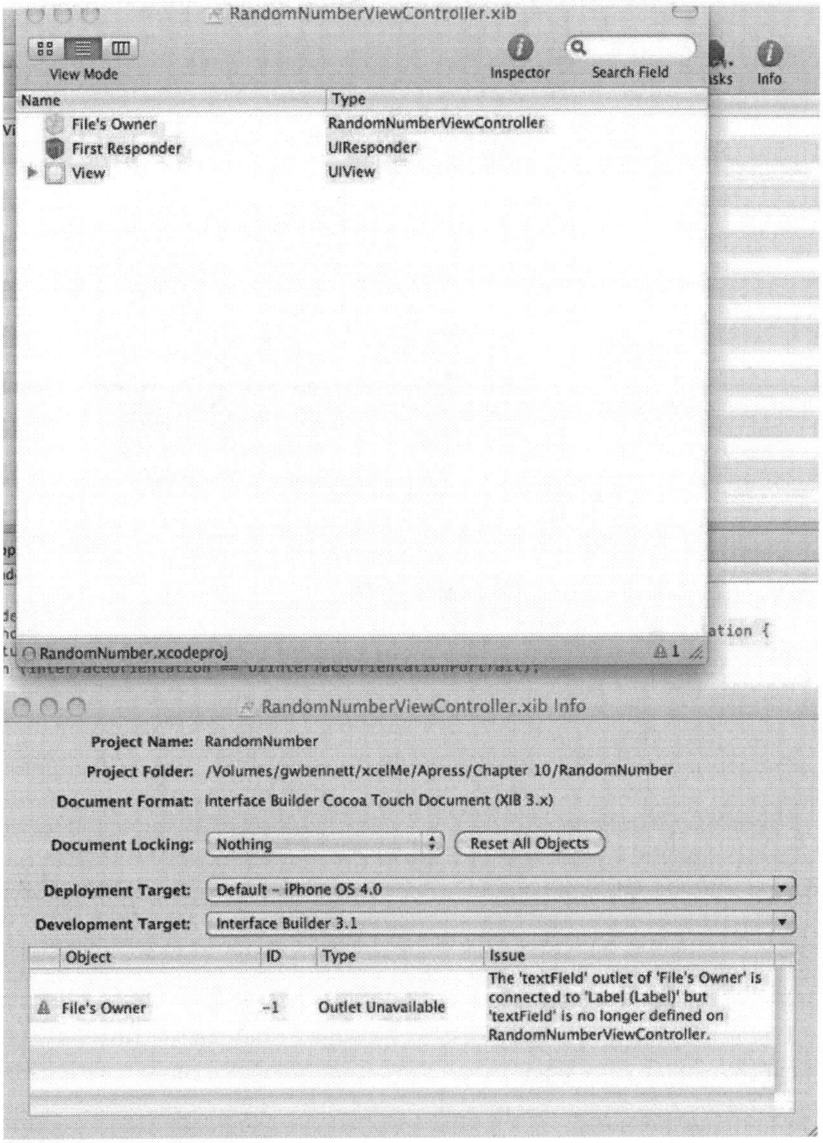

Figure 10–22. *Detecting Interface Builder warnings*

To find the offending actions or outlets, right-click on the File's Owner, and look for the yellow warning triangle(s). See Figure 10–23.

To fix the warning, simply delete the connection and connect the correct outlet or action, if applicable.

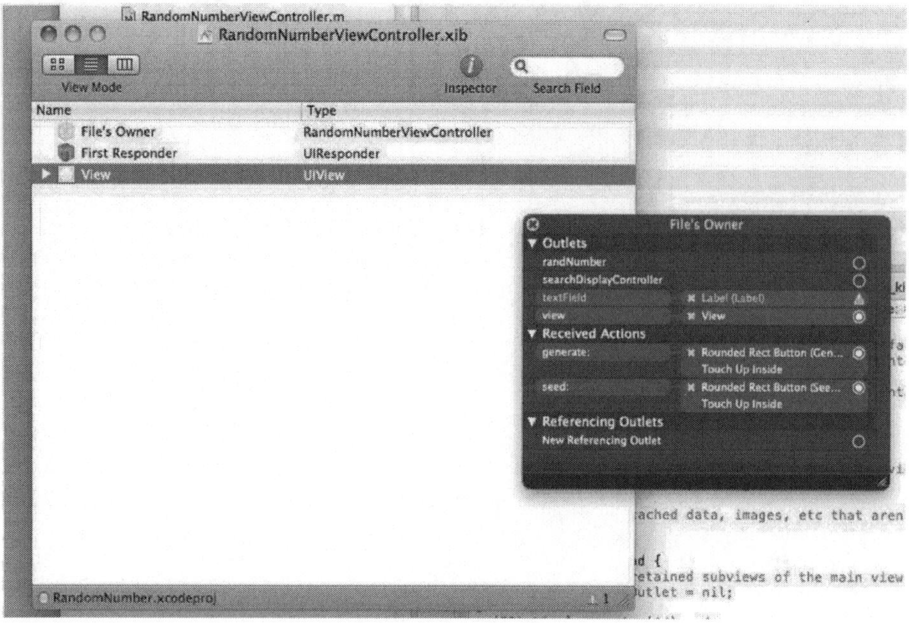

Figure 10–23. *Finding and fixing Interface Builder warnings*

Summary

Great job! Interface Builder saves a ton of time when creating our User Interfaces. You have a powerful set of objects to use in your application, with a minimum of coding. Interface Builder handles many of the details you would normally have to deal with.

You should be familiar with the following terms:

- NIB and XIB files
- Model-View-Controller (MVC)
- Architectural pattern
- Human interface guidelines (HIGs)
- Outlets
- Actions

Exercises

- Extend the random number generator app to show a date and time in a Label when the app starts.
- After showing a date and time label, add a button to update the data and time label with the new time.

Chapter 11

Memory, Addresses, and Pointers

Computers, just like you and me, need a place to work and store things. Think of computer memory like space on a desk, for example. Someone who needs to work on many projects at once needs to have enough desk space to place all the papers and documents so they can be quickly and easily accessed. If the desk space is too small for the number of projects being juggled, some projects may have to be filed back into drawers so they can be quickly pulled back once there is more space on the desk. Making sure the desk space is used efficiently also very important.

Dealing with a computer's memory is one of the more complicated areas of programming. Why is this the case? Surely these problems have been solved by now, right? Well, yes and no. Some languages have taken the approach to remove the need for programmers to manage memory at all. Some internal magic (and a little something called garbage collection) handles all the management of how memory is used and released when it is no longer being used. The negative side to this approach is that garbage collection does not give the programmer the ultimate say-so on how the memory should be used in all cases. Why is this important? Generally speaking, the issue is performance. With full control of memory management, the programmer also has full control over the performance (or lack thereof) of the program.

This chapter will introduce the ideas of working with the memory of the Mac, iPhone, or iPad. Working with memory on any device has its challenges. For example, the iPhone and iPad, being smaller devices, have less memory to work with, which means that it is important that their memory is used efficiently. Fortunately, Objective-C provides mechanisms that keep managing memory from being a chore. You will learn about how to allocate and deallocate memory as well as about the retain/release (or reference counting) model of memory management.

Understanding Memory

While many people may have associated computer memory with that of the human brain, I prefer to compare computer memory to physical space that you, as a person, have to work. You are like the computer's CPU, the part that actually processes information and does something with it. The more space you have to work, the easier it is to organize things and the quicker you can actually accomplish your tasks. Of course, we all reach that place where, no matter how much more space, we get we won't be able to work any faster.

To a computer, memory is the workspace where certain programs (or parts of programs) as well as data are stored. On the Mac, iPhone, and iPad, the most basic unit of memory is a **byte**. If you think of memory as nothing more than a grid of boxes, a byte would simply be a single box.

Figure 11–1. *Bytes are like a row of boxes.*

Of course, there are generally billions of these boxes, or bytes, of memory in a typical modern computer. While it does seem like a vast, almost limitless amount, memory is the most important resource that a computer has at its disposal. Only programs that reside in memory can be executed; only data loaded from disk can be inspected or acted on. Also, on the iPhone or iPad, there is much less memory than on a typical PC or Mac computer. A certain degree of memory conservation is always a good practice.

Okay, so memory is like a grid of boxes that each holds a byte of information. What good is it at this point? How does the computer put each byte in its place and how does it pull it back out? Certainly, if my garage was full of boxes, I would have a very difficult time figuring out where, for example, all of my old video games were stored. A computer has exactly the same problem, so it goes about solving that problem in a very organized way. Before we go into how the computer solves this problem, you need to understand the basics of units of memory and addresses.

Bits, Bytes, and Bases

In Figure 11–1, each box represents one byte, or memory space. Each byte can hold a total of 8 bits. A **bit** is simply a number that can be either a zero or a one—off or on. It is this sequence of zeros and ones that give the byte its value. These zeros and ones represent a **binary** numeral system; that is, each digit can have a maximum of two values, zero or one. This is sometimes referred to as base-2 numbering system (verses the base-10 or decimal numbering system that we all use in our every day lives). Before we get into more specifics of memory, it's very important that you understand the numbering systems that are typically used on modern computer hardware.

> **NOTE:** Modern computers use 8 bits per byte. In the early days of computing, different manufacturers of computers sometimes had different byte sizes. For example, Control Data Corporation's CDC-6000 often used 12-bit bytes for display codes, and the DEC PDP-10 operated on bit fields, so a "byte" could be anything from 1 bit to 36 bits. IBM, with its popular System/360, set the standard on the 8-bit byte as did the microprocessors of the 1970s.

Generally speaking, people use base-10 numbering for pretty much everything; from money to measurements, base-10 is the standard. However, in the realm of the modern computer, the base-10 system is rarely used. Instead, the computer typically uses base-2 (binary) or base-16 (hexadecimal).

> **NOTE:** Base-8, commonly referred to as octal, is also used but is not as common as hexadecimal.

Converting Base-10 (Decimal) to Base-2 (Binary)

A typical everyday number may look like this: 1101. Now, most people would consider this number to be "one-thousand, one-hundred, and one." However in base-2 numbering, this number would represent the decimal number 13. Let's look at how this can be.

As shown in Figure 11–2, in base-10 numbering, each digit represents a power of 10; that is, each column increases by a power of 10 (10, 100, 1000, etc.) right-to-left. We add the 1000s column (10^3), 100s column, and the 1s column to get $1,101_{10}$ (the subscript means "base-10").

10^3	10^2	10^1	10^0
1	1	0	1

Figure 11–2. *Base-10 numbering system*

Now, let's look at the same number in base 2 in Figure 11–3.

2^3	2^2	2^1	2^0
1	1	0	1

Figure 11–3. *Base-2 numbering system*

In base-2 numbering (shown in Figure 11–3), the columns all increase by a power of 2 (2, 4, 8, 16, 32, etc.) right-to-left. We add 8, 4, and 1 to reach a value of 13_{10} (in base-2 that is). Also note that a series of 4 bits, which represents half of a byte, is typically referred to as a **nibble**.

Of course, it was mentioned earlier that *eight* bits (numbered 0 to 7) make up a byte. Figure 11–4 shows an example of an entire byte consisting of 8 bits. To get the value, add up all of the columns as follows:

$128 + 16 + 8 + 4 + 1 = 157_{10}$

Bit 7			. . .				Bit 0
128	64	32	16	8	4	2	1
1	0	0	1	1	1	0	1

Figure 11–4. *An entire byte showing base-2 and base-10 values.*

Using Base-16 (Hexadecimal) Numbering

The last base that is worthy of mentioning, used quite ubiquitously in modern computers, is the base-16, or the **hexadecimal**, numbering system. In base-2, each digit can have one of two values, 0 and 1. In base-10, each digit can have one of ten values, 0–9. In base-16, each digit can have one of 16 values, 0–F. Yes, you read that correctly; the last value is **F**. To represent 16 values in a single column, it became necessary use letters to represent values. In the case of base-16, the numbering goes from 0 through 9 and A through F. It takes two hexadecimal (**hex** for short) digits to represent a single byte; each hex digit represents 4 bits as show in Figure 11–5.

Hex	Dec
0	0
1	1
2	2
3	3
4	4
5	5
6	6
7	7
8	8
9	9
A	10
B	11
C	12
D	13
E	14
F	15

Upper Nibble				Lower Nibble			
Bit 7			. . .				Bit 0
128	64	32	16	8	4	2	1
1	0	0	1	1	1	0	1
9				D			

Figure 11–5. *On the left, two nibbles make a byte. A simple hex to decimal conversion chart appears on the right.*

So the hex number 9D is equal to the binary number 10011101, which is equal to the decimal number 157. As shown in Figure 11–5, a byte can be any value between 0000 0000 and 1111 1111 (base-2), which is 0xFF in hex.

NOTE: In "0xFF," the "0x" that precedes the "FF" is used in programming to indicate that the number is a hex number. While FF seems obvious, because there are only letters, a number like "10" is less clear, is it 10 or 16? Well, 0x10 makes it clear.

Hexadecimal takes some getting used to, but learning it is time well spent. This is because when dealing with memory, pretty much everything is expressed in hexadecimal. Just like in base-10, each numeric column is an exponentially larger that the previous, as shown in Figure 11–6.

0010	0001	1010	0010
16^3	16^2	16^1	16^0
2	1	A	2

Figure 11–6. *A 16-bit hexadecimal number*

In base-10, each column is 1, 10, 100, 1000, and so on. In hexadecimal, the columns are base-16, so you have 1, 16, 256, 1024, and so on—each column is a multiple of 16. However, once you understand hexadecimal, you may want to express the number in decimal as well. Figure 11–7 is an example of how a 16-bit hexadecimal number is converted to a decimal one.

2	1	A	2
2×16^3	1×16^2	10×16^2	2
2 x 4096	1 x 256	10 x 16	2
8,192	256	160	2

Figure 11–7. *Converting a 16-bit hex number to decimal*

If we add all of our columns together we will have our answer:

8,192 + 256 + 160 + 2 = 8,610
So 0x21A2 equals 8,610.

Figure 11–7 represents a 16-bit number. Calculating 32- and 64-bit numbers means just simply increasing the columns to the left.

TIP: If you find yourself calculating 32- and 64-bit values a lot, just use the calculator on the Mac (in the Programmer view) or spend a few bucks and buy a scientific calculator that can do hex.

We hope you haven't been scared off. Understanding computer memory at its lowest level is actually not that bad, and it's something that won't be necessary all the time. The important thing is to remember is that when dealing with memory, it may be necessary to understand binary (Base-2), decimal (Base-10), and hexadecimal (base-16) values. This will become clearer when debugging an application, as discussed in Chapter 12.

Understanding Memory Address Basics

Memory, just like buildings on a street, has addresses, except that, in some ways, memory addressing is much simpler. Earlier in this chapter, we mentioned that computer could solve a problem of keeping track of boxes of old video games in a garage—virtually of course. The first part of this process is to be able to keep track of certain locations in memory, called **addresses**. From a program's perspective, these addresses are stored into variables for later reference.

Memory in a computer is a linear set of bytes (or boxes) that store information. If you were to simply start labeling these boxes as 1, 2, 3, 4, and so on, you would have a set of boxes starting at 1 and end with some very large number. These numbers are referred to as a **memory address**.

Figure 11–8 provides a simple example of addressing memory.

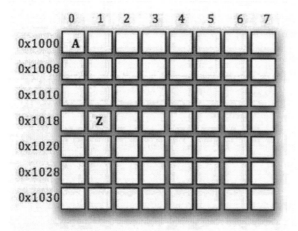

Figure 11–8. *A simple example of addressing.*

If each block is one byte the first byte starts at address 0x1000 and ends at 0x1037. Remember that the "0x" that precedes the number indicates that the number, in this case, the address, is expressed in hexadecimal. So address 0x1000, for example, is really 4096 and not 1000. The number 0x1000 represents the start of our memory example. At this location is the letter "A". Also in the example is the letter "Z". The value of "Z" is located at the memory address of 0x1019. The address 0x1000 is an example of a simple 16-bit address. A 32-bit iPhone address would look like 0x03C06D80. A 64-bit address would be double the 32-bit size.

> **NOTE:** If our program were given access to the memory in Figure 12-8, it would store the starting point of the memory, 0x1000, into a variable. This variable is commonly referred to as a **pointer**, since the value of the variable (the address 0x1000, which is just a number) points to the data we are interested in, like an arrow on a map.

Another way to think of this grid of memory is to consider it an array. If you recall, an array is declared like the following:

In this example, a variable has been declared as an array. The array size is 56 characters in length, the exact same size as our example in Figure 11–8. Whenever a variable is declared as an array, like `myArray`, the variable resolves to an address, or pointer. Just for argument's sake, let's assume that `myArray` has an address of 0x1000, just like our grid in Figure 11–8. If you were to look at the variable `myArray`, it would have a value of 0x1000. Remember, the value of an array resolves to an address. So how do we access the memory in the array?

```
char myArray[56];
```

> **NOTE:** In C and Objective-C, all arrays are **zero-based**. This means that the first element in the array is at element zero, not one. An array of 30 elements would start at element 0 and end at element 29. Element 30 is outside of the bounds of the array

Since C and Objective-C use zero-based arrays, if the program need to access the first element in the array it would be done like the following:

```
char letterA = myArray[0];
```

In this case, `letter` would be set to the first element in the array, which would be the letter "A" (using **Figure** 12-8 as the array). What's really happening under the hood is that the computer is simply using the array index and adding it to the address. Again, if the address is 0x1000, adding 0 result in a new address of 0x1000, which is where the letter "A" resides.

```
char letterZ = myArray[25]; // or myArray[0x19] if you
                            // getting into this hex thing!
```

In the preceding example, `letter` would be set to the value at element 25, which is the letter "Z." The computer adds 25 (0x19) to the base address of 0x1000, resulting in a value of 0x1019. This is where the letter "Z" is. Remember, arrays are zero-based so "Z" is at element 25 because "A" started at element 0; "Z" is still the twenty-sixth element (using natural numbers, or counting numbers, that start at one).

Using the brackets ([ ]) after a pointer makes it very simple to access elements within that array of memory. There is a different way to do this that will yield the same result.

This example will hopefully help the understanding of pointers and addresses even more.

Listing 11-1. *Using Pointers*

```
1   int main(void)
2   {
3       char myArray[] = "ABCDEFGHIJKLMNOPQRSTUVWXYZ";
4       char *aPointer;
5       char letter;
6
7       aPointer = myArray;
8       letter = myArray[25];    //  letter == 'Z'
9       letter = *(aPointer+2);  // letter == 'C'
10      letter = aPointer[3];    // letter == 'D'
11  }
```

In Listing 11-1, line 3 declares a new array. The brackets ([ ]) are empty because we're assigning the array a value of the alphabet. In this case, since we provide the values, the compiler knows what size the array is going to be. So, our new array is just like **Figure** 12-8, the first value at element 0 is the letter "A," and the last value at element 25 (0x19) is the letter "Z." myArray is a pointer, and it points to memory that has the alphabet in it.

Line 4 declares a variable that is a pointer. aPointer is a pointer to data of type char, if line 4 were int *aPointer, then aPointer would be a pointer to data of type int. In out case, we'll keep it as char. Remember, a pointer is just an address, and an address is just a number.

On line 5, the program is declaring a character variable. We'll be using this variable to store data from the array.

Line 7 looks a little strange but what it's doing is assigning the aPointer variable, the value of myArray. As mentioned previously, a variable that is an array always resolves to a pointer. So, myArray is a pointer, which is an address, which is just a number. That number is assigned to aPointer. The program is not copying the array to aPointer; its just setting the value of aPointer to what myArray is. At this point in the program, myArray and aPointer both have the same value.

Line 8 adds 25 to the address of myArray and returns the value that is 25 bytes into the array, which results in the letter "Z."

Line 9 adds 2 to the value of aPointer. Remember, aPointer is equal to myArray. aPointer + 2 now points to the letter "C." If this seems a little off mathematically, remember zero-based arrays:

- aPointer+0 points to "A"

- aPointer+1 points to "B"

- aPointer+2 points to "C"

Hopefully, you are getting used to zero-based arrays. Line 9 also makes use of the **dereference operator**, the asterisk (*), more about this in the next section.

Line 10 is equivalent to line 8. Both myArray and aPointer are pointers, and both point to the same memory, so the array operator works.

Using the Dereference Operator

Line 9 looked a little different from the other lines, so let's examine it a little closer:

```
letter = *(aPointer + 2);
```

First, let's consider what's inside the parenthesis:

```
aPointer + 2
```

This should be pretty straightforward: we are adding 2 to the pointer aPointer. If aPointer was 0x1000, the resulting value would be 0x1002. The pointer now *points* to the letter "C." Using a pointer this way is very different from using the brackets in line 8 or 10. We're manually adjusting the pointer so that it results in a new value. Next, we need to ask the computer, "What does the pointer point to?" With the array operator on line 8 and 10, that question is implied, and the program responds. But when we simply change an address by adding, subtracting, or whatever, the program needs to explicitly ask this question. This is where the asterisk (*) comes into play.

Using an asterisk in front of a pointer *dereferences* the address and returns what value the pointer is pointing to. So, if our pointer is 0x1000 and at 0x1000 is stored the letter "A," we can get to the letter "A" by dereferencing the pointer. *(0x1000) would return the letter "A" if our example was pointing to real memory (don't actually do this because 0x1000 is not a real address, just an example is used to simplify the problem!). Remember, a pointer is an address, and an address is just a number. The asterisk asks the computer to return what stored at the address rather than to return the address itself.

> **NOTE:** In most common programming the programmer rarely gets to tell the system, for example, at location 0x1000 is our data. The reason for this is that memory is **virtualized**. Virtualized memory allows more memory to be used than is physically present on the machine *(Vitual memory is out of scope of this book)*. Because of this, the operating system manages where the data is stored. As a result, the computer tells the program where its memory is, rather than the program telling the computer. Regardless, the concept is the same.
>
> When developing software at the hardware or device driver level, using hard-coded addresses is much more common. Typical programs in Mac OS X or iOS will never use hard-coded addresses.

Requesting Memory

In modern operating systems, the program requests memory, and the operating system complies by returning a pointer to the requested memory. In C and Objective-C, a **pointer** is declared by preceeding the variable name with an asterisk (*), for example:

```
char *theData;
NSString *theString;
```

Don't confused the asterisk here with the ***dereference operator***. Only when declaring a variable does the asterisk identify the variable as a pointer.

Here are some more examples of requesting memory:

```
1.   char data1[100];
2.   char *data2 = malloc(100);
3.   NSString *myString = [[NSString alloc] init];
```

In example 1, memory is allocated in the form of an array declaration. The program now has a pointer (data1) that points to 100 bytes of memory. In C, any variable that is declared as an array is referenced as a pointer.

Example 2 is a little more complex. data2 is declared as a pointer to a char data type. We can tell it's a pointer because the variable name is preceded by an asterisk. The next part of the line is malloc(100), which is a standard C library function call. This function allocates the requested amount memory and returns a pointer to it. In our example, malloc is passed the value 100. This requests that 100 bytes be allocated. When the function returns, data2 contains a *pointer* to the 100 bytes of memory.

Example 3 is a more traditional Objective-C type memory allocation. First, the program declares a pointer to an NSString class named myString. Next, the following code is executed: [[NSString alloc] init]. This will allocate the necessary memory for the object and return a *pointer* to it.

In all these examples, memory is requested from the operating system and returned to the program via a pointer, even in example 1—except example 1 is just a little different from the rest.

Working with Automatic Variables and Pointers

Any variable created within a function or block is considered an **automatic variable**, or **auto-variable**. In our previous examples, example 1 allocates 100 characters as an array. It does so automatically since, as you learned, all variables are auto-variables by default. Because we define all the space up front via an array declaration, all of this memory is managed automatically for us. Examples 2 and 3 are also auto-variables but they allocate just enough space to hold a pointer to memory—that's all. Recall that a pointer is just a variable that holds an address to memory; it's not the memory itself. So, char* data2 and NSString *myString are really just variables that hold a number, which represents an address to memory.

TIP: Think of pointers this way: a *pointer* is like a ticket to a concert the allocated memory is like the seat. The ticket has the information on how to get to the seat. If the ticket card is discarded (or lost), the ability to find the seat is also lost. However, the seat (allocated memory) still remains.

Examples 2 and 3 are auto-variables that hold the "ticket" to the memory, not the memory itself (see Figure 11–9). This means that, when the function exits and the variables go out of scope, the pointers to the memory will be lost; the "ticket" is lost. The problem with this is that the program needs to also release, or deallocate, the memory that the pointer points to before it is lost. The manually allocated memory does not go out of scope with the pointer; allocated memory is global to the program and doesn't get released until the program exits.

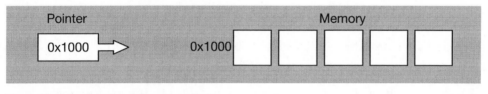

Figure 11–9. *A pointer is not the memory itself.*

What's very important to remember is that memory that is manually allocated must be deallocated at some point and depending on how the memory is used. Some memory might be allocated at the start of the program and doesn't have to be released until the program exits. However, the most common memory allocations happen many, many times throughout the life program, and it becomes critical that the associated memory be deallocated as soon as the object is no longer being used.

Deallocating Memory

When a program allocates memory, it needs to ensure that it's released, or **deallocated**, once the program is finished using the memory. Using the examples again, example 2 allocates memory with the `malloc` command. When the program is finished with that memory, it needs to be deallocated. Failing to deallocate memory is a common programming mistake and goes by the descriptive name of **memory leak**.

To prevent memory leaks (which eventually lead to program crashes), allocated memory must be managed with care. Listing 11–2 shows the code could look when properly deallocating memory for examples 2 and 3.

Listing 11–2. *Memory Allocation and Deallocation*

```
1    int main(void)
2    {
3        char *data2 = malloc(100);
4        NSString *myString = [[NSString alloc] init];
5        ... // standard "doing-stuff" ellipse
6        ...
7        free(data2);  // Deallocate the 100 bytes
8        data2 = NULL;
9        [myString release];  // I'm done using this string.
10       myString = nil;
11   }
```

In Listing 11–2, data2 is allocated on line 3. This type of allocation is plain old standard C and is not typical in an Objective-C program, but its still very important to know and understand.

Line 4 declares and allocates an Objective-C object, NSString.

Line 7 deallocates the block of memory allocated from line 3.

Line 8 sets the pointer to NULL. This is a good practice that is going to be explained in the next section.

Line 9 releases the object that was allocated on line 4. The release message is a request to deallocate the object. The reason that release message is a *request* to deallocate memory has to do with the mechanism of how memory is managed for Objective-C objects. This mechanism is referred to as the **retain/release model**, or sometimes as **reference counting**. Reference counting makes using memory a little more efficient, because it allows the objects to know when it should be deallocated. It's a slightly better mechanism than completely managing memory manually.

Line 10 is equivalent to line 8. Objective-C pointers *can* be set to NULL but its much better to set the pointer to nil. A nil object in Objective-C has a special meaning and can actually respond to a message. NULL does not have that same property.

Using Special Pointers

As you've learned, a pointer is just a number that represents an address to memory. There are two special pointers that are worth mentioning. They really aren't pointers per se, but they represent an empty pointer—a pointer that doesn't point to anything. These two pointers are NULL and nil. NULL is nothing more than zero, zilch, nada. Since pointers are just numbers that represent an address, an address of 0, or NULL, represents a pointer that logically points to nothing. Using an address of zero is a convention that modern computers use; computers do not allow any program to store something at the address 0 which makes using NULL to represent an empty or unused piece of memory much more meaningful. This is important to know because if memory allocation fails, the resulting pointer returned is NULL. NULL is also useful to indicate that the pointer is no longer valid or is simply empty. This is true for all of standard C. Here's how NULL can be used to initialize a pointer:

```
char *data = NULL;
```

It should also be used in comparisons like the code fragment in Listing 11–3.

Example 11–3. Using NULL to Verify and Clear a Pointer

```
1    char *data = malloc(100);
2    if (data != NULL) {
3        // Do something with the memory.  It's valid.
4        free (data);   // Deallocate the memory, we're done with it.
5        data = NULL;  // Set the pointer to NULL indicating that its empty.
6    }
7
```

In Listing 11–3, line 2 checks to make sure that the `malloc` function worked by checking the pointer with NULL. If the pointer is not NULL, the allocation worked, and the program can use the returned value. The memory is then deallocated on line 4 and set to NULL on line 5 to indicate that the pointer is no longer pointing to anything.

When we are dealing with Objective-C objects, the equivalent of NULL in Objective-C is nil. Like NULL, nil is a special pointer to nothing. However, in the case of Objective-C, nil is actually an empty object. Since Objective-C is heavy on sending messages to an object, an empty pointer should respond to message sent to it, even if that pointer is empty—the nil empty object fulfills this purpose. Listing 11–4 is a sample code fragment that is similar to the standard C version.

Listing 11–4. Using nil to Verify and Clear an Objective-C Pointer

```
1    NSString *data = [[NSString alloc] initWithUTF8String: "Hello World!"];
2    if (data != nil) {
3        // Do something with the memory.  It's valid.
4        [data release];   // Deallocate the memory, we're done with it.
5        data = nil;  // Set the pointer to NULL indicating that its empty.
6    }
```

TIP: Using the ticket metaphor for deallocated memory, here is something to watch out for: If a ticket is a pointer to a seat in a theater, what happens when the show is over? Well, the ticket still points to that same seat, but it isn't valid anymore; the show is over. The same is true with memory. If the memory that a pointer points to is deallocated, that memory is now free to be used by another memory allocation. However, the pointer still points to that old memory. It's important to clear the pointer so it isn't mistakenly used. The practice of checking to see if the pointer is not NULL before using it paired with the practice of setting a pointer to NULL or nil when the object is deallocated is a "best practice" that should be strictly followed.

Managing Memory in Objective-C

As mentioned earlier, Objective-C handles allocated memory in a slightly different way than most applications written in standard C. Recall that the Objective-C system uses something called the retain/release model. With this model, memory that has been allocated by an object gets counted every time the application that is interested in the memory sends a `retain` message to the object. At various stages of the application, the program indicates that it's finished using the memory and sends a `release` message. When the number of releases equal the number of retains, the memory associated with the object is finally deallocated. Let's see how this model looks like in practice. Listing 11–5 is a very basic example.

Listing 11–5. *Allocating an Objective-C Object*

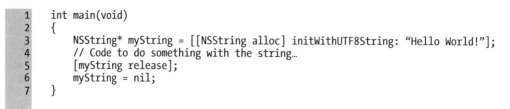

```
1    int main(void)
2    {
3        NSString* myString = [[NSString alloc] initWithUTF8String: "Hello World!"];
4        // Code to do something with the string…
5        [myString release];
6        myString = nil;
7    }
```

In this example, Line 3 allocates a new string object using `alloc`. This line is actually very important in this situation; the reason will be explained in a bit. So line 3 created the new string. As its created, the Objective-C system automatically sends a `retain` message to the object. At this point, the `myString` variable points to an object that has one `retain` so far.

Line 5 issues a `release` to the `myString` object. The release subtracts one from the current retain count (which is 1). As mentioned before, once the retain count reaches zero, the object is deallocated. So, once Line 5 has finished, the `myString` variable points to deallocated memory.

Line 6 sets our original variable to nil to indicate that the pointer is empty.

Using the Retain/Release Model

The process of retaining and releasing memory is something that Objective-C uses extensively to manage memory. The alternate name of this process, reference counting, is a little more descriptive, because the process of retaining and releasing memory is a way of counting how many times the memory has been retained rather than. released. Note the term "memory" is used here generically. Memory management in Objective-C allocates memory for *objects* instead of just blocks of memory. The Objective-C base class `NSObject`, which most Objective-C objects are derived from, keeps track of the retain count.

NOTE: If you are looking for exactness, the NSObject protocol group actually defines the reference counting messages. NSObject implements that protocol.

So far, things sound fairly simple: for every retain, there needs to eventually be a release. This doesn't sound too tricky, right? Well, it's not always straightforward to know when an object is retained. Consider the example in Listing 11–6.

Listing 11–6. *A Retain Count*

```
1    NSMutableDictionary *dict = [[NSMutableDictionary alloc] init];   dict retainCount = 1
2    NSDate *today = [[NSDate alloc] init];                            today retainCount = 1
3
4    [dict setObject: today forKey: @"TODAY"];                        today retainCount = 2
5    [today release];                                                 today retainCount = 1
6    today = nil;
7    [dict removeObjectForKey: @"TODAY"];                             today deallocated
8    [dict release];                                                  dict deallocated
```

Looking at Listing 11–6, the retain counts of the dict and today objects are shown. The dict object looks pretty normal: it has a retain count of 1 whenever the object is created. The same is true for the today object on line 2.

At line 4, things look a little odd. For some reason the today retain count is now 2. What happened? Well, if we look closely at the NSMutableDictionary documentation for the setObject: forKey: method, we see, in the documentation for the setObject: part of the message, and the anObject parameter is the value for the key and that "the object receives a retain message before being added to the receiver."

According to the documentation, before an object is added to the dictionary, the object is sent a retain message. This is why today had a retain count of 2.

Why does the dictionary do this? Well, the answer is quite simple. If we add an object to the dictionary, the dictionary should be responsible for it now; we basically handed it over to that class. We can release any local variables to objects we added to the dictionary. The dictionary now becomes the owner of the objects. To ensure this, the NSMutableDictionary class sends all of the data it stores a retain message so that the system knows that someone is using that object.

Since dict is managing the object, line 5 is used to release our object. The dictionary still has the same memory that the today object has; we've just told the system that we're finished with it. Had the dictionary object *not* sent a retain message, line 5 would have actually deallocated the message. The rule is pretty simple: Once the retain count of an object reaches zero by way of a release, the object is sent a dealloc message, and the memory to that object is actually deallocated.

Line 6 is a simple convention to indicate we're finished with the pointer.

Line 7 removes the object by way of the key "TODAY". When an object is removed from a dictionary, the object is automatically sent a release message. At this point, the object that today used to point to is sent a release message. Since this now makes the retain count of the object zero, the object is also sent a `dealloc` message to deallocate its memory.

Line 8 simply sends a `release` message to the `dict` object. This will deallocate the memory of the object, since nowhere else is the object retained.

Working with Implied Retain Messages

How do we know which objects need to be released and which don't? The answer basically falls under the rule of object ownership. If an object is created that has `alloc` or `new` in the message name, you own the object, and it, therefore, needs to be released once the program is finished using it. There are other examples but no hard and fast rule unfortunately. Properly deallocating memory takes an understanding of the objects and what messages result in an explicit `retain`.

While an object can be sent an explicit `retain` message, in the examples so far there isn't one `retain`, because there are automatic or implied retain messages. For example, whenever the message `setObject: forKey:` is sent to the dictionary object, the object we add is automatically sent a `retain` message. As mentioned previously, whenever we are allocating an object a `retain` is implied:

```
NSMutableDictionary *dict = [[NSMutableDictionary alloc] init];
```

Other calls are not so obvious, for example:

```
NSDate* today = [NSDate date];
```

In this case, `alloc` was *not* called, but we get a new `NSDate` object. The key is to read the Apple Developer Documentation on the `NSDate` class and the `date` class method that states that the method will return a *new* date object.

The key is that the return value is a `new` date object. Because it's a new object, it receives an implied `retain`. The program could just have also been written like so:

```
NSDate* today = [[NSDate alloc] init];
```

This code would yield the exact same results. The difference is that, in the second example, we are explicitly allocating the memory. Based on the Objective-C memory management rules, if we explicitly use a method that begins with `alloc` or `new` or contains the word `copy`, or if we send the object a `retain` message, we are then responsible for releasing the allocated memory. If we don't specifically deallocate that memory, the Objective-C system will automatically release the memory. While it's nice to have the system automatically release memory on your behalf, it's inevitable that you will eventually have to deallocate your own objects.

Sending the dealloc Message

Under normal circumstances, your program should never send a `dealloc` message to another object. There are some rare exceptions. One of these is when handling the `dealloc` message itself. You will be dealing with the `dealloc` message only for objects you create. Listing 11–7 is a snippet of code that shows how a typical dealloc message is coded. Every object that you create should implement a `dealloc` message.

Listing 11–7. *A Typical dealloc Implementation*

```
1    - (void)dealloc
2    {
3        self.iVar1 = nil;        // If we had instance variables, make sure they are
     deallocated.
4                                 // This instance variable was a property (Chapter 10)
5        [iVar2release];          // Another example.  We release an instance variable that we
6                                 // were using - it wasn't a property.
7        [super dealloc];// We finally tell our parent to deallocate itself.  This is one of the
8                        // rare times dealloc will be called explicitly.
9    }
10
```

Listing 11–7 is strictly an example, and the instance variable names are completely fabricated.

Line 3 sets an instance variable to `nil`. Not only is this common practice but also, in our example, the instance variable is a property. If it were created with the `retain` keyword like this:

```
@property(retain) NSDate* iVar1
```

Setting the property to `nil` automatically sends a release message to whatever object iVar1 was pointing to first. It's a very clean way to release an object.

Line 5 shows how a nonproperty instance variable would be released. We've used this method in many of our examples so far.

Line 7 is one of the rare cases in which you would send a `dealloc` message to an object. In this case, the program is telling its parent (the superclass) to deallocate itself. The parent would end up doing the same, sending a `dealloc` to its parent and so on until the base object is finally deallocated. Also note that `[super dealloc]` is the last thing the method does—it's not a good idea to deallocate the parent class and then continue to do more things.

Dealing with the retain/release model will take some time to get used to but overall is a fairly straightforward system of managing memory. Here's a word of caution though: even though our examples talked about the `retainCount` method of an object, do not rely on this value. Since you have no idea what parts of the framework have an interest in your objects, the retain count could be higher than you expect. However, knowing about the `retainCount` is beneficial in troubleshooting a potential memory leak. Continue to practice working with the retain/release model, and make sure that you read the developer documentation when sending or receiving objects so that you know how the object in question is being handled.

If Things Go Wrong

Allocating memory either through the standard C mechanisms or the Objective-C object allocation methods works most of the time. However, the programmer cannot assume that allocating an object or allocating memory works *all* the time. When memory allocation fails it's generally a sign that bigger problems are at hand, and the program may not be around too much longer (it will crash because of memory issues). However, even though the program may be getting into a bad state because it can't allocate memory, the program should ignore the signs. Here are some conventions that are used to test if memory allocation has failed:

```
1   int main(void)
2   {
3       char *data2 = malloc(100);
4       if (data2 == NULL) {// Malloc returns NULL (0x00000000) if allocation fails.
5           // Application has detected a major failure.
6       }
7   }
```

In this standard C example, if the malloc function fails, a NULL pointer is returned. Recall that NULL pointer is nothing more than a pointer that points to location 0x00000000. Memory never starts at this location, so NULL can be used to indicate a *bad* memory allocation.

In Objective-C, there are two main areas that we need to perform validity checks. Here's the first:

```
1   int main(void)
2   {
3       MyObject* obj = [[MyObject alloc] init];
4       if (obj) {    // If the object is valid….
5           // Application has detected a major failure.
6       }
```

In this example, we try to create an object, but we check to see if the pointer returned is nil or not. Recall that a nil object is basically a default empty object used as a placeholder to mean "empty," or "nothing." Don't confuse this with an empty MyObject, because that it is not.

The second validity check only applies to objects we've created. This check is done in the init method of the class:

```
1   - init
2   {
3       self = [super init];
4       if (self != nil) {
5           // Do object initialization here on a valid self object.
6       }
7       return self;
8   }
```

In this example, in the object's init method, the program explicitly tests to see if self returns a value that is not nil. If self is not nil, things are OK, and the method can continue initializing the object. The method then returns self, which can be either nil or not. The important thing to note here is that we are testing to ensure that the call to [super init] works before preceding to work on self.

Summary

We've covered quite a bit in this chapter. Hopefully, you now have a clearer understanding of how memory, addresses, and pointers work. In this chapter, we covered the following:

- Defining "memory"
- Using base-2, base-10, and base-16
- Defining and using memory addresses
- Defining and using pointers
- Defining and using the dereference operator
- Allocating memory
- Using auto-variables are and watching out for pitfalls so as not to cause a memory leak
- Deallocating memory and preventing memory leaks, including using the dealloc method
- Using the special pointers NULL and nil
- Managing memory using Objective-C and its retain/release model
- Detecting when things go wrong with memory allocation.

This chapter definitely covered a lot of ground, but congratulate yourself on making it through. Understanding how memory works on a Mac, iPhone, iPad, or any computing device is very important.

Exercises

- In the following memory space, how large is the memory block? What is the address of the very last byte in this block of memory?

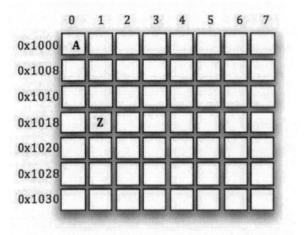

- Using the code from Listing 12-1, try to determine what these statements will do and why:

  - `*(aPointer + 2) = '1';`

  - `(aPointer + 2) = '1';`

- Look at the Apple developer documentation for the method addObject in the NSMutableArray class.

  - What differences are there between the addObject method of the NSMutableArray class and the NSMutableDictionary class's addObject:forKey: method?

  - How would using an NSMutableArray change, if at all, the code in Listing 11–1

Chapter 12

Debugging Programs with Xcode

Xcode is fantastic! Not only is this tool provided free of charge from Apple's developer site but it is actually really, really good! Aside from being able to create the next great Mac OS X, iPhone, or iPad app, Xcode has a fantastic debugger built right into the tool.

So, what exactly is a debugger? First of all, let's get something straight – programs do *exactly* what they are written to do. Sometimes, what is written isn't exactly what the program is really meant to do. Sometimes, this means that the program crashes or just doesn't do something that is expected. Whatever the case, when a program doesn't work as planned the program is said to have **bugs**. The process of going through the code and fixing these problems is the process known as **debugging**.

There is still some debate as to the real origin of the term "bug," but one well-documented case from 1947 involved Grace Hopper, a Naval reservist and programmer at the time. Hopper and her team were searching for a problem with the Harvard Mark II computer. One of her associates found a moth in the circuitry that was causing the problem with one of the relays. She was later quoted as saying, "From then on, when anything went wrong with a computer, we said it had bugs in it."[1]

Regardless of the origin, the term has stuck and programmers from all over the globe use debuggers, like Xcode, to help find bugs in programs (people are the real debuggers. Debugging tools help the programmer locate the problem. No debugger, whatever the name might imply, fixes problems all on its own).

This chapter will highlight some of the more important features of the Xcode debugger and how to use them. Once you are finished with this chapter, you should have a good enough understanding of the Xcode debugger and of the debugging process in general to allow you to search for and fix the majority of program issues.

---

[1] Michael Moritz, Alexander L. Taylor III, and Peter Stoler, "The Wizard Inside the Machine," *Time* Vol. 123 No. 16: pp.

Getting Started with Debugging

If you've ever watched a movie in slow motion just so you can catch a blooper or detail that you can't see when the movie is played at full speed, you've used a tool to do something a little like debugging. The idea that playing the movie frame-by-frame will reveal the detail you are looking for is the same sort of idea that we will apply to debugging a program. With a program, sometimes it becomes necessary to slow things down a bit to see what's happening. The debugger allows us to do this with two main features: setting a breakpoint and stepping through the program line by line—more on these two features in a bit. Let's first look at what how to get to the debugger and what it looks like.

First, we need to load an existing program. Our examples in this chapter use the MyBookstore project from Chapter 10, so open Xcode and load the MyBookstore project.

Second, make sure that the **Debug** configuration is chosen, as shown in Figure 12–1. **Debug** is the default selection, so you'll most likely not have to change this. This step is important, because if the configuration is **Release**, debugging will not work at all!

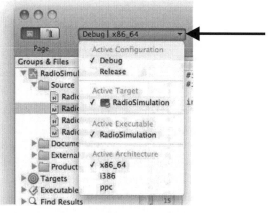

Figure 12–1. *Selecting the Debug Configuration*

While we won't discuss Xcode configurations in this book, just know that, by default, Xcode provides both a **Release** and a **Debug** configuration option for any Mac OS X or iPhone OS project you create. The main difference as it pertains to this chapter is that a release configuration doesn't add in any program information that is necessary for debugging an application, whereas the debug configuration does.

Setting Breakpoints

To see what's going on in a program, we need to make the program pause at certain points that we as the programmer are interested in. A **breakpoint** allows us to do this. In Figure 13-2, we've set a breakpoint on line 14 of the program. To do this, simply place the mouse cursor over the line number (not the program text but the number "14" to the left of the program text), and click once.

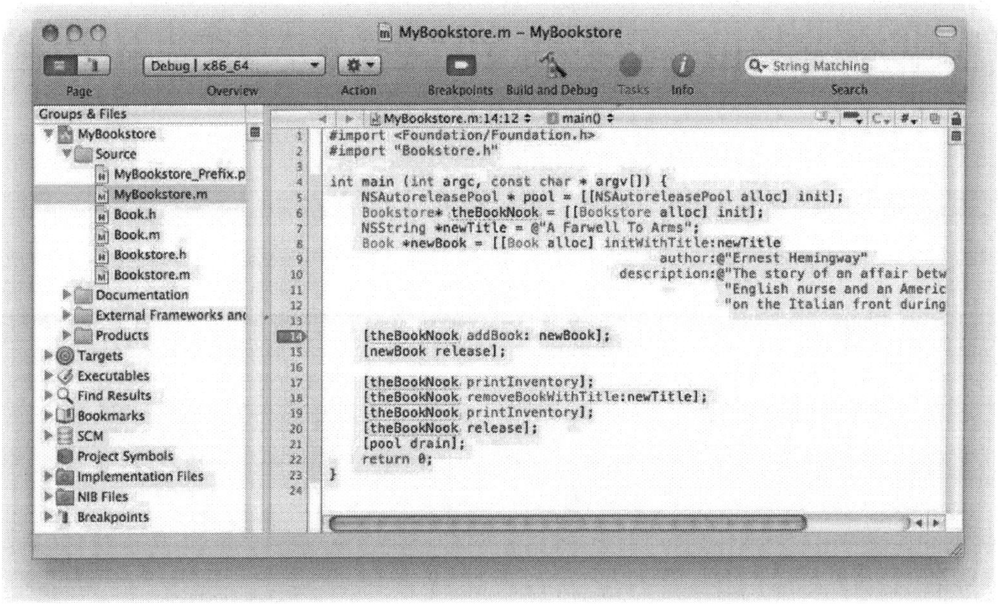

Figure 12–2. *Our first breakpoint*

We can also remove the breakpoint by simply dragging the breakpoint to the left or right of the line number column and then dropping it. In Figure 12–3, the breakpoint has been dragged to the left of the column. During the drag-and-drop process, the breakpoint will turn into a puff of smoke.

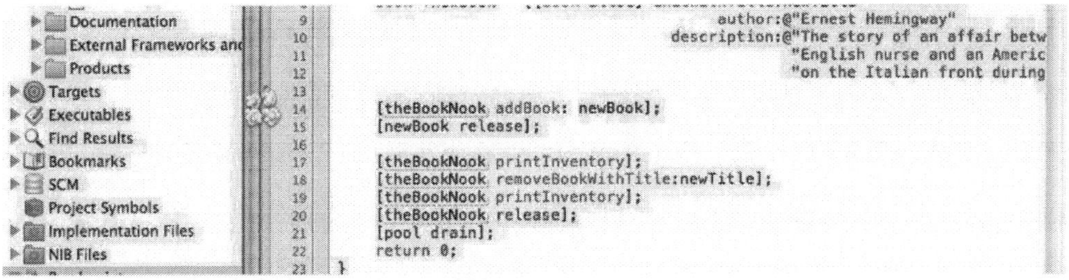

Figure 12–3. *The breakpoint disappears in a puff of smoke*

Setting and deleting breakpoints are pretty straightforward tasks. There are other ways to delete breakpoints, but this way is the most entertaining!

Debugging Basics

Set a breakpoint on line 14 like in Figure 12–2. Next, as shown in Figure 12–4, click the **Build and Debug** button to compile the project and start running it within the Xcode debugger.

Figure 12–4. *The Build and Debug button in the Xcode toolbar*

Once the project builds, the debugger will start; the screen will change to the debugging view, and the program will stop execution on line 14, as shown in Figure 12–5.

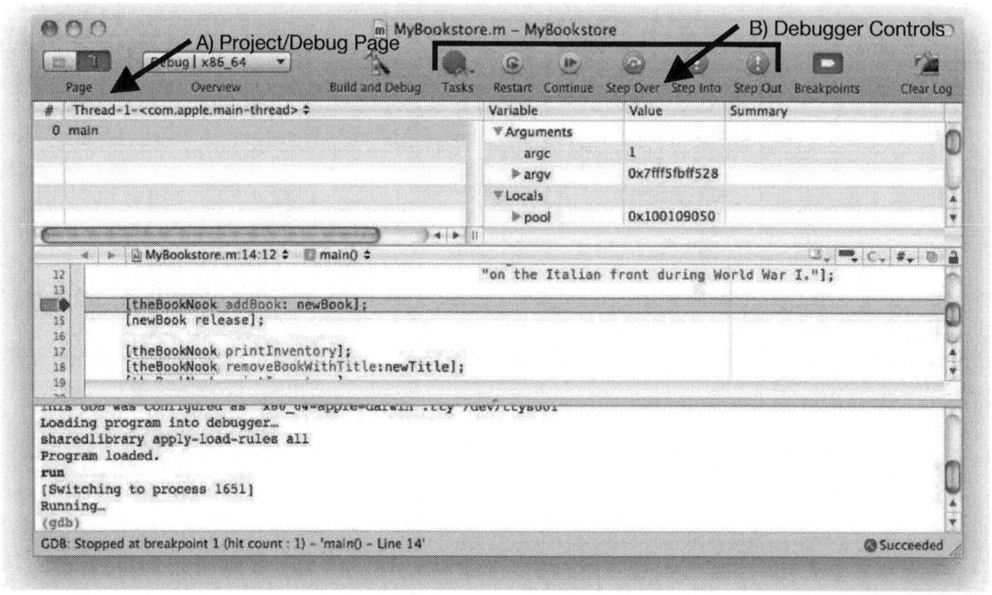

Figure 12–5. *The Debugger view with execution stopped on line 14*

The debugger view looks a lot different from the project view. Let's go over the different parts of the debugger shown in Figure 12–5.

1. **Project/debug page**: These two buttons switch between the project and debugger views. You can change to the project view while the program is being debugged, but the debugging controls change slightly.

2. **Debugger controls**: The debugging can be stopped, restarted, continued, or stepped through. The stepping controls are used most often.

Working with the Debugger Controls

As mentioned previously, once the debugger starts, the view changes. What appears are the debugging controls (item B in Figure 12–5). The controls are fairly straightforward and are explained in Table 12–1.

Table 12–1. *Xcode debugging controls*

Control	Description
	Clicking the **Tasks** button will stop the execution of the program. if the iPhone or iPad emulator is running the application, it will also stop as if the user pressed the Home button on the device. The Xcode project will stay in the debugger view. To get back to the regular text view, click the project button at the top-left of the project window (see item A in Figure 12–5.
	If the program is stopped at a breakpoint, the **Continue** button will appear next to the stop sign. Clicking this causes the program to continue execution. The program will continue running until it ends, the stop sign is clicked, or the program runs into another breakpoint. While the program is running, this icon will turn into a **Pause** button, and clicking it will cause the application to effectively stop as if on a breakpoint wherever it is.
	When the debugger stops on a breakpoint, clicking the **Step Over** button will cause the debugger to execute the current line of code and stop at the next line of code. If the debugger encounters a breakpoint while stepping over code, the debugger will go to the breakpoint instead of skipping over it. In Figure 12–5, clicking this icon will cause the debugger to the next line, line 15.
	Clicking the **Step Into** button will cause the debugger to go into the specified function or method. If we clicked this control, the debugger would go into the addBook method in Figure 12–5. This is very important if there is a need to follow code into specific methods or functions. Only methods for which the project has source code can be stepped into.
	The **Step Out** button will cause the current method to finish executing, and the debugger will go back to the caller. Using Figure 12–5 as an example, if we were to step into line 14 and then immediately click **Step Out**, the addBook method would finish executing, and the debugger would then stop on line 15, effectively finishing the current functions and stepping back out.

Debugging a Program

Your debug console should look very similar to Figure 12–6. The cursor should be positioned in the text editor on line 14, which is where our breakpoint was set.

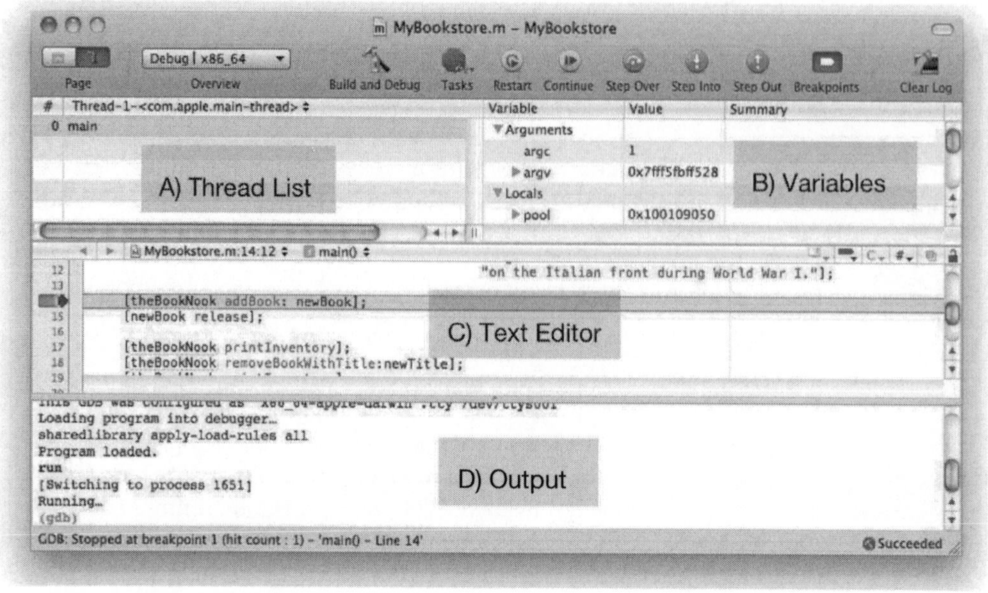

Figure 12–6. *The debug window*

Here is a description of the various panes:

1. **Thread list**: This pane shows all the threads that are executing. There is always at least one thread, which is our application. This is where the call stack is viewed (more in 'Looking at the Thread Window and Call Stack' section).

2. **Variable**: All of the variables currently in scope are displayed in this pane.

3. **Text**: This is the text editor that is seen in the project view. Hovering the mouse over variables will show their contents. To a limited extent, the code can be changed while the program is being debugged.

4. **Output**: Program output, like the output from NSLog, is displayed here. If the program encounters a failure, the system may also display information in this window.

Using the Step Controls

To practice using the step controls, let's step into a function. As the name implies, the **Step Into** button follows program execution into the method that is highlighted. Click the **Step Into** button at the top of the screen; this will cause the debugger to go into the addBook method. The screen should look like Figure 12–7.

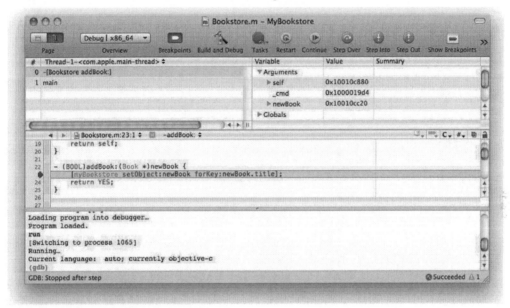

Figure 12–7. *Stepping into the addBook method*

It's important to note that the not only is the debugger in the Bookstore object but the debugger has also moved to the Bookstore.m file (we used to be in the MyBookstore.m file).

The control **Step Over** continues execution of the program but doesn't go into a method. It simply executes the method and continues to the next line. **Step Out** is a little like the opposite of **Step Into**. If the **Step Out** button is clicked, the current method continues execution until it finishes. The debugger then stops on the very next line after the method call. For example, if the **Step Into** button is clicked on the line shown in Figure 12–6. and then the **Step Out** button is clicked, the debugger will return to the MyBookstore.m file on line 15—the line *after* the method call.

Looking at the Thread Window and Call Stack

As we mentioned earlier, the thread window displays the current thread (there is only one in our program) but it also displays the **call stack**. If we look at the difference between Figure 12–6. and Figure 12–7 as far as the thread window goes, we can see that Figure 12–7 now has the addBook method listed, because main calls the addBook method.

Now, the call stack is not simply a list of functions that *have* been called; rather, it's a list of functions that are currently *being* called. That's a very important distinction. Once the addBook method is finished and returns (line 24), addBook will no longer appear in the call stack. You can think of a call stack almost like a breadcrumb trail. The trail shows us how to get back to where we started.

Debugging Variables

Not only are the variables listed in the top-right window but their details are easily visible by and hovering the mouse over variables you wish to know more about, as shown in Figure 12–8.

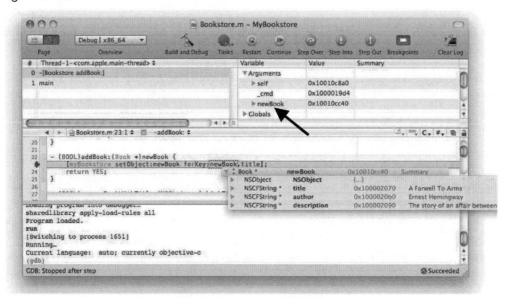

Figure 12–8. *Hovering over the newBook variable reveals much information.*

Moving the mouse over the newBook variable reveals its information. This variable is a local variable passed into the function. It can also be seen in the top-left Variable window. If this variable were to be expanded, it would show the same information that we can see by hovering.

The information that is pertinent in the newBook are the NSCFString variables. To simplify things, just know that NSCFString (Core Foundation String) is still the NSString classes we used in building the Book class. The "Core Foundation" is simply the base library of classes that Apple provides the programmer. The information to the far right (red colored text in the debugger) is the actual string information being passed in to this method. When a variable's contents change, the debugger highlights the variable's new contents in red. Since this is a new variable being passed into the addBook method, the values are new and red. For values that are unchanged, the debugger leaves the values' colored black.

Clicking the Value part of the variable (the information at the far right) will allow you to actually modify the contents of the variable. This is sometimes useful if it becomes necessary to force a certain condition to test. Here is a simple example.

First, Click the **Tasks** stop sign to stop debugging the application. Next, change the addBook method to what appears in Figure 12–9. We are making the return value of the method a variable instead of hard-coding the value YES.

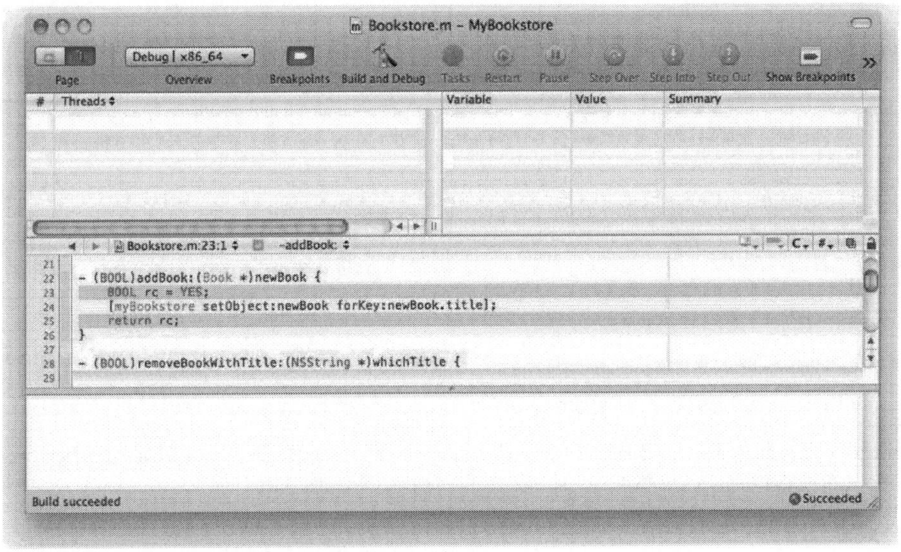

Figure 12–9. *Updated addBook method*

Lines 23 and 25 have been added to the addBook method as shown in Figure 12–9. Next, set a breakpoint on line 25, as shown in Figure 12–10.

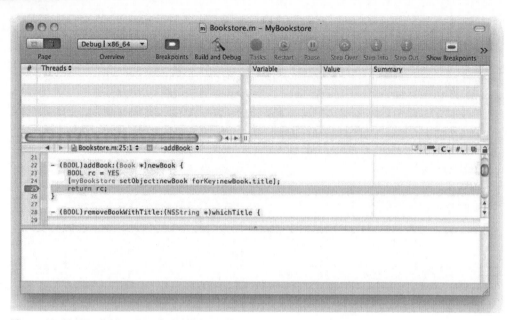

Figure 12–10. *Breakpoint set on the addBook method*

Setting the breakpoint on line 25 will cause the debugger to stop right before we return the value to the caller. Let's run the program now and see how we can modify a variable.

Click **Build and Debug** to build the app and start the debugger. Our first stop will be in the main function on the MyBookstore.m file as shown in Figure 12–11.

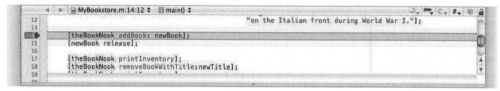

Figure 12–11. *Our first breakpoint*

At this point, we could click **Step Into** to go into the addBook method, or we can simply click **Continue** to continue running the program. Since we added the second breakpoint in the addBook method, continuing the program will simply cause the debugger to break at the next breakpoint, which just happens to be where we want to be (see Figure 12–12). Go ahead and click **Continue**.

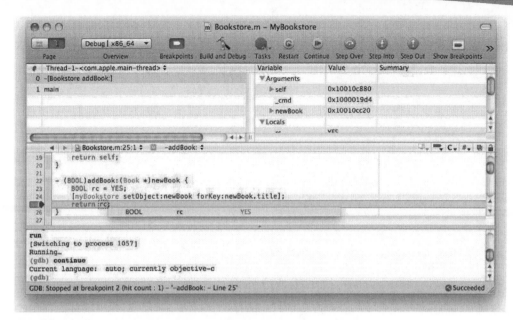

Figure 12–12. *Stopped at line 25 with the mouse hovering over the rc variable*

The debugger will stop on line 25 of the addBook method. Next, move the mouse over the rc variable to display the quick view of the variable and its value. We can see that the value is YES. To change the value of the variable, move the mouse over the value of the variable (YES) and left-click once. The value of the variable will open into an entry field and allow you to change the value of the variable, as shown in Figure 12–13.

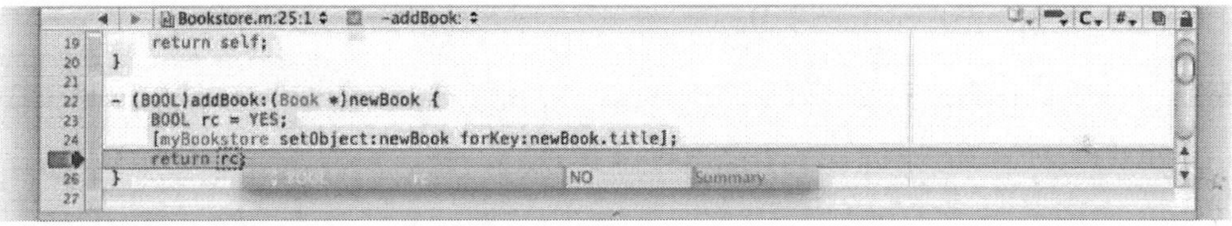

Figure 12–13. *Changing a variable's value*

Change the value to NO (use capital letters, because the debugger is case-sensitive) and then press Enter. Looking closely at the Variable window (it might take a little scrolling of the window) you can see that the value of rc has indeed changed to NO, and it has changed to the color red, indicating that the value has changed as shown in Figure 12–14.

Variable	Value	Summary
_cmd	0x1000019d4	
►newBook	0x10010cc20	
▼Locals		
rc	NO	
►Globals		
►Registers		

Figure 12–14. *The updated rc variable's value*

Now, when the addBook method returns, it will be returning NO to the caller instead of YES. In our case, the caller doesn't use the return value, so changing it from YES to NO will have no effect to the caller. This exercise was just to show how to change the value of a variable.

Deleting Multiple Breakpoints

Before we continue to the next section, let's delete the existing breakpoints. Earlier in this chapter, you learned that dragging and dropping a breakpoint to the left or right of the line number column would delete the breakpoint. However, if we have many breakpoints, this process will take too much time. Plus, once we put breakpoints all over our code, we might actually miss one. There is another way of deleting a breakpoint with which it's possible to delete more than one at a time.

First, press ⌘ + 0 (Command + zero) to return to the normal project view. In the **Groups & Files** pane, find the **Breakpoints** group and expand it. There will be two types of breakpoints: **Project Breakpoints** and **Global Breakpoints**, as shown in Figure 12–15.

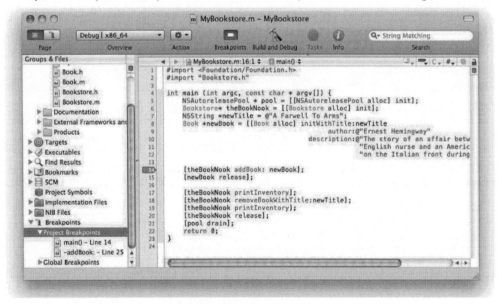

Figure 12–15. *The project view showing project breakpoints*

Expand the **Project Breakpoints** Option. At this point, there should be two breakpoints listed: one in the `main()` function and the other in the `addBook:` method. Simply Command-click (press ⌘ and click the mouse button) each breakpoint, and right-click any of the breakpoints. This will bring up a context menu that will allow you to delete only those breakpoints that have been selected, as shown in Figure 12–16.

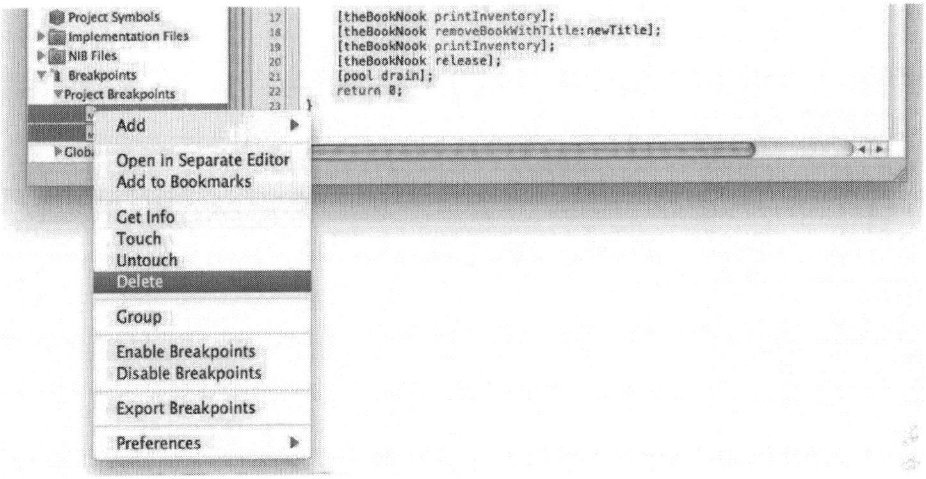

Figure 12–16. *Context menu used to delete the breakpoints*

Once you've finished, the two breakpoints are now deleted. You can use this trick on any number or any specific breakpoint that you want to remove.

Disabling Breakpoints

We've talked about adding and deleting breakpoints, but there is a third option: disabling a breakpoint. It is sometimes handy to disable a breakpoint instead of deleting it, especially if you plan to put the breakpoint back in the same place again. Disabling a breakpoint is actually quite simple. Just click the existing breakpoint, and the breakpoint will turn from a dark blue color to a very faded blue. The debugger will not stop on these faded breakpoints, but they remain in place so that they can be conveniently enabled as well as act as a marker to an important area in the code. To enable a disabled breakpoint, simply click once on the disabled breakpoint.

A Larger Call Stack

Up to this point, the thread window, which also contains the call stack, has been pretty empty. At most, in our little program, you've seen only two entries. We're going to introduce a small bug into our program. Not only will this bug present a real problem for the program, but you'll also be able to see what a longer call stack looks like. Add `[myBookstore anUnknownMessage]` to the program (`Bookstore.m`) file, as shown in Figure 12–17.

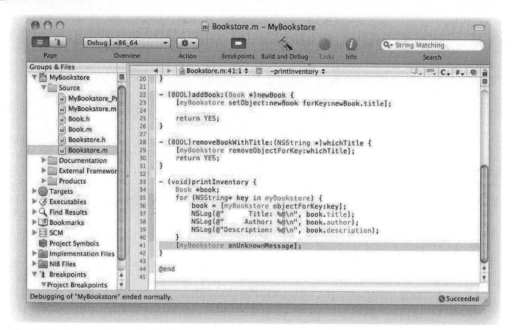

Figure 12–17. *A bug has been added to our program.*

This code is a bug is because neither the `myBookstore` object nor any of its parent objects implement the message anUnkownMessage. In fact, when the program is compiled, a warning message will be flagged on line 41—just a warning message, not an error. Let's click **Build and Debug** for this updated program and examine the results.

> **TIP:** Since Objective-C is dynamic, an object may be able to respond to a message that is not defined in any interface file. This is why this particular line is a warning and not an error.

Unsurprisingly, the program doesn't run very will. In fact, the program aborts due to an uncaught exception. Here is where a debugger becomes invaluable. Notice now, as shown in Figure 12–18, that our call stack has a lot more information than you've seen up to this point. The text edit area has a lot of unintelligible numbers and letters, which is very typical whenever the debugger stops in a part of the program that we don't have any source code to (i.e., stuff we didn't write).

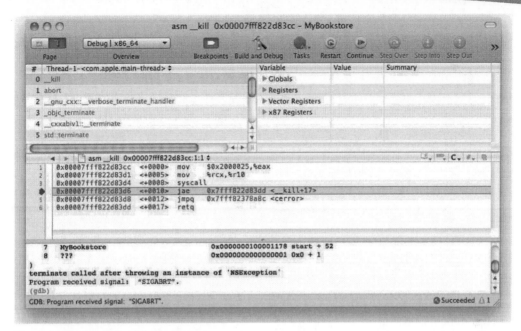

Figure 12–18. *A well-populated call stack*

At this point, the call stack in the thread window shows a lot of functions that are unfamiliar which is because these are system level functions and not from our code. Scroll down in the call stack until something from our program can be seen.

If you scrolling down the call stack, you see that the only messages that are recognizable from our program are main() and -[Bookstore printInventory]. main() is the entry point to our program, which then sends the printInventory message to our Bookstore object, theBookNook.

Click the line in the call stack that contains -[Bookstore printInventory] listed (line 11). As Figure 12–19. shows, the debugger highlights the line in the program that is being executed. From this, we know that our program is sending a message to theBookNook object. Somewhere in the printInventory method, things have gone awry.

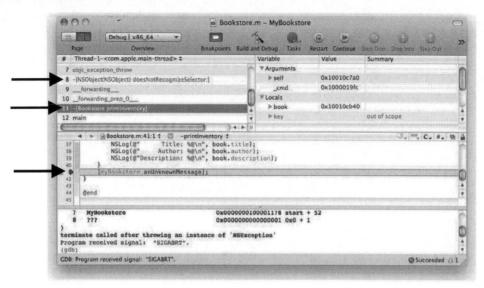

Figure 12–19. *Here is what caused the program to fail.*

The final piece of this puzzle is on line 8 of the call stack: the system is calling the doesNotRecognizeSelector: method on NSObject (in an earlier chapter, you learned that a selector and a method are, for all practical purposes, the same thing). This message is sent to NSObject (the parent of the Bookstore class) whenever, as you can probably guess, the message is not recognized by our object or its parents. An exception is thrown, and since we are not handling exceptions (nor have we even discussed what an exception is!), the program simply aborts. To the user, the program simply disappears from their iPhone, iPad, or Mac. I'm sure you've personally seen this happen once or twice!

In our particular case, the bug is easily resolved by simply removing the line [myBookstore anUnknownMessage] from the Bookstore.m file. Not all bugs are as simple to fix that way, unfortunately. Debugging programs takes patience and practice. The more you play with the Xcode debugger, the better you will get at finding and fixing bugs and the more you will understand what the Xcode debugger has to offer—which is a lot!

Summary

In this chapter we covered the high-level features of the Xcode debugger that freely available from Apple. Regardless of price, Xcode is an excellent debugger. Specifically, in this chapter, you learned the following:

- The origins of the term "bug" and what a debugger is
- The high-level features of the Xcode debugger.
    - Breakpoints
    - Stepping through a program

- Using the debugging controls
    - Tasks (stop sign)
    - Restart and Continue (Pause)
    - Step Over
    - Step Into
    - Step Out
- Working with the various debugger views
    - Threads (call stack)
    - Variables
    - Text editor
    - Output
- Looking quickly at a variable and changing its value
- Adding a bug to watch how the debugger handled the problem

Exercises

- Our addBook method has been set up to use a variable to return its return value. Modify the calling function so that if the return value is NO, an error message is printed (hint: use the NSLog function to print the error message).

- Restart the program and step through the code. Practice stepping into, stepping out of, and stepping over these methods. Stop and start the application as many times as necessary.

- Experiment with breakpoints. Set them in the MyBookstore.m file as well as the Book.m and Bookstore.m files.

Chapter 13

Storing Information

As a developer, you will run into many different situations where you will need to store data. Users will expect your application to remember many things each time you launch it. In previous chapters, we discussed the Book Store app. With this app, users will expect your application to remember all of the books in the bookstore and default database location. Your application will need a way to store this information, retrieve it, and possibly to search and sort this data. Working with data can sometimes be difficult. Fortunately, Apple has provided methods and frameworks to make this process easy.

In this chapter, we discuss two different formats in which data will need to be stored. We will start by discussing saving preferences for the Mac and the iPhone, and then move on to using a SQLite database in our application to store and retrieve data.

Storage Considerations

There are some major storage differences between the Mac and the iPhone, and these will affect how you work with data in each environment. Let's start by first discussing the Mac and how you will need to develop for it.

On the Mac, by default, applications are stored in the Applications folder. Each user has his or her own home folder where preferences and information related to that user are stored. Not all of the users will have access to write to the application folder or the application itself.

On the iPhone, we do not need to deal with different users. There are some other factors to consider with the iPhone, though. Every application on the iPhone is in own "sand box." This means that files written by an application can only be seen and used by that individual application. This makes for a more secure environment on the iPhone, but it also presents some changes in the way we work with data storage.

Preferences

There are some things to consider when deciding where to store certain kinds of information. The easiest way to store information is with the preferences file, but this method has some downsides. One, all of the data is both read and written at the same time. If you are going to be writing often or writing large amounts of data, this could take time and slow down your application. As a general rule, your preference file should never be larger than 100K. If you start to fall into that category, consider using Core Data as a way to store your information. The preference file is really nothing more than a standardized file and accompanying classes and methods to store application specific choices. A preference would be, for example, the sorting column and direction (ascending/descending) of a list. Anything that is generally customizable within an app should be stored in a preference file.

Writing Preferences

Apple has provided developers with the NSUserDefaults class that makes reading and writing preferences very easy on the iPhone and Mac OS X. The great thing is that, in this case, you can use the exact same code for the iPhone and Mac OS X. The only difference between the two implementations is the location of the preference file.

> **NOTE:** For Mac OS X, the preference file is named com.yourcompany.applicationname.plist and is location in the /Users/username/Library/Preferences folder. On the iPhone, the preference file is located in your application bundle in the Library/Preferences folder.

All you need to do to write preferences is to obtain an NSUserDefaults object. This is done with this line

```
NSUserDefaults *prefs = [NSUserDefaults standardUserDefaults];
```

This instantiates the object prefereces, which you can now use to set preference values. Next you need to set the preference keys for the values you would like to save. Because we have been working with a bookstore example all along, we will continue to do that. As a bookstore, you might want to save a username or password in the preferences. You also might want to save things such as a default book category or recent searches. The preference file is a great place to store this type of information.

Also, on the iPhone, it is often necessary to save your current state. If a person is using your application and then gets a phone call, when they are done, you want to bring them back to the exact place they were before they left your application.

Once you have instantiated the object, you can just call setObject forKey to set an object. If we wanted to save the username of sherlock.holmes, we would just call the following line of code

```
[prefs setObject:@"sherlock.holmes " forKey:@"username"];
```

You can use setInteger, setDouble, setBool, setFloat, and setURL instead of setObject depending on the type of information you are storing in the preferences. Let's say you store the number of books a user wants to see in the list. Here is an example of using setInteger to store this preference.

```
[prefs setInteger:10 forKey:@"booksInList"];
```

Once you have set all of your preferences, you will need to tell the app to write them. You can do this by using the synchronize function. This function should be called automatically after a certain period in your application, but we prefer to make sure it gets saved and call it after any change:

```
[prefs synchronize];
```

With just four lines of code, we are able to create a preference object, set two preference values, and then write the preference file. It is all very easy and clean. Here is all of the code together:

```
NSUserDefaults *prefs = [NSUserDefaults standardUserDefaults];
[prefs setObject:@"sherlock.holmes " forKey:@"username"];
[prefs setInteger:10 forKey:@"booksInList"];
[prefs synchronize];
```

Reading Preferences

Reading preferences is very similar to writing preferences, and is just as easy. Just like writing, the first step is to obtain the NSUserDefaults object. This is done in exactly the same way as it is in the writing:

```
NSUserDefaults *prefs = [NSUserDefaults standardUserDefaults];
```

Now that we have the object, we are able to access the preference values that are set. For writing, we use the setObject syntax; for reading, we use the stringForKey function. In the writing example, we set preferences for username and for the number of books in the list to display. We can read those preferences out by using the following simple lines of code

```
NSString *username = [prefs stringForKey:@"username"];
NSInteger booksInList = [prefs integerForKey:@"booksInList "];
```

Notice what we do in each of these lines. We start out by declaring the variable username, which is an NSString. This variable will be used to store the preference value of username. We then just assign it to the value of the preference username. You will notice that in the read example we do not use the synchronize function. This is because we have not changed the values of the preferences, and therefore we do not need to make sure it is written to disk.

Databases

We have discussed how to store some small pieces of information and retrieve them at a later point. What if you have more information that needs to be stored? What if you need to search this information or put it in some sort of order? These kind of situations call for a database.

Let's start by discussing what a database is. A database is a tool for storing a significant amount of information in a way that is easily searched or retrieved. Many applications you use in your daily life are based on databases of some sort. Your online banking application retrieves your account activity from a database. Your supermarket uses a database to retrieve prices for different items when you are checking out. A simple example of a database is a spreadsheet. You may have many columns and many rows in your spreadsheet. The columns in your spreadsheet represent different pieces of information you want to store. In a database, these are considered attributes. The rows would be different records in your database.

Storing Information in a Database

Databases can be an intimidating subject for a developer. Many people will think of enterprise database servers such as Microsoft SQL Server or Oracle. These applications can take time to set up and require constant management. For most developers, a database system like Oracle would be overkill. Apple has included a small compact database engine on the Mac and iPhone. SQLite will provide you with a lot of flexibility with storing information for your application. It stores the entire database in a single file. It is fast, reliable, and easy to implement in your application. The best thing about the SQLite database is that there is no need to perform any installation of software. Apple has taken care of that for you.

SQLite, however, does have some limitations that you should be aware of as a developer.

SQLite was designed to be used as a single user database. You will not want to use SQLite in an environment where more than one person will be accessing the same database. This could lead to data loss or corruption.

In the business world, databases can grow to become very large. It is not surprising for a database manager to handle databases as large as 500GB, and in some cases databases can become much larger than that. SQLite should be able to handle smaller databases without any issues, but you will begin to see performance issues if your database starts to get too large.

SQLite lacks some of the backup and data restore features of the enterprise database solutions.

For the purposes of this book, we will focus on using SQLite as our database engine. If any of the mentioned limitations are a problem for the application you are developing, you may need to look into an enterprise database solution, which is beyond the scope of this book.

Apple has worked to iron out a lot of the challenges of database development. As a developer, you will not need to become familiar with SQL, as Apple has taken care of the direct database interaction for you. Apple has created a framework called Core Data that makes interacting with the database much easier. Core Data has been adapted by Apple from a NeXT product called Enterprise Object Framework, and it will handle all of the database interaction for you. Working with Core Data is a lot easier than interfacing directly with the SQLite database. Directly accessing a database via SQL is beyond the scope of this book.

Getting Started with Core Data

Let's start by creating a new Core Data project. Open Xcode and select **File ➤ New Project**. To create a Mac OS X Core Data project, select Application from the left-hand menu underneath the Mac OS X header. In the options, be sure to check both Use Core Data for Storage and Create Document-Based Application. See Figure 13–1.

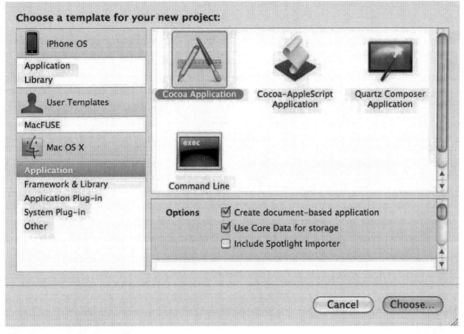

Figure 13–1. *Creating a new project*

Click on the Choose button when done. The next screen will allow you to decide where to save your poject and the name you want to use. For the purposes of this chapter, we will use the name Bookstore. Once you are done with that, your new project will open. It will look similar to a standard application, except that now you will have a Models folder.

The Model

If you click on the triangle next to the folder, you will see a file called MyDocument.xcdatamodel. This file will contact information about the data you want stored in the database. Double-click on the Model file and it will open. You will see a window similar to to the one shown in Figure 13–2.

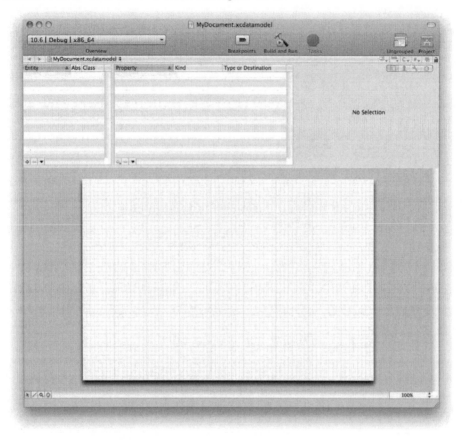

Figure 13–2. *The blank model*

The window is divided into three sections. One the top left you have your entities. In database terms, these are your tables. In more common terms, these are your objects or the items you want to store in the database. The top right window contains the attributes. Attributes are pieces of information about the entities. For example, a book can be an entity and the title of the book would be a attribute of that entity. The bottom window will show you all of your entities and allow you to create relationships across your entities.

Let's create an entity. Click on the plus sign in the bottom left corner of the top left window, or select **Design ➤ Data Model ➤ Add Entity** from the menu. See Figure 13–3.

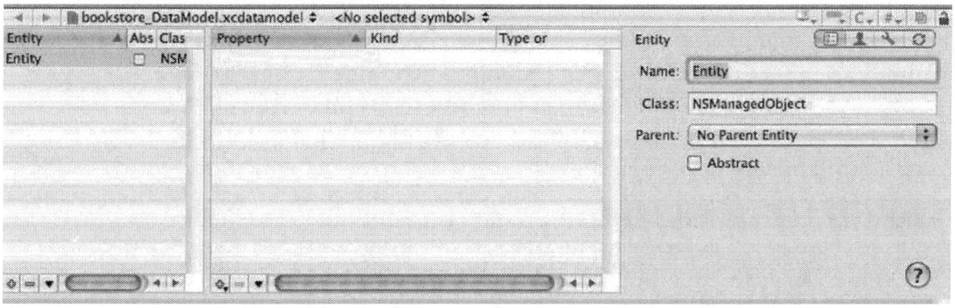

Figure 13–3. *Adding a new entity*

On the right hand side, you will now have the option to name the entity. We will use the name Book for this entity. It is generally considered good practice to capitalize your entities' names.

Now let's add some attributes. Because we are describing details of a book, we will store the title, author, price, and year published. Obviously in your own applications, you will want to store more information such as publisher and page count, among others, but we want to start out simple. Click on the plus sign in the bottom left of the top center pane, or select **Design ➤ Data Model ➤ Add Attribute**, as shown in Figure 13–4. If you do not see the option to add an attribute, make sure that you have selected the Book entity on the left-hand side.

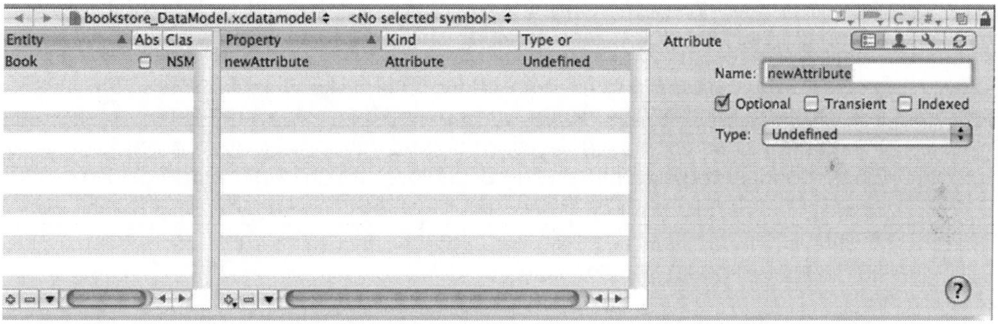

Figure 13–4. *Adding a new attribute*

You will be given several options relating to your attribute. Let's call this attribute "title." Unlike entities, Atribute names should be lowercased. For now, uncheck the check box next to Optional and check the check box next to Indexed. Here's an explanation of the choices you see:

> **Optional**: This check box decides whether an attribute can be blank. All books should have a title, so we will not allow this to be optional.

Transient: Checking this check box will cause data in this field not to be stored in the database. This is used for values that you want reset every time the data is read or the application is launched. We need to store the book's title, so we will not select this. Transient data are generally data that can be calculated. For example, having a list of purchase amounts stored in the database is fine, but the total of all those purchases is something that can be calculated, so it shouldn't be stored in the database.

Indexed: This is a database term. When an attribute is indexed, two things happen. One, search speed on that attribute is increased dramatically. Two, the database size is increased slighly. For future expansion of this app, we will check this box to increase search speed. A database index is much like an index to a book. Finding a topic in the index and then going to the page in the book is much faster than having to read through the book page by page trying to find the information. An index improves database performance in the same way.

Now we will need to select a data type. Selecting the correct data type is very important. It will affect how your data is stored and retrieved from the database. The list has 12 items in it and can be very daunting. We will discuss the most common options and, as your become more familiar with Core Data, you can experiment with the other options. The most common options are String, Integer 32, Float, and Date. For the title of the book, select String.

String: This is the type of attribute used to store text. This should be used to store any kind of information that is not a number or a date. In this example, the book title and author will be strings.

Integer 32: There are actually three different integer values possible for the attribute. Each of the integer types only differ in the minimum and maximum values possible. Integer 32 should cover most of your needs when storing integer without being overkill on the amount of storage. An integer is a number without a decimal. If you try to save a decimal to an integer, the decimal portion will be truncated. In this example, the year published will be an integer.

Float: A float is a type of attribute that can store numbers with decimals. A double is another type of attribute and is similar to a Float. It differs in the minumum and maximum values, similar to the integers. A float should be able to handle any values you will need. In this example, we will use a float to store the price of the book.

Date: A date attribute is exactly what it sounds like. It allows you to store a date and time and then perform searches and lookups based on dates and times. We will not use this type in this example.

Now let's create the rest of the attributes for the book. Select String for the type. Now add Price. Make it not optional, not transient, and indexed. It should be a float. Now add year published. For two-word attributes, it is standard to make the first word lowercase and the second word initial capped. For example, an ideal name for year published would be something like yearPublished. Make it optional, not transient, and indexed. Select Integer 32 as the attribute type. Once you have added all of your attributes, you screen should look like Figure 13–5.

NOTE: Attributes names cannot contain spaces.

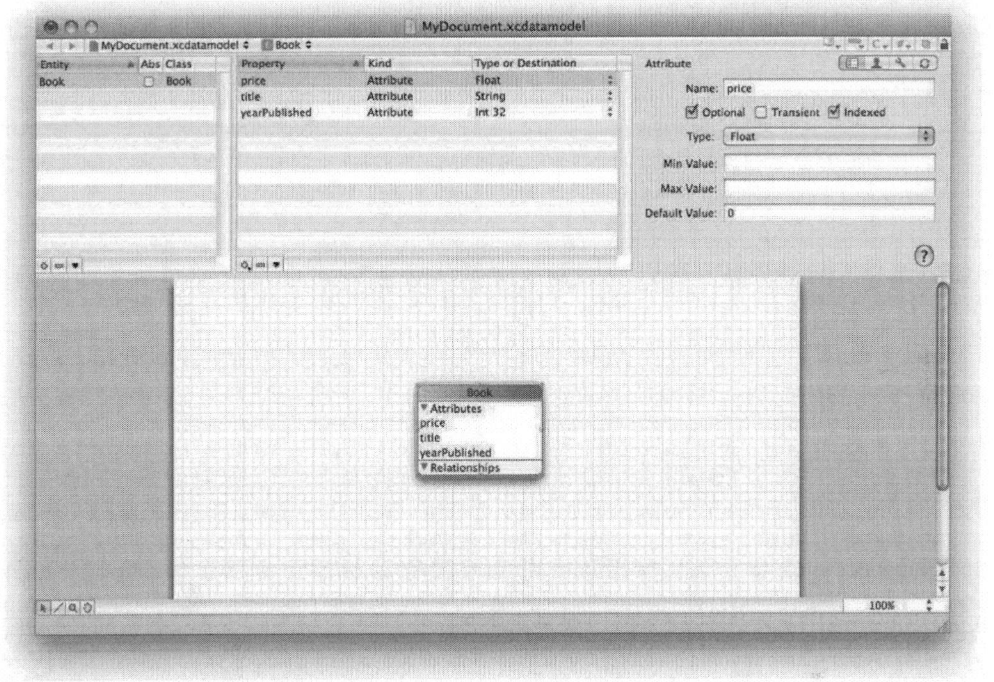

Figure 13–5. *The finished book entity*

NOTE: If you are used to working with databases, you will notice that we did not add a primary key. A primary key is an arbitrary field (usually a number) that is used to uniquely identify each record in a database. In Core Data databases, there is no need to create primary keys. The framework will manage all of that for you.

Now we have finished the Book entity. Let's add an Author entity. It would be nice to be able to select the Author from a drop-down menu rather than having to enter author information every time. Add a new entity and call it Author. To this entity, add lastName and firstName, both strings. Once this is done, you should have two entities in your relationship window. Now we need to add the relationships. Click on the Book entity, then click on the plus sign in the bottom left of the attribute area. Select Add Relationship, as seen in Figure 13–6.

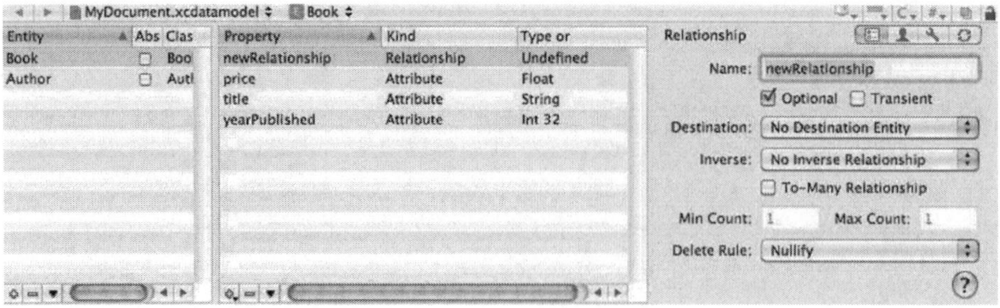

Figure 13–6. *Adding a new relationship*

You will now be given the opportunity to name your relationship. We usually give a relationship the same name as the entity to which is points. Type in "author" as the name. From the drop-down menu, select Author. Currently we do not have an inverse relationship, so leave that alone for now. The To-Many Relationship check box can be a little more complicated. To determine if you need to select it, ask yourself how many authors a book can have. If the answer is one and only one, then you do not need to check this box. For the purposes of this project, we will assume there can only be one author per book, so we will leave it unchecked.

The Delete Rule drop-down can be a little complicated. If you delete a book, what would you like the system to do with the author record? Nullify means that the relationship is deleted only and the author remains in the system. Cascade means that the relationship will be deleted and the author record will be deleted. Deny means that the system will not allow you to delete a record with an author. For this project, we will use Nullify, the default.

Now we have created one half of our relationship. To create the other half, click on the Author entity. Now click the plus sign and select Add Relationship. We will use the entity name that we are connecting to as the name of this relationship, so we will call it "books." We will add an "s" to the entity name because an Author can have many books. Under Destination, select Book, and under Inverse, select the relationship you made in the previous step. For the To-Many Relationship, we will assume that one author can write many books, so check it. We will leave the Delete Rule on Nullify. Your model should now look like Figure 13–7.

NOTE: Sometimes in Xcode, when working with models, it is necessary to hit the tab key for the names of entities, attributes, and relationships to update. This little quirk can be traced all the way back to WebObjects tools.

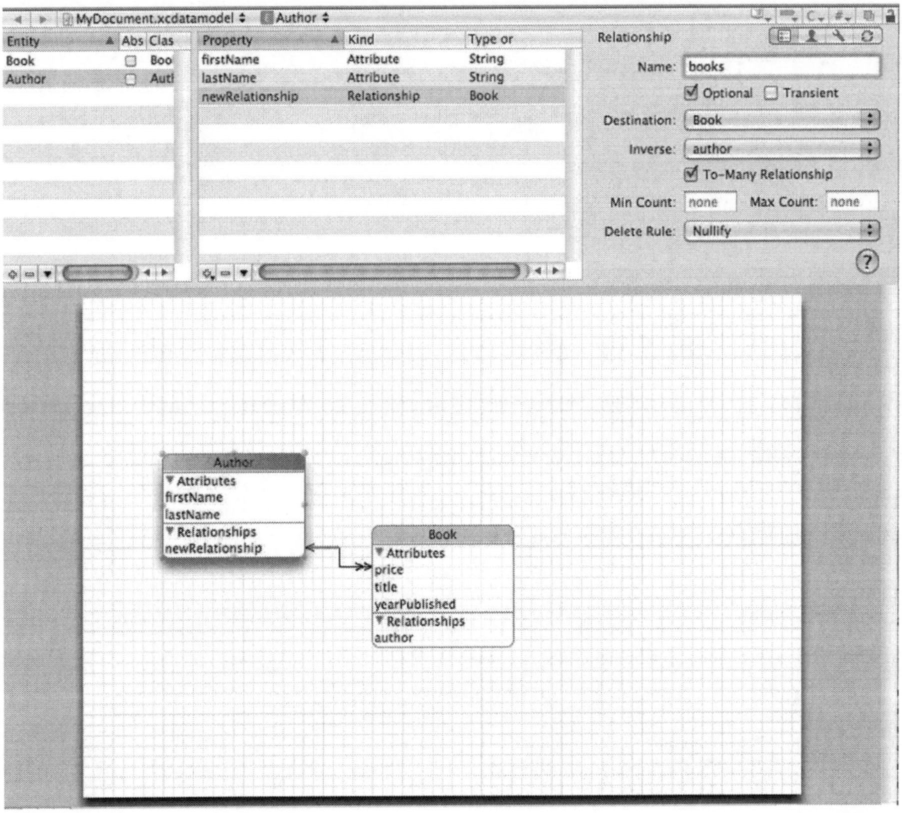

Figure 13–7. *The final relationship*

Now we need to tell our code about our new entity. To do this, select the Book or the Author entity and then select **File ➤ New File**. Under Mac OS X, select Cocoa Class, and then select Managed Object Class, as we see in Figure 13–8.

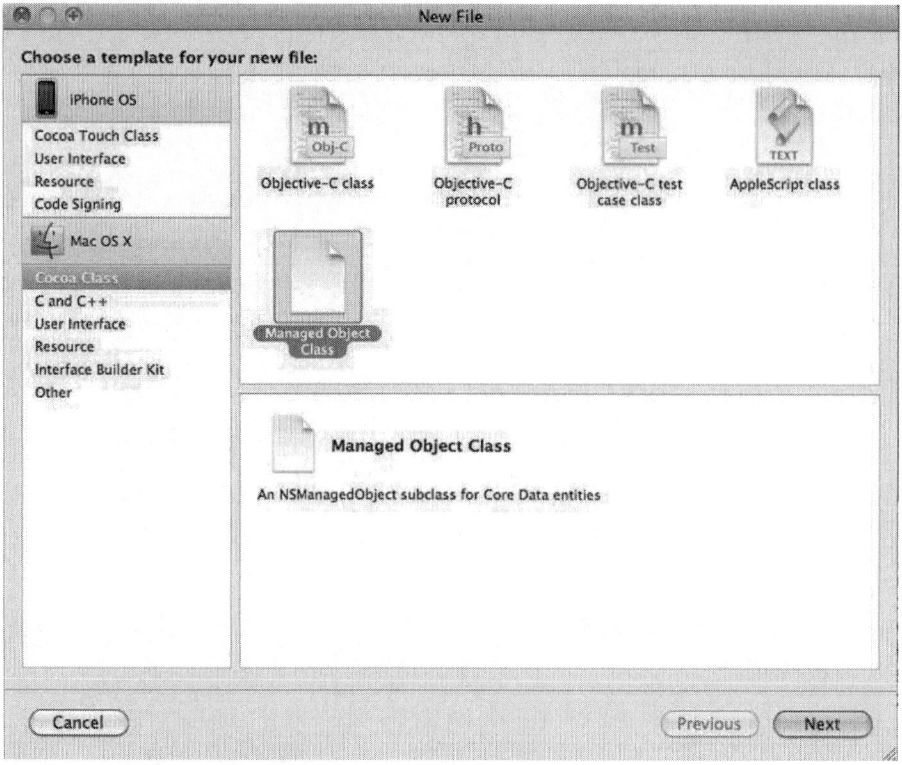

Figure 13–8. *Adding the Managed Objects to your project*

Select the storage location and add it to your project. You should not need to change any of the defaults on this page. Then click Next. Check the box next to your entities and click Finish. See Figure 13–9.

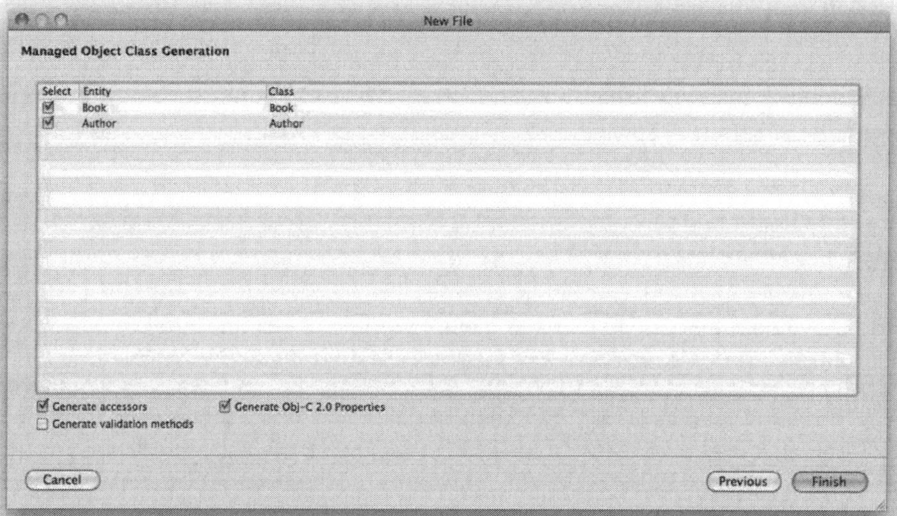

Figure 13–9. *Adding our entities to your project*

You will notice that four files have been added to your project. Book.h and Author.h contain the header information about your book, and Book.m and Author.m contain the actual implementation. These files are fairly simple, as Core Data will do most of the work with them. You should also notice that, if you go back to your model and click on Book, it will have a new class. Instead of an NSManagedObject, it will have be a Book class.

Let's look at the contents of some of Author.h.

```
#import <CoreData/CoreData.h>

@class Book;

@interface Author :  NSManagedObject
{
}

@property (nonatomic, retain) NSString * firstName;
@property (nonatomic, retain) NSString * lastName;
@property (nonatomic, retain) NSSet* books;

@end


@interface Author (CoreDataGeneratedAccessors)
- (void)addBooksObject:(Book *)value;
- (void)removeBooksObject:(Book *)value;
- (void)addBooks:(NSSet *)value;
- (void)removeBooks:(NSSet *)value;

@end
```

You will see that the file starts out including the Core Data framework. This is necessary in each of these files in order to allow Core Data to manage your information. Further down, you will see the three attributes you created with the mode. Finally, under the interface, you will see there are now methods for adding and removing books from the author. In this project, you will not need to directly access these methods, but if you go more in-depth with Core Data, they will be invaluable.

Managed Object Context

We have created a managed object called Book. The nice thing with Xcode is that it will generate the necessary code to manage these new data object. In Core Data, every managed object should exist within a Managed Object Context. The context is responsible for tracking changes to objects, undo operations, and writing the data to the database. In this example, we will not have to write code to create or manage the Object Context, but as you explore using Core Data in your own projects, you will need to be aware of it. For now, the base funtionality of what is provided with the generated classes will work fine for our example.

Setting Up the Interface

In the Resources folder in your project, you should have a MyDocument.xib. Double-click on this file and Interface Builder should open with a window. If there is text in the window that says "Your document contents here", select and delete it. On the left-hand side of Interface Builder, you should have a library window. If you do not have this window, to go Tools ➤ Library and it should appear.

Scroll down to find the Tab View. Drag the tab view to your document window. Resize it to take up most of the screen. Double-click on one tab and change the name to Books. Double-click on the other and change the name to Authors. See Figure 13–10.

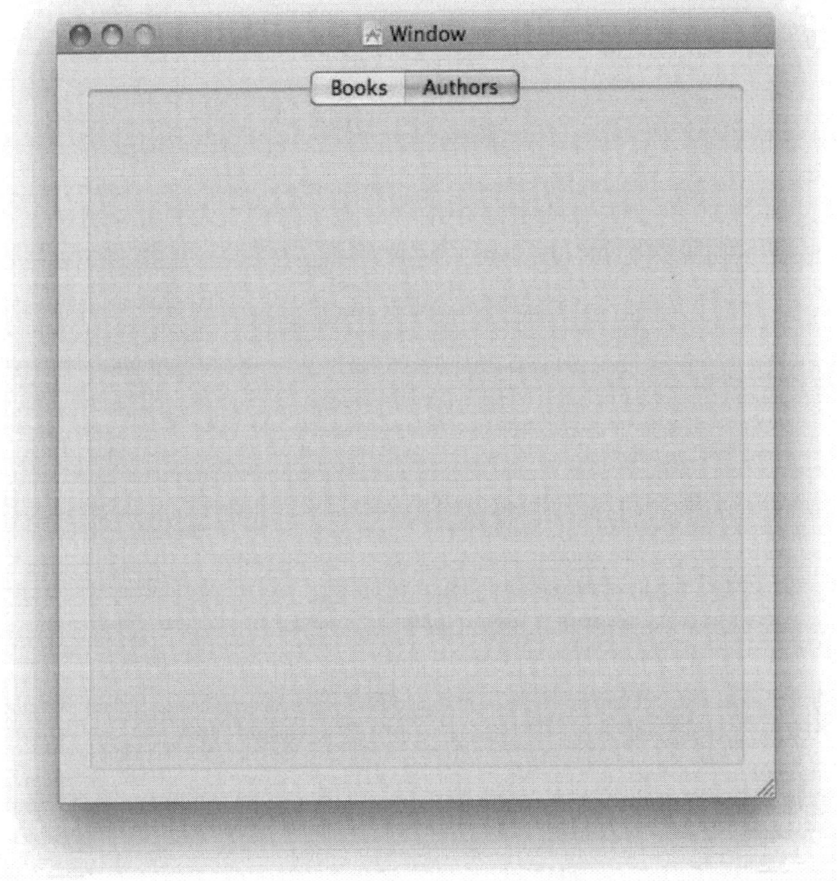

Figure 13–10. *Creating the interface*

Click on the Books tabs and scroll down in the Library to the the the category of **Library ➤ Cocoa ➤ Object Controllers ➤ Core Data**. Within the Core Data category, you should see a Core Data Entity. Drag that to your window. You will be prompted to select your object. Traverse through your project and select Book. Click Next. See Figure 13–11.

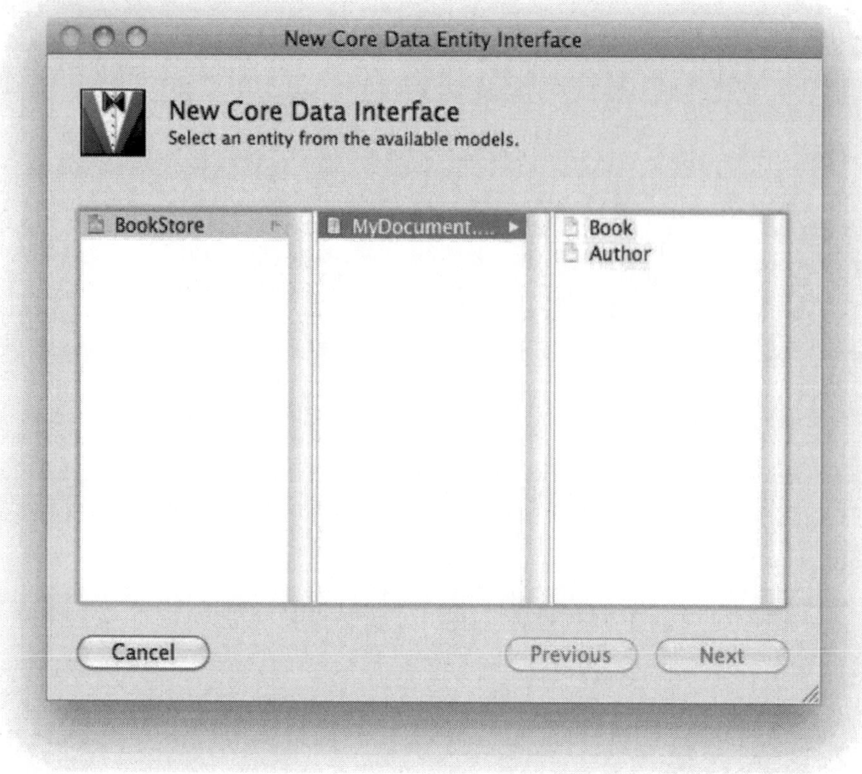

Figure 13–11. *New Core Data interface*

You will now be promted to decide on the type of interface for your Core Data object. We suggest selecting Master/Detail View, as it is the most complete. Check all of the boxes to create a Search Field, Detail Fields, and Add/Remove. Click Next. See Figure 13–12.

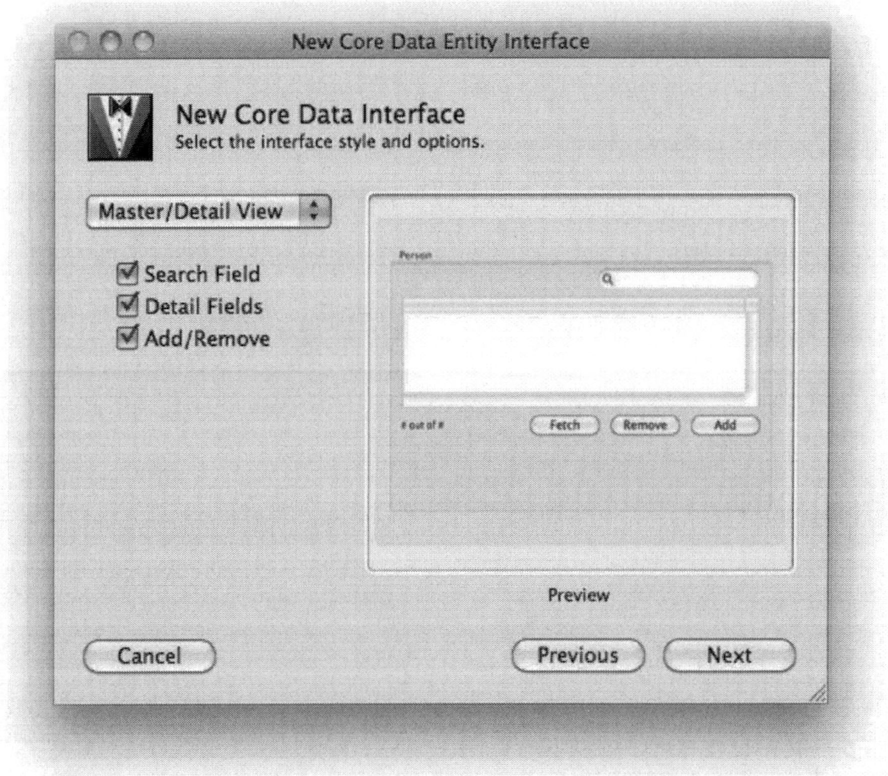

Figure 13–12. *Customizing the Core Data interface*

Now you will be given the option to select the attributes you want to include in your application. Check all of them for the purposes of this project. Once selected, click Finish. See Figure 13–13.

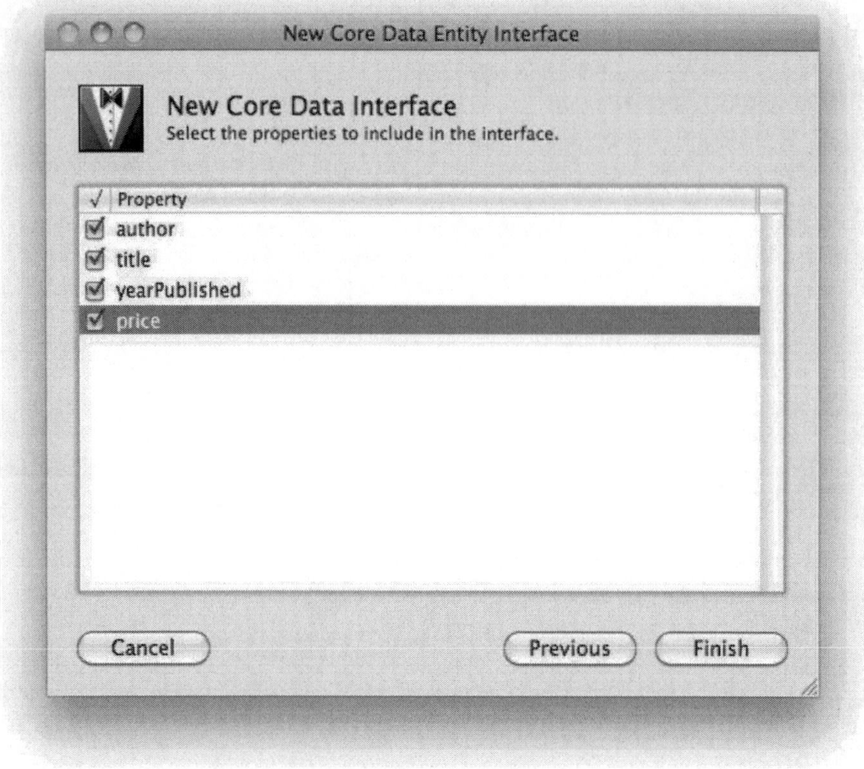

Figure 13–13. *Selecting the attributes to include in the interface*

Your window will now be populated with an inteface to your Core Data application. It will be divided into two sections. You have a list section at the top with a search button above it. You also have a bottom section that will allow you to edit the values of the entity.

Go ahead and repeat the same steps for the Authors tab. You will then have two different tabs, each with a similar interface on them.

Quit Interface Builder and, in Xcode, click on the Build and Run button. This should launch your application. Click on the Authors tab and add a new author. Now go to the Books tab and add a book. You should see your author's name in the drop-down list. You should be able to add books and sort them by clicking on the column titles. You can also go into Interface Builder and make changes to the layout of the window and the individual items. We will cover more about Interface Builder in a later chapter.

Summary

We've finally reached the end of the chapter! Here is a summary of the things that we covered.

- Preferences

  You learned to use NSUserDefaults to save and read preferences from a file, both on the iPhone and a Mac OS X computer.

- Database

  You learned what a database is and why using one can be preferable to saving information in preferences.

  You learned about the database engine Apple has provided on the Mac and iPhone, and the advantages and limitations of this database engine.

- Core Data

  Apple provided a framework for interfacing with the SQLite database. This framework makes the interface much easier to use.

- Book Store Application

  You created a simple Core Data application.

  You used Xcode to create a data model for your Book Store application. You learned how to create a relationship between two different Entities.

  You used Interface Builder to create a simple interface to your Core Data model.

Exercises

- Add more fields to the Book entity. Try adding publisher, pages, and ISBN number.

- Change the layout of the Book tab. Reorder the columns. Make the title column first.

- Add a default value to the author's first and last names.

- For the daring and advanced:

- Add a new entity to store the publisher of the book. Change the interface to allow the user to select the Publisher from a drop-down menu similar to Author.

- Add a new interface to allow the author's full name to be shown in the drop-down menu.

Chapter 14

Protocols and Delegates

Congratulations, you have acquired the skills to become an iOS developer! However, there are two additional topics that iOS developers need to understand to be successful: protocols and delegates. It is not uncommon for new developers to get overwhelmed by these topics, so we thought it best to introduce the foundation topics of the Objective-C language first and conclude this book with protocols and delegates.

Multiple Inheritance

We discussed object inheritance in Chapter 1. In a nutshell, object inheritance means that a child can inherit all the characteristics of its parent. See Figure 14–1.

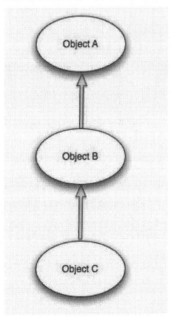

Figure 14–1. *Typical Objective-C inheritance*

Java and C++ have a feature called multiple inheritance. **Multiple inheritance** enables a class to inherit behaviors and features from more than one parent. See Figure 14–2.

However, problems can arise with multiple inheritance because it allows for ambiguities to occur. Because of this, Objective-C does not implement multiple inheritances. Instead, it implements something called a **protocol**.

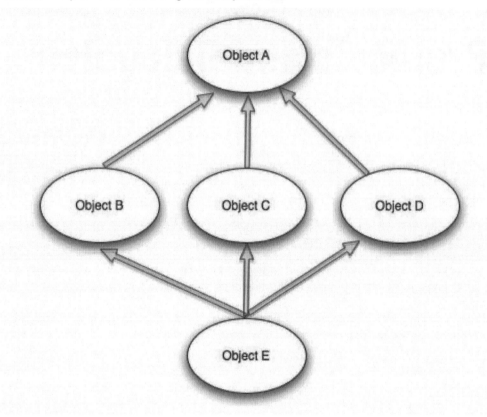

Figure 14–2. *Multiple inheritance*

Understanding Protocols

Apple defines a protocol simply as a list of methods declarations, unattached to a class definition. The methods listed for protocols are suppose to be implemented by you. For example, these methods that report user actions for the mouse could be placed into a protocol. See the following example:

```
- (void)mouseDown:(NSEvent *)theEvent;
- (void)mouseDragged:(NSEvent *)theEvent;
- (void)mouseUp:(NSEvent *)theEvent;
```

Any class that wanted to respond to mouse events could adopt the protocol and implement its methods.

Protocol Syntax

The interface example for a protocol is

```
@protocol WebServiceDelegate
- (void)connetionURL;
- (void)connectionComplete;
@end
```

The implementation file for this protocol example would be

```
@interface MyClass : SomeSuperClass < WebServiceDelegate >
@end
```

Any object that wants to implement the WebServiceDelegate protocol would include < WebServiceDelegate > after object definition.

It is not uncommon for iOS developers to have multiple protocols for their objects. This adds real power to your objects when needed.

```
@interface MyClass : UITableViewController  <CLLocationManagerDelegate, WebService,
UITextFieldDelegate, UITextViewDelegate, UITableViewDataSource>
{
}
```

This example illustrates the power of delegates. MyClass is able to handle all methods from CLLocationManagerDelegate, WebService, UITextFieldDelegate, UITextViewDelegate, and UITableViewDataSource.

This means that MyClass is able to use all the methods in these protocols. This includes the following:

- GPS information
- Our custom web services
- Text field handling
- Table view handing

The methods from these protocols are called **delegates methods**.

Understanding Delegates

Delegates are helper objects. They enable us to control the behavior of our objects. The methods listed in the protocol become **helpers** to our MyClass.

We can now use these methods in our object. For example, including the <CLLocationManagerDelegate> protocol in our MyClass enables our object to get notified by the iPhone's GPS of our new location. The following example shows the method that we will include and define inside our object's implementation file:

```
- (void)locationManager:(CLLocationManager *)manager didUpdateToLocation:(CLLocation
*)newLocation fromLocation:(CLLocation *)oldLocation
```

```
{
......
}
```

The `locationManager` delegate method automatically gets called as our GPS location changes, allowing your code to process the new and old coordinates. Listing 14–1 is an example of how to implement `didUpdateToLocation` and `didFailWithError` delegate methods from `CLLocationManagerDelegate`.in our class `MyCoreLocationController`

Listing 14–1. *Core location delegate example*

```
@implementation MyCoreLocationController //our own controller
@synthesize locationManager;

- (id) init {
    self = [super init];
    if (self != nil) {
        self.locationManager = [[CLLocationManager alloc] init];
        self.locationManager.delegate = self; // send location updates updates to myself
    }
    return self;
}

- (void)locationManager:(CLLocationManager *)manager
    didUpdateToLocation:(CLLocation *)newLocation
            fromLocation:(CLLocation *)oldLocation
{
    NSLog(@"Location: %@", [newLocation description]);
}

- (void)locationManager:(CLLocationManager *)manager
            didFailWithError:(NSError *)error
{
        NSLog(@"Error: %@", [error description]); //print error description
}

- (void)dealloc {
    [self.locationManager release];
    [super dealloc];
}
@end
```

Next Steps

You now have a great Objective-C foundation. You should be able to dive right becoming a great iOS developer. Two great books that we recommend to students as they progress to becoming iOS developers are *Learn Objective-C on the Mac* by Mark Dalrymple and Scott Knaster, and *Beginning iPhone Development* by Dave Mark and Jeff LaMarche, both published by Apress.

You will be well prepared for these books and writing your iOS apps. However, don't take time off – keep moving forward. Get started with these books and writing your apps. The faster your start using what you have learned, the better you will get. Whatever you do, don't stop now!

Summary

You made it! In this chapter we covered why multiple inheritance is not used in Objective-C and how protocols and delegates work.

There is still a lot to learn and know on your iOS journey. Keep it up and help others along their way.

You should be familiar with the following terms:

- Multiple Inheritance
- Protocol
- Delegate

Index